UTOPIAS
OF THE CLASSICAL WORLD

ASPECTS OF GREEK AND ROMAN LIFE

General Editor: Professor H. H. Scullard

UTOPIAS
OF THE
CLASSICAL
WORLD

John Ferguson

THAMES AND HUDSON

J.A.C.
sodali amicissimo

PRINTED IN GREAT BRITAIN BY
COX & WYMAN LTD
LONDON, FAKENHAM AND READING

ISBN 0 500 40027 X

CONTENTS

UTOPIAS OF THE CLASSICAL WORLD

PREFACE

It was Martin Charlesworth who first interested me in ancient Utopias, and in this as in almost every aspect of my classical training and interest I owe him a great debt. I did much of the basic work for this study during the year which immediately followed my Cambridge Part II, and am grateful to the electors to the Henry Carrington and Bentham Dumont Koe Studentship and the Denney Studentship for making this possible. It is thus an old love. I have modified my views on many aspects in the subsequent quarter of a century, but not my enthusiasm.

Utopia *is* an enthusiasm. 'We were all a little mad that winter,' wrote Emerson of 1840. 'Not a man of us did not have a plan for some new Utopia in his pocket.' More's *Utopia*, Campanella's *City of the Sun*, Morris's *News from Nowhere*, Bellamy's *Looking Backwards*, Skinner's *Walden Two* do not lose their fascination. I have sternly eschewed any temptation to wander down those later paths. Those who wish to ramble in that direction should look at Marie Louise Berneri's *Journey through Utopia* (London 1950) and read at first hand some of the books to which she refers. (Others too. She does not mention John Macnie who in *Diothas* in 1883 foresaw a horseless carriage with a speed of 20 mph and even imagined a 'white line running along the centre of the road. The rule of the road requires that line to be kept on the left, except when passing a vehicle in front. Then, the line may be crossed, provided the way on that side is clear.') The name of course means 'no-where': *ou* + topos (though More intended a pun on Eutopia); we can if we like distinguish between eutopias and dystopias (or something such: favourable or unfavourable), but they are all alike utopias.

Perhaps more reprehensibly, I have equally not allowed myself to be drawn into speculation about the social or psychological basis of Utopianism. Toynbee suggested that all Utopias were an attempt to peg back history, as Plato tried to peg back history at the city-state stage, Mercier to return to the days before printing, Morris to stem the tide of the Industrial Revolution. Lamartine, by contrast, thought Utopias were premature truths. Engels and Karl Mannheim offered a sociological analysis. Mannheim in his well-known *Ideology and Utopia* (London 1936) suggested that every utopian movement needed a class interest to sustain it. Herbert Marcuse, Norman Brown and others have seen Utopia as an escape from sexual repression. All these views, to my mind, have enough interest to make them worth examining and testing, but they will hardly stand as universal generalizations. It seemed better to tell the tale of ancient Utopianism and let readers draw their own conclusions.

For the tale has, oddly, never been told, though most modern Utopians nod or shake their heads in the direction of Plato. It is an absorbing story, partly because it is such a varied one, partly because theory and practice, philosophy and politics, idealism and pragmatism are so closely intertwined.

And herein is the perennial fascination. It consists precisely in the relation between vision and reality. For the vision is in the strict sense Utopian unless it affects reality; and reality is the idle tinkering of a social garage mechanic unless it is informed by a vision.

Among many debts of gratitude four must be here acknowledged. First, to Professor Howard Scullard, editor of the series, for his friendly co-operation and encouragement. Secondly, to my friend and secretary, Marilyn Grootes, for her good humour and skill in coping with an unwieldy and untidy manuscript, and to her successor Margaret Bartlett, and Georgina Coleman, for their help with the proofs. Finally, to my wife, for more things than I can say, but specifically and concretely for yet another admirable index.

J.F.

CHAPTER I

HOMERIC BEGINNINGS

GREEK POLITICS ARE INEXPLICABLE apart from Greek geography.[1] 'The political organization of Greece,' writes Rostovtzeff, 'was dictated by the geographical and economic conditions. Nature had divided her into small economic units, and she was incapable of creating large political systems. So it had been during the prevalence of the Aegean culture, and so it still remained. Each valley was self-centred, and its inhabitants jealously guarded their pasture and arable land. The best parts of the country, especially its rich valleys, are open to the sea and shut in by land – separated from the central high valleys and plateaux by formidable barriers. They are more in touch with those neighbours from whom the sea divides them than with those whom the land brings near them. It is easier for them to exchange goods and ideas by sea than by land. Hence civilization develops quickly on the coast but slowly in the centre of the country. This type of life is however the same in all parts. Stocks, and portions of stocks, form petty political units which keep jealous guard of their independence. To protect themselves and their property against attack they built fortified refuges on the hill-tops and these by degrees are converted into cities (*poleis*), which offer markets for their produce, a centre of religious life, and a residence for their kings, leaders in war, and priests. The city becomes a focus of a larger or smaller territory, inhabited by farmers and shepherds who live either in detached houses and cottages scattered over the country, or together in villages (*demes*).'[2] 'The country,' says Ehrenberg, 'was divided into many small areas which were separated by mountains, and the Greek tribes, differing among themselves in character and history, were in addition split into innumerable political communities, all of which were bound to be rather weak. Not only were the natural regions severed from one another by nature, but also each one was again subdivided into mountains and plains, which in their continual alternation created many opportunities both for settlement and traffic, and made possible many varieties of political growth.'[3] Hence 'the Greeks found the fulfilment of their political aims within small, even tiny, areas.'[4] Attica, the territory of Athens, as Ehrenberg points out, is little larger than Luxemburg. A Roman, Sulpicius Rufus, citizen of a world power, sailing in Greek waters, reflects with amazement that he can see around him four states which once were prosperous and independent.[5] But this was the prime characteristic of Greek political development – the small, independent city-states, and until the time of Alexander the vision of even her most farsighted dreamers was almost without exception circumscribed within those limits.

In *The Iliad* we have a memory of the dominance of Mycenae towards the end of the second millennium BC. Agamemnon, commander-in-chief of the Greek forces, rules over 'many islands and all Argos.' He appears as king of kings, and Menelaus, Odysseus, Achilles and the rest of them, kings in their own right, are subordinate to him. Indeed, we now know, through Ventris's decipherment of Linear B, that the Mycenaeans owned a supreme *wanax*, and the *basilewes* sometimes seem little more than mayors. The organization of the army as a whole reflects the political organization of any single state, with the king supreme, but advised by a council of elders, and incipient democracy represented by the voice of the people assenting to the decisions of the king. Here the commanders of the local contingents, each of whom has in fact his own 'companions', act as the supreme council of elders, and the voice of the people is expressed through the army assembly. The kingship is hereditary. Agamemnon's had been handed down from his grandfather, Pelops, and Pelops had been granted his sceptre, the work of Hephaestus, by the king of the gods.[6] But though he is a hereditary monarch his position is maintained by his dominance on the battlefield, as Sarpedon makes clear in referring to the kings of Lycia.[7] The scenes in Olympus reflect precisely the terrestrial organization. Zeus is supreme, he rules at the last by strength and power, and when he asserts himself he is a figure of fear and awe to the rest. The great gods, Poseidon, Athene, Apollo and their fellows, are his counsellors and represent the barons. At the beginning of the twentieth book we see the general assembly of the divinities, rivers and nymphs and all. They are not summoned to give counsel but to hear the dictates of their overlord. The Athenians of the fifth century, with unpleasant memories of a comparatively recent dictatorship in their minds, stressed the supremacy and isolation of the monarch, as they looked back to the heroic age. This is clear in Aeschylus' *Agamemnon*, where the elders, for all their proud words, are helpless before Clytemnestra and Aegisthus. A very little reflection on the position of Oedipus or Creon will amply reinforce this judgement.

The Odyssey displays society at a somewhat later stage of development than *The Iliad*. The cities are still ruled by kings, each assisted by his council of elders, but there are significant changes. The idealized ruler of the fictitious community of Phaeacia is called Alcinous; his name implies that his supremacy is intellectual not physical, and we are specifically told that the gods had given him wisdom.[8] He has his council, and it soon appears that he, like Agamemnon, is lord of lords, for some, though not all, of his counsellors are described as sceptred kings.[9] In the ideal community Alcinous has the confidence of his barons. He does not act without consulting them, but in fact his plans are already cut and dried and no one questions them. The people however are at no time consulted, and Alcinous coolly remarks that he will recoup the expenses of entertaining Odysseus by a tax upon the people.[10] The author of *The Iliad* placed his sympathy firmly by the side of his aristocratic masters upon whom he after all depended.

This is to be clearly seen in his account of the army assembly in book two, and his treatment of Thersites,[11] who is described as ugly, misshapen and foul-mouthed, and summarily silenced by Odysseus when he offers some pertinent criticisms of the High Command. This is not the place to argue in detail the authorship of the Homeric poems. The debt of *The Odyssey* to *The Iliad* is obvious, and if they be not by the same hand they at least reflect the same pattern of thought. The author's standpoint is firmly that of the aristocrats. There may be sympathy for individuals such as Eurycleia or Eumaeus, but it is the sympathy of condescension and there is no question of politics being seen from the popular side. But there is a change in the balance of power among the aristocrats, well to be seen in the second book of *The Odyssey*. There Telemachus summons the assembly at Ithaca. Aegyptius, an elderly baron, is the first to speak: 'Listen to what I have to say, gentlemen. There has been no session of the assembly since Odysseus sailed. Who has summoned this meeting? One of the younger men or one of the older generation? What is the emergency?'[12] Telemachus, the heir to the throne, sits in the president's chair, but he does not open the business, and he does not have the sole right of summoning the assembly, which any of the nobles may do. Further when he makes his request for a ship, the barons refuse it. The power has shifted from the royal house to the barons. Webster treats this as a council meeting. That it is not, for the people are summoned as well as the nobles, though they have no voice or part in the proceedings. But Webster's summary of the political state of Homeric society is succinct and accurate: 'Thus at the beginning of Greek literature in the ninth century BC in a small feudal world of kings, princes, and retainers, we can already see the germ of later development. First, the king of kings disappears when he can no longer justify himself as a warlord; then the individual kings in their turn, unable to justify special privileges by special services, sink to the level of their "companions", and the forms of government by an aristocratic council are moulded. Thersites, cruelly caricatured and ruthlessly manhandled, is the beginning of a democratic opposition to aristocratic misuse of power.'[13]

Even in the Homeric poems we can trace an element of aspiration as well as of reflection; this is particularly true of *The Odyssey*. The political organization of the gods, as we have already remarked, reflects the political organization of men, but it is enacted on a higher plane. In *The Iliad* little distinction can be drawn in quality between the councils of the gods and the councils of men. The king is there with his barons. He is supreme, but supreme by strength, not heredity.

> Come and try, gods – you'll soon learn.
> Stretch a rope of gold down from the sky.
> Grip it, every one of you, gods and goddesses.
> Never could you drag Zeus, the lord of wisdom,
> from sky to ground, labour as you will.
> But the moment I took a mind to pull,
> I would pull you up, earth, sea and all.

> Then I would fasten the rope about the peak
> of Olympus, and leave everything dangling in mid-air.
> So much am I stronger than any gods and men.[14]

At his solemn nod all Olympus shakes. But powerful though he is, he can be outwitted. At the start of *The Iliad* he goes off to feast with the blameless Ethiopians, in apparent ignorance of the storm that will break over the Greek camp before his return.[15] His attention can be distracted, a situation of which Poseidon is not slow to take advantage.[16] Further, in a famous episode Hera uses her sex appeal, somewhat heightened by supernatural cosmetics, and for the moment completely outmanoeuvres him.[17] In all this we seem to be seeing the king from the standpoint of the barons. Among the barons themselves there are, however, party differences,[18] which Zeus does not take very seriously. Zeus in fact stands above the quarrels, there is no challenge to the institution of kingship. For the rest the supernatural accoutrements of the gods, which may be taken as representing the natural aspirations of humans, are power, which is merely a human quality magnified, the sustenance of nectar, a wine-like drink, and the use of ambrosia, which is not yet differentiated as food, and which conveys to its users the substance of immortality.

One further point merits comment; that is the exaltation of the 'blameless' Ethiopians.[19] They are a vague and distant people to the far south. Völcker's comment is intelligent: 'The Ethiopians are with Homer a general name for the last inhabitants of the earth, the most remote people he knew of: to whom he might send the gods, in order to gain time for events which according to his plan must occur. The epithet *blameless* rests perhaps on grounds similar to those on which certain Scythians are elsewhere denominated the most just among men (the Abii), viz., a confused notion of the innocence and justice of semi-savage nations that are but little known, which has in all ages been cherished, when an opposite opinion, a belief in their utter wildness and ferocity, has not yet been formed.'[20] This particular view is taken up in *The Odyssey*, where the Ethiopians are described as long-lived[21] and is to be traced surviving in the pages of Herodotus.[22] The idealization of a primitive nature-people as early as *The Iliad* is worth noting; it is a formative element later.

In *The Odyssey* there are certain well-marked differences. There is a more intense Utopianism, to be seen in the description of Olympus.

> No winds stir there, no rain drizzles,
> no snow assails; the sky is clear
> and cloudless; it is bathed in pure light.[23]

This is Tennyson's

> island valley of Avilion,
> Where falls not hail nor rain nor any snow,
> Nor ever wind blows loudly.

It is the beginning of that Utopianism of nature which invested so much subsequent political idealism with an air of unreality. Furthermore the councils of
the gods are idealized, as they are not in *The Iliad*. It is true that divisions
remain. Poseidon is hostile to Odysseus, just as Athene supports him. But there
is no quarrelling in council, where indeed Poseidon does not appear; his one
appearance before Zeus is private and amicable.[24] For the rest Zeus appears as a
wise and benevolent monarch, perhaps a little under Athene's thumb. We have
already seen that the social conditions of *The Odyssey* show a period when the
power of the monarch has been effectively challenged by the barons. We are
bound to add that that situation is viewed from the standpoint of the monarch –
and his daughter.

Furthermore we have, in the terrestrial adventures of Odysseus, encounters
with two forms of society which might be called Cacotopian and Eutopian.

> We reached the country of the Cyclopes, a fierce,
> lawless people. They leave everything to the gods;
> they lift no finger to plant or plough.
> Their crops grow, unsown, untended –
> wheat and barley and vines, heavy
> with bunches for wine, ripened by rain from Zeus.
> The Cyclopes have no political assemblies, no laws,
> but live on the heights of the mountains
> in caves, each exercising authority over his own
> wife and child, ignoring all the others.[25]

The poet proceeds to say that the land is naturally fertile, but is inadequately
exploited, and that the Cyclopes lack craftsmen and shipwrights and do not
trade with other peoples. The negative criticism here has its positive implications. We have the inkling of Aristotle's doctrine that man is a social animal;
atomic individuals are barbarous and uncivilized. We have a typically Utopian
treatment of nature, curiously and unusually redeemed by a doctrine of skill
and work almost worthy of *The Georgics*. Above all the blame attached to the
statement that each Cyclops is the source of his own *themis* implies a doctrine of
communal law and morality. If the aspiration of the author of *The Odyssey* is
towards monarchy, it is towards constitutional monarchy.

This can be seen, as we have already observed, among the Phaeacians. The
contrast with the Cyclopes is deliberately drawn by the poet whose statement
that they were once neighbours is otherwise without point.[26] It is important
that the Cyclopes persecuted the Phaeacians because of their greater strength.
Strength is no longer the criterion of leadership. Odysseus outwits Polyphemus,
and the Phaeacians are ruled by wisdom. This is exemplified also in the emphasis upon skill, the men with ships and the women at the loom.[27] The Utopian
treatment of nature directly influenced later composers of ideal commonwealths, to their detriment, for they did not always note the correlative
emphasis on skill.

Outside the courtyard, near the door is a large
four-acre orchard, with a fence on either side.
Here trees grow tall in rich profusion,
pears, pomegranates, glowing apples,
luscious figs, olives in profusion.
Their fruit never goes rotten, never runs short,
winter or summer, all through the year. Always
the west wind's breath is bringing growth or ripeness.
Pear after pear, apple after apple, grape
after grape, fig after fig grow ripe.
There his fruitful vineyard is planted.
In one part currants are drying in the sun
on a level exposed patch, in another they are gathering
or treading the grapes. Close by is young fruit
with freshly-shed blossom, or the first tinge of purple.
Beyond the farthest row are neat beds
of various vegetables, green all through the year.
There are two springs. One irrigates the whole
garden; its fellow gives water to the citizens,
then gushes under the gate to the great house.
These were the gods' glorious gifts to Alcinous.[28]

The patronal behaviour of the spring is noteworthy! These magical powers
extend to their ships, which are propelled by oars in the normal way, though
with superlative skill, but require no steering; the ships respond directly to the
will of the sailors.[29] In the perfection of external circumstances the Phaeacians
live at ease. They are not boxers or wrestlers – there is a slight imputation of a
tendency to softness, which reminds us of Toynbee's claim that civilization
emerges in response to a challenge which is sufficient but not excessive; if the
challenge of some hardship is absent, civilization either does not emerge or
stagnates. But they are first-rate sailors; the magical properties of their ships
should not lead us to forget that. They run well, and they take especial delight
in 'feasting, music, dancing, clean clothes, hot baths and bed'.[30] The political
constitution we have already examined. One of Alcinous' counsellors, Echeneus,
speaks freely in rebuke of him.[31] Equally, the counsellors seem to have full
confidence in him. He may require an occasional reminder, even from his
daughter, to keep him up to scratch, but his judgement is unquestioned. In
general we see the court of Phaeacia through the eyes of Alcinous and Nausicaa,
just as we have seen the court of Olympus through the eyes of Zeus and Athene.
The ideal is a monarchy. The monarchy is not arbitrary and absolute, however.
It is benevolent and paternalistic. It depends on intellectual and spiritual qualities, not on physique. If it be not under the rule of law, it is at any rate dictated
by custom and convention. It is sustained by the free consent of the governed,
who treat Alcinous' words like those of a god.[32]
    This is the first surviving Utopia in European literature. Toynbee's view that
with rare exceptions Utopias are devised during periods of decay, and are the
work of those who wish to arrest the march of events and peg back history at

a stage which it is rapidly outstripping, is here helpful. The picture of Phaeacia is an attempt to peg back society at the monarchical stage and to suppress the power of the barons and oncoming oligarchy. The episode is incidental to *The Odyssey*, and its historical significance peripheral. But in seeking to present the best possible case for these ideals, the poet idealized nature, and the later popularity of the poem meant that more serious political thinkers tended to present their political ideals in unnatural natural surroundings.

CHAPTER II

THE NOBLE SAVAGE[1]

WE HAVE SEEN ALREADY in the Homeric poems some tendency to idealize imaginary people such as the Phaeacians or dimly known people such as the Ethiopians. This tendency recurs throughout ancient literature, and since it in measure reflects those parts of Utopian thinking which permeated through and made their appeal to the ordinary reading public, and in measure the aspirations of the man in the street which in turn affected the constructions of the Utopians, it is worth essaying some analysis of these ideas before we turn to historical developments or theoretical construction.

In the first place there is the frequently repeated idealization of nature, with the spontaneous or toilless production of food. Horace will provide an instance in his description of the Isles of the Blest:[2]

> You, who have manhood, stop moping like women,
>   speed past Etruria's coasts.
> Encircling Ocean is awaiting us. Let us make for
>   the Fields of the Blest, the Isles of Prosperity,
> where each year the land unploughed produces corn,
>   unpruned the vine blossoms,
> the shoots of the olive unfailingly burst into bud,
>   the dark fig graces its native tree,
> honey oozes from the hollow oak, on the high hills
>   the water lightly leaps with sounding step.
> There the she-goats come to the milk-pail unherded,
>   the flock is happy to bring its swelling udders home.
> No bear growls round the sheepfold in the evenings,
>   the ground does not swell high with snakes.
> There will be more for us to marvel at in our fortune. No east wind
>   rain-laden drowns the fields with showers.
> The seeds swell and do not wither and parch in the baking earth.
>   The king of the gods keeps heat and cold under control.
> No pestilence attacks the flocks, no planet's
>   torrid fury burns up the herds. . . .
> Jupiter set these shores apart for a people of righteousness.

There is a similar description in Plutarch's life of Sertorius:[3] 'They enjoy a light rainfall, and that not too frequently. Generally they have light breezes with a bit of moisture in the wind. These make the soil rich and good for ploughing and planting; in fact they produce crops spontaneously, delicious and sufficient to feed the people without any effort on their part.' So too Isidore:[4] 'The islands of their own accord bear fruits of the most valued trees. The ridges of the hills are clothed with untended vines, and everywhere crops and vegetables grow instead of weeds.' The benefits of this imaginary paradise were extended in imagination to more or less historical peoples – to the Hyperboreans,[5] the Gabii:[6]

> where no plough cleaves the soil
> nor mattock delves the earth
> but seed grows without toil
> and plenty springs to birth

or the Albanians. These last are described by Strabo:[7] 'Now a people of this kind has no need of the sea. Nor do they use the land to the full extent of its value, the land which bears every kind of fruit, even the type which normally requires cultivation, and every kind of plant. In fact its fruits are everlasting. It does not require the slightest attention, "but all things grow there untilled and unsown", as the soldiers say, living a sort of Cyclopean life. For in many parts, after sowing once, they reap two or three times, and the first sowing multiplies itself fifty times over, and these crops are not produced by cutting the land with iron, but with a wooden plough. The whole plain is watered, even more than those of Babylonia and Egypt, by rivers and other streams, so that it always keeps its grassy appearance; it is, therefore, excellent pasture land. Besides, the Albanians enjoy a better climate. The vines never need hoeing, and pruning only once every five years. When new, they produce so much that the people leave much of it unpicked. They have wild and domesticated cattle, both very sleek.' Vergil of course uses a similar conceit not merely in his picture of the golden age which shall return with the birth of the child – a picture therefore of an idealized past and an idealized future, with a land needing no tilling, free from lethal animals and poisonous plants, where the sheep have their fleeces ready dyed[8] – but also in his passage in praise of Italy with its perpetual spring, freedom from wild animals and poisonous plants, and fruit trees and herds bearing twice a year.[9]

Sometimes there is the suggestion that the primitive peoples owe their high qualities to a difference of diet. This seems implied in the awed references to milk-drinkers in the lands of the north and north-east;[10] the association of justice and milk is difficult to justify, but may be due in part to scorn of the effect of meat on the mind.[11] The inhabitants of the Hebrides are also said to have a diet of fish and milk.[12] Elsewhere it is realized that the people who live from untilled soil are probably living from herbs or berries, but this may itself lead to toughness.[13] In general, whether by reason of favourable conditions leading to ease of life or (less frequently) unfavourable conditions leading to hardihood, primitive peoples were thought to live longer than those in the known world. Thus in Pindar the Hyperboreans are free from disease and destructive old age,[14] and Pliny says of the race *annoso degit aevo*.[15] Callimachus calls them a very long-lived race.[16] Agatharchides, who specialized in the exotic,

speaks of one people who lived to 120.[17] Similarly Scylax has a passage in praise
of the physique of the Ethiopians: 'These Ethiopians are the tallest race we
know, with heights more than six feet, and in some cases seven and a half. They
have long hair and beards and are the handsomest of mankind. They take as
king the tallest among them.'[18] Strabo also describes the Albanians as tall and
handsome.[19]

Vegetarianism is an aspect which plays some part in the idealization of the
simple life.[20] Thus Porphyry looks back with admiration to the pre-pastoral
stage before men began doing violence to animals, and argued that it was as a
result of doing violence to other animals that he came to do violence to his
fellow humans.[21] On the whole this appears as a feature of primeval man rather
than of contemporary nature-peoples, though the Rhizophagi, Spermatophagi
and Hylophagi show that there were contrary accounts,[22] and we should not
forget Homer's Lotus-Eaters.[23] Thus in Hesiod's five ages of man,[24] the Golden
Age enjoys the fruits of the earth growing freely; by the time we get to the
Bronze Age they have degenerated into meat-eating. After his catalogue Hesiod
returns to praise the way of life which depends on acorns and wild honey.[25] It
is a way of life which Herodotus seems to attribute to the Arcadians in historical
times.[26] The Epicureans similarly in their remarkable anthropological speculations postulated a simple livelihood from acorns and arbute-berries in the
earliest stages of human existence,[27] and Vergil with his Epicurean background
echoes the thought.[28] The same existence is attributed in an Orphic source to
the mysterious Macrobians, but that is likely to be controlled by the vegetarianism of the Orphics themselves.[29] Ovid makes his Pythagoras refer his
vegetarianism back to the Golden Age.[30] Porphyry attributes vegetarianism to
a number of leading non-Greek nations, or to groups within them, the Egyptians, Jews, Syrians, Persians and Indians.[31]

Secondly, primitive peoples are regarded as peculiarly just. This is the
idealization of the 'blameless Ethiopians' over again. Thus Homer's Abii are
'supremely upright',[32] and Aeschylus' Gabii, who may be the same, are
'supremely just and generous to strangers'.[33] In another fragment Aeschylus
calls the milk-drinking Scythians *eunomoi*, obedient to law.[34] Dio Chrysostom,
in a passage more governed by philosophy than fact, similarly eulogizes the
Scythians:[35] 'The nomadic Scythians, though they have neither houses nor
plant nor cultivate the soil, conduct their government justly and according
to law.' In some analyses law does not enter into the situation. 'Justice is
served by the tribe's inherent respect for it, not by laws. Theft is the
most serious crime in their eyes, since, if it were permitted to steal what
would men whose flocks and herds are in the woods unprotected by a
roof have left?' So Pompeius Trogus, also on the Scythians, perhaps having in
mind the philosophical notion of the Social Contract.[36] Legendary figures like
Anacharsis and Abaris emerge from the darkness of the north to take their place
among saints and sages. Sometimes justice is regarded as the result of simplicity;
the complexities of civilization and business corrupt.[37] Agatharchides, writing
in the second century BC, gives an interesting analysis of the 'Fish-eaters':[38]

'While the life which we pursue is divided between superfluities and necessities, the tribes of the Ichthyophagi, already mentioned, are said to have limited all useless things and lack nothing which is fitting, all endeavouring to follow the divine way of life, and not the way which tries to surpass nature by false opinions. For since they do not crave power, they are not involved in contentious and unhappy strife. And since they do not love superfluity, they do not do many things to others nor suffer many things from others which are unnecessary. And since they do not start great feuds so as to do bodily injury to their enemies, they are not undone by the misfortunes of their kinsmen. They do not endanger their lives by navigation for the sake of gain, thereby meting out pain through fatal shipwrecks. But needing little, they have few griefs. Gaining a sufficiency, they do not demand superfluities. None is troubled by the absence of what is beyond his ken, but only of that for which he wishes when he falls short of the satisfaction of some urgent desire. Therefore, having all that he wants, he is happy according to the logic of nature, not according to that of opinion. These people moreover are not governed by laws. For why need one be subservient to ordinances who is able to be honest without instruction.' Besides these we may note a description of the Ethiopians: 'They are pious and just, and their houses are without doors, and though many things lie about on their streets, nothing is ever stolen.'[39] Favorinus suggests that the Ethiopians were the first people to invent laws.[40] Again there are the Illyrians: 'Some of them are obedient to royal authority and some to monarchical' (an obscure distinction) 'while some are self-ruled. They are said to be god-fearing and exceedingly just and generous to strangers; they delight in good fellowship and advise a well-ordered life.'[41] Again the Scythian Tibareni are said to be the justest of men.[42] The Arcadians are notable for their hospitality and humanity.[43] Tacitus asserts that the earliest generations of humans were free from guilt or crime.[44]

Sometimes this justice is rooted in communism. At its lowest this means that where there is no property there can be no theft, at its highest it comes to the admission of a common social purpose where all things are held in common. Dicaearchus, himself much inclined to pacifism,[45] was one of those who idealized primitive man for his absence of private property; he evidently believed positively that a communal state led to happiness and peaceability, and negatively that private property led to economic competition, dissension and war.[46] The Arcadians had a common board, masters and slaves sitting at one table and sharing the same food and drink.[47]

One aspect of communism has left a particular mark upon the constructors of artificial Utopias, and that is communism of wives and, sometimes, children. This is partly a recognition of the way in which family ties and family prejudice can corrupt a society, partly the working out of a Freudian preoccupation with sex. We find it first in Herodotus. Among the Massagetae each man marries a wife, but the wives are common to all.[48] He denies that the Scythians have wives, children and families in common, as is generally supposed, and as Ephorus later asserts.[49] The Agathyrsi practise promiscuity so that they may all be brothers and a single family and avoid mutual jealousy and suspicion.[50] The Ausees also practise promiscuity, not cohabiting, but having intercourse like cattle. When a woman's child is well grown within three months, the men foregather and assign it to the man it most resembles.[51] Aristotle similarly says of the tribes of Upper Libya that some have community of wives and assign the children to different fathers on the basis of likeness.[52] Another African tribe of whom the same is said are the Garamantes;[53] it makes the single-minded devotion of Iarbas to Dido more poignant. Nicolaus of Damascus, contemporary of Augustus and friend of Herod the Great, is a good source of such stories. He tells, for example, that the Abii or Galactophagi, a Scythian tribe, have a great concern for justice, holding property and wives in common. They address their elders as father, their juniors as son and their contemporaries as brother.[54] The Liburnians too are said to have their wives in common and their children up to the age of five. In their sixth year the children congregate and are distributed to the men by likeness, being thereafter accounted sons by the men to whom they are allotted.[55] Another source is the Peripatetic Agatharchides, who tells of the Ichthyophagi (fish-eaters) that the men and women wear no clothes and the procreation of children is promiscuous. At periods of festivity the men lie with any women they happen to meet, and hold their women and children in common just like flocks and herds.[56] So too with the Hylophagi (tree-eaters),[57] and the Spermatophagi (seed-eaters).[58] The Trogodytes have a different pattern. They hold wives and children in common, except for the ruler's wife, who is sacrosanct, and reserve the name of parent not for any of their fellow humans, but for the animals who give them sustenance.[59] The Hyrcanians, according to Plutarch, learned marriage from Alexander; previously he implies that they practised some kind of group marriage or community of wives. One curious example comes from a late authority writing on the Hebrideans. He does not say that they practise conjugal communism as a people, but writes of their king: 'He has no wife of his own, but from time to time he takes to himself as a loan her towards whom he may be drawn. Hence he has neither the promise nor hope of children.'[60] There are even similar stories about more familiar peoples. For example, Xanthus records that the Magi hold their wives in common and have no objection to incest. There is no rape or stolen adultery, but if a woman is living with one man his agreement is secured before another takes her.[61] Theopompus tells us that the Etruscans hold their wives in common by law. These exercise together with the men, appear naked, sit at meals not next to their own husbands but where they will; they are hard drinkers and lovely to look at. All the children born are reared, but the fathers remain unknown.[62] Clearchus of Soli says that in the early days of Athens promiscuity was rife and marriage communal until Cecrops came and taught the principle of monogamy.[63] Varro adds that women in those days enjoyed equal status with men, and children were named after them.[64] Finally we may note that a late Greek inscription from Egypt, dating to the third century AD, attributes to Isis the invention of marriage, and suggests that the Egyptians regarded mankind as originally promiscuous.[65]

Happily we are not here concerned with the anthropological conclusions to be drawn from this evidence. Modern anthropologists deny an era of promiscuity in the history of human sexual relationships, and hence either deny the above statements or interpret them differently. Thus the statement about the Athenians may be a true reflection of what they themselves believed, but is unlikely to be historical. Varro's remark shows the clear link between children and mother, and if it reflects anything reflects a matriarchal society which by no means excludes marriage. The statement about the Galactophagi is loose: this can be paralleled from the Andaman islands, where within relatively recent times every woman belonged to every man in the tribe, and resistance to any of them was a crime severely punished. This appears to indicate promiscuity: in fact there was a succession of short monogamous conjugal unions extending until the child was weaned in each case of maternity. Happily too we need not embark on a full examination of non-classical examples, the Kourumbas and Iroulas, Zaporog Cossacks and Ansarians, Nairs and Teehurs, Kamilaroi and the rest, though it is worth comparing with Clearchus' statement the Chinese tradition that wives were held in common until the reign of Fouhi. The significant point is that, whether or not community of wives was at a certain stage and in certain places a historical fact, the ancient Greeks certainly believed that it was. They believed too that it was purposed to express the solidarity of the people concerned, to avoid hate and envy, and to realize the as yet inarticulate philosophical ideal of Concord. And, though community of children is not found as commonly as community of wives, they believed that too to have been practised. Furthermore, these tales are found before the formulation of similar philosophic principles: they are not the projection of these upon history but their predecessors, and in the current Greek belief about primitive tribes we see one source from which the idea may have entered into the mind of Plato, and a very potent and attractive source for those Cynics and Stoics who might find in such peoples an approximation to the life lived according to nature.

Finally, it is not to be expected that the idealization of primitive tribes will include much in the way of culture; the preoccupation of the Utopian philosophers with education is quite absent from these more popular writers. But there is some account of a natural talent for music. This is most marked among the Hyperboreans. So Pindar depicts them as they dance to the sound of flute and lyre, free from work and fighting.[66] Aelian gives an account of the Hyperborean devotion to Apollo, and the choir singing hymns with lyre accompaniment. It is here that the swans learn to sing in Apollo's praise.[67] Diodorus Siculus too speaks of the musical skill of the Hyperboreans.[68] There is something similar in Polybius' picture of the Arcadians.[69] Here are an idealized people, shepherds and acorn-eaters, pious and virtuous, who had escaped the evils of urbanization. Polybius says that music was with them an actual necessity, and that the boys were trained from their first lisping to sing hymns and paeans. The state fostered military music for parades, and at private entertainments the people made their own music and did not depend on hired professionals. This in Polybius' eyes was not a matter of luxurious living but a necessary alleviation of manual labour and a harsh climate.

The other cultural aspect which is emphasized is that of religion. Again the Hyperboreans, with their association with Apollo, spring to mind at once.[70] So too the Arcadians. They welcome men and welcome strangers, but their predominant characteristic is their piety and Polybius links their music with religious festivals and sacrificial duties.[71] The Ethiopians also were honoured for their piety, and were said to be the first to worship gods.[72] When Philo, a Hellenized Jew, portrays the Essenes, there is an element of the Hellenic idealization of simple people in his picture of their piety.[73] Other holy people include Herodotus' Argippaeans,[74] and Mela's Aremphaeans.[75]

It is important to see however that not all Greeks and Romans idealized the primitive. Thus Aeschylus' Prometheus claims that it was in pity for man's hard condition that he stole the fire which was the key to civilization;[76] and the *Protagoras* myth celebrates urbanism and political philosophy as the salvation of man.[77] The Hippocratic doctors speak of the progress achieved through scientific advance.[78] The Epicureans too saw the life of primal man as nasty, brutish and short, and only slowly emerging to civilization.[79] Cicero, despite his hostility to the Epicureans, shares their anti-primitivism.[80] An amusing passage from the comic dramatist Athenio plays on speculations of this sort; in his play the invention of cookery raises man above the beasts.[81] In this way we can see that the myth of the fall is balanced by a myth of progress. Not all savages were regarded as noble.

CHAPTER III

THE GREAT DEBATE

DREAMS MUST ALWAYS BE SEEN AGAINST THE BACKGROUND of reality. It is possible to give a generalized picture of political development in the Greek city-states, provided that it is realized that it *is* a generalized picture and one subject to infinite variations.[1] It is right to concentrate on the city-state (*polis*). The Greeks were also familiar with what they called the tribal state (*ethnos*), which survived in classical times in the western and central parts of Greece, where Mycenaean civilization was less strong, Aetolia, Acarnania, Elis, Arcadia, Locris, Achaea. Here settlement took the form of isolated farmsteads and villages. Any strongly centralized political organization fell away. Except in Macedon in the north, kingship was not even a memory, and there was no central *polis*. Elsewhere the Hellenic immigrants might take over a central citadel. Even so the diffusion was strong, and, as in Attica, there were traditions of *synoecism*, the drawing together of scattered villages into a single centralized city-state. On the coast of Asia Minor, faced with a potentially if not actually hostile population inland, the Greek settlers were virtually driven to a central fortified *polis*. The *polis* was the determinative factor in Greek history, and it affected the development of the *ethnos*.

The Hellenic kingship never had the rigid power that it possessed in the Mycenaean age. Indeed it is significant that the words for king, such as *basileus*, are of non-Greek derivation. We must remember that we are dealing originally with marauding tribes driven down from the Balkans. What they needed was a warlord, commander-in-chief in battle, but also priest and judge. We are not to think of him as ruling by arbitrary fiat. From the start there were three major factors in the constitution: first the warlord himself; second the Council of the Elders, the heads of the 'patrician' families; third the Assembly of the Army or People, free members of the tribe, whose acclamation was needed to establish the initial authority of the overlord and the subsequent acceptance of his policies. In this way the 'mixed' constitution was there from the start, and the participants in the great debate were already assembled. A substructure of slavery was at all times taken for granted.

The king then was an overlord among lords. The ruling class ruled by a combination of birth and economic power. They owned the land. They might breed horses; they were potent in war. Words which later become the terminology of ethical philosophy, in early times denote social effectiveness: such are *arete* ('virtue') or *agathos* ('good').[2] In Hesiod *arete* walks hand in hand with wealth;[3] in Tyrtaeus *agathos* means 'courageous in battle'.[4] Pindar, who reflects the values of a conservative aristocracy, continually insists on the importance of breed and wealth.[5] In contrast to these stand the toiling labourers, living close to the bone.

The talons of the overlord were soon clipped, or he himself was eliminated altogether. At Athens the name survived for a state official charged with the traditional cult practices; he also presided over murder trials. The title also survived in other Greek states, Elis,[6] for example, and Mytilene.[7] Aristotle comments on the general use of the word for a magistracy.[8] Over much of Greece the kingship was sunk without trace. In Sparta, military Sparta, the institution survived, hedged about with checks and balances, there being two kings to keep an eye on each other. But Sparta was by any standards a 'sport'.

The power in the hands of the nobles – whether a single clan like the Bacchiadae at Corinth, or a wider group like the Eupatridae at Athens – they did their best to hold it within their strictly limited group. Among themselves they fostered the catchword of equality. At Sparta the ruling class were known as the *Homoioi* ('equals'): in Homer the word had been used as a term of disapprobation for those forces, such as war, death, old age, which blot out the proper distinction between one man and another; now it is turned to a virtue. Similarly Herodotus in the fifth century speaks of the equality in power (*isokratia*) among the Corinthian oligarchs.[9] As their power was challenged, so the need for social solidarity became more self-conscious. This was the age of a great expansion in the words compounded with *syn* (with) and expressive of togetherness.[10] An exclusive ruling class then. It is important to see that the great conflicts to come between oligarchy and democracy were relative not absolute. They were about the right of more people to 'belong to the club', not about abolishing the club. This is why the aristocratic catchword of equality can be taken over by the democrats. It is not an assertion of the equality of all men, only of those knocking at the doors of power with those inside. Neither group would have dreamed of extending the equality to women, slaves or foreigners: that was left to a few Utopians.

The monolithic solidarity of the ruling class began to crack. Probably the main factors were economic. Already the state was divided between the large landowners and the smallholders, whose hardships are so eloquently described by the Boeotian poet Hesiod. On this situation supervened the expansion of industry, trade and transport. The combination of land hunger and trade development led to a wave of colonization. The immediate result of this was to give an outlet for political discontent. In the long term the wider contacts tended to loosen the old order, and economic developments led to an aristocracy of wealth secured from trade challenging the aristocracy of wealth based on land. Meantime discontent grew among those who were economically deprived and politically disfranchised.

The phenomenon known as tyranny or dictatorship,[11] which was widespread in the Greek world during the seventh and sixth centuries, is sometimes treated as a period of incipient democracy for which the extended ruling class were not ready. In one sense this is right: it was a period which paved the way for democracy. But negatively rather than positively: what power did the people have under the dictators? Plato in treating dictatorship as logically an outcome of democracy has effectively confused that issue.[12] The dictators contributed to the rise of democracy by weakening the power of the ruling class. They were not democrats, and they were not precipitated into power by a democratic uprising. They were disaffected aristocrats, who lacked a base for power in their own class and went outside it.

The dictatorships did not last long, for the most part not more than a generation and a half, before the oligarchy re-established itself. But from this point the pressures were continually felt towards the broadening of political power. Monarchy, so far as Greece was concerned, apart from remote Macedon and unique Sparta, was a thing of the past. Monarchy now conjured up the oriental rulers of Persia, and stood in sharp contrast, in the minds of Greeks, to their own institutions both as empire to city-state and as the autocracy of an individual to the corporate decision of the citizens whether few or many. But within Greece itself numbers of states saw a democratic revolution, and often a constitutional seesaw as the power fluctuated between the many and the few. The changes might be bloody. They are the theme of some of Thucydides' bitterest pages,[13] in which he suggests that the catchphrases, *isonomia* (equality under the law) for the democrats and *aristokratia* (government by the best) for the oligarchs, were specious covers for personal ambition.

There is thus a logical and generally chronological progression through Greek history from the power of the overlord, first to the power of the barons, then to the usurping of autocratic power by a disaffected member of the upper class, then to a restored but weakened oligarchy, to the extension of political power to the poorer citizens in a full democracy. Oligarchic constitutions were frequently characterized by the accession of power to a Council easily controlled by the ruling class, and the limitation of any real voice in politics to a small proportion of the citizens, usually on a property basis.[14] Sometimes, as at Massilia, the limitation was so severe that it is hard to tell the Council from the Assembly. In democracy the power lay with the Assembly.[15] The Council and magistrates, who at Athens were for the most part chosen by lot, were there to prepare the business for the Assembly and to fulfil their decisions. At the end of their term of office they were liable to indictment before the popular courts, which were again controlled by the people. The typical watchword of the oligarch was *eunomia*, good government; the democrat spoke of equality and freedom.

It is illuminating to watch the movement of political power at Athens in the three years from 413 to 410. The disaster to the Athenian expedition sent against Syracuse occasioned a political crisis. The majority of the citizens still believed in democracy, but were willing to concede the need for a small group to take prompt action, especially in securing aid from Persia. Ten elder statesmen were appointed with special powers, and their commission was expanded by the addition of twenty others over the age of forty. A small group of oligarchic conspirators by a packed meeting and a coup d'état now introduced a new constitution. The power was in the hands of a Council of 400; the real power lay with an inner cabinet of ten. An Assembly of 5,000 was chosen from the three upper property classes only: even so this was only about half of those eligible from these classes. It is doubtful whether the small group with whom the power lay ever intended this to be an effective body, but it formed a rallying point for a more moderate, but still anti-democratic opinion, represented by Theramenes. For nearly a year the 5,000 held the power. It was a compromise between oligarchy and democracy, and Thucydides regarded it as a successful compromise.[16] Aristotle also approved, implicitly and perhaps explicitly.[17] But at Samos the sailors' democracy remained triumphant, and their successes made possible the restoration of the democracy in 410.

The debate over the merits of different forms of government appears for the first time in writing in Herodotus, though Aeschylus' play *The Persians* draws a sharp comparison between the autocratic power of the Persian monarchy and the freedom of the Athenians.

ATOSSA: Who is their shepherd, their army's overlord?
CHORUS: They own themselves slaves and subjects to none.[18]

So when the news of Salamis arrives, one of the watchwords of democratic propaganda, freedom of speech, is ruefully wrung from the chorus.[19] Herodotus implausibly places his debate in Persia.[20] A usurper has been assassinated, and the conspirators have no fixed plans. They debate the merits and demerits of democracy, oligarchy and monarchy. Otanes speaks for the sovereignty of the commons (he does not use the word 'democracy'). Monarchy is subject to two defects. First the monarch is not answerable to anyone; second, he is bound to be corrupted by power. (Otanes sounds like Lord Acton.) Popular power means the allocation of office by lot, officials answerable to the people for their tenure of office, and political decisions taken by the whole people. It has a glorious name – equality before the law (*isonomia*). Megabyzus agrees with the critique of autocracy, but argues that the people also act with irresponsible violence, and they are ill-educated and ill-informed; democracy is one stage worse than dictatorship. The answer is government by the educated few; the fruits of it good counsel (*euboulia*: not essentially different from *eunomia*, but used here because the oligarchs favoured the Council or *boule*). Darius finally argues for monarchy. He claims that it is right to take each of the forms of government at its best: in this way he foreshadows the later analysis of constitutions into six, the good forms monarchy, aristocracy, democracy, the bad forms tyranny, oligarchy, ochlocracy. The best individual is the best possible ruler; there can be only one best. Further, he is the most effective in practice; either of the other forms will sooner or later degenerate into chaos, and an individual be called in to set matters right. It is of course quite impossible that such a debate took place in Persia in 522 BC; it represents the current controversies of 450 or thereabouts, and no one knows precisely what was Herodotus' source.

For a second contrast let us take two views of Athenian democracy. The first comes from the anonymous author we know as the Old Oligarch, a work of uncertain date.[21] It is a writing heavily slanted in terms of the language used. Those who take the oligarchic view are rich, noble and respectable; they are 'the best'. The commons, the democracy, are called the worst elements, the lower classes, the rabble, the mob. The writer takes it for granted that the essential division in society is between the rich and the poor, and that it is entirely natural for the group in power to follow their own self-interest. (Aristotle similarly is inclined to think that government by a rich majority would still be oligarchy.[22]) From this he deduces freedom of speech, lawlessness, the rejection of tradition, the oppression of the allies and especially of their upper classes, litigation and shifts of policy. By contrast an aristocracy will stand for the authority of law. But he grudgingly admits that not many have, in fact, suffered unjustly under the democracy.

For a defence of democracy we may look at the Funeral Speech attributed to Pericles by Thucydides.[23] Athens is a democracy because the power is with the many not the few. This gives equality under the law, together with acknowledgement of individual merit. The keynote of society is freedom, but freedom within the law. Pericles emphasizes the rule of law, including protection for the oppressed, and the existence of moral sanctions as well as legal control. There is leisure, openness, an absence of militarism, an encouragement of culture. The stress of the speech is that the freedom of the individual to run his own life leads to the greatest degree of communal happiness, provided that there is the overriding power of the law. It should be remembered that there were those who saw in Periclean Athens a mixed constitution. It was constitutionally without doubt a radical democracy, but there were those to denounce Pericles as an autocrat, and others to say that he guided the workings of the constitution so that the real aristocrats maintained their influence.[24]

Complementary to this is a speech attributed to a Syracusan democrat named Athenagoras.[25] He sees danger to democracy from rich young men who object to *isonomia*, that is to say who object to being placed on the same legal footing as others, and who want to attain exclusive power, and that at an age before the constitution entitles them to hold any power at all. They claim that democracy puts no premium on intelligence. They even turn the democrats' catchphrases against them. Democracy does not mean real equality, which would not be identity of treatment but that appropriate for each individual; and they claim that the propertied classes have experience, education, judgement and are best equipped to rule. Athenagoras answers that democracy alone makes appropriate use of all its citizens. The propertied classes may well be best for the protection of property; their qualifications extend so far and no further. The intellectuals may well be the best at preparing the business and executing the decisions, even on advising about them; the speaker pointedly distinguishes them from the property-owners. The people are the best at listening to the arguments and coming to the decisions. Athenagoras' arguments are valid against a famous simile of Plato's, the ship of state. Plato argues by analogy from the ship's captain that politics is an expert job to be left to the experts. But the passengers, not the captain, decide on the destination; the destination once fixed, there is room for expertise in getting there, and the passengers have no further say.[26] Athenagoras claims that democracy is comprehensive, oligarchy exclusive.

Two more fragments of the great debate may here be mentioned.[27] One is indeed a fragment only, in dialogue form, criticizing the view that oratorical skill is more important under democracy than under oligarchy. Plainly it comes from some discussion of the detailed merits of different constitutions. A summary of a similar discussion is attributed not very plausibly by Xenophon to Socrates.[28] It is a *pericope* with no connection with its surroundings, and it is impossible to say where he found it. It consists of the definition of five forms of government. Monarchy is the rule of one man, constitutionally and by consent. Tyranny or dictatorship is the rule of one man, unconstitutionally and without consent. Aristocracy is when political office falls to those who perform the duties prescribed by tradition. Plutocracy is when political office falls to the wealthy. Democracy is when political office is open to all.

In all this we see a ferment of discussion. Which is the best constitution of all? This was the question the Utopians set out to answer.

CHAPTER IV

THE MIRAGE OF SPARTA[1]

THE MODERN CHILD engages in play warfare between Goodies and Baddies, and
for those who encounter the study of ancient history before they have shaken
off this approach, look at things through the eyes of literate Athenians, and
write off the Spartans as Baddies, it is nearly always a salutary shock to find
the philosophers uniting in a paean of praise for the Spartan constitution.[2] It
starts perhaps with the Pythagoreans, though the evidence is shaky.[3] It is certainly there in Socrates. 'Before you founded your city,' says the herald to
Peisthetaerus in Aristophanes' play, 'everyone was Sparta-mad – long hair,
empty bellies, grubby, Socratizing, staff in hand.'[4] The association of Socrates
with Sparta was politically significant. He was known to be unsympathetic to
the democracy, and Aeschines says that this was the reason for his execution.[5]
Socrates had in a marked degree the power of being all things to all men, but it
is noteworthy that of those whose names are linked with his, Alcibiades went
over to Sparta for a period, Critias wrote of Sparta as the ideal commonwealth,
Xenophon retired there, Antisthenes showed some admiration of the Spartans,
and Plato's ideal commonwealth evinced some affinities with Sparta. Of the
later thinkers Aristotle, who has trenchant criticisms of some aspects of the
Spartan system, shows general approval, and the Stoics are emphatic in their
praise.

What attracted them was the massive stability of the thing, a stability which
made the break-up all the more dramatic when it eventually came.[6] Elizabeth
Rawson puts it well, though she is thinking primarily of later Utopias. 'But
there can be little doubt that she (Sparta) contributed to the authority of such
ideas as those of state restriction of, or control over, private property, the use of
money, industry, commerce and foreign contacts; a measure of equality
between the sexes, with the regulation of sex and marriage in the service of the
community, particularly by the laying down of minimum ages higher than
was usual; public and primarily moral education, common meals, and simple
uniform clothing – especially the restriction of the young to a single garment;
regulations against luxury in building . . .; the insistence on few and simple
laws . . .; and the tendency to make the imaginary state a republic headed by
variously elected magistrates and councils with members of great age and
experience; to make it, too, . . . a city-state with a small territory . . .; and lastly,
the view that susceptibility to change was a mark of imperfection.'[7]

Toynbee classified Sparta as an 'arrested civilization'.[8] He compared it with the Ottoman system of the Osmanlis. There the ruling institution comprised the Sultan and his family, his household officers, the executive, and the military together with trainees for these duties. The curious feature of the régime was that the free-born Ottoman aristocracy were not permitted to participate in the power or the tasks of government. The governing power rested with the Sultan's slaves, many of whom were the children of Christian homes, all of whom were wrested from their family, deprived of the ties of kin and property, and educated under rigid discipline for the responsibilities of office. For centuries the system worked and it collapsed only when the principle of exclusiveness was broken, all demanded the privileges and power and pressed into the Janissaries. As long as the system was rigid it succeeded. When circumstances changed its rigidity proved its downfall.

The parallels with Sparta are obvious – 'caste and specialization' says Toynbee, and elaborates the latter to include supervision, selection, specialization and the competitive spirit. He quotes an interesting parallel between a remark by Busbecq on the Turks and one by Plutarch on the Spartans. Busbecq, who was Habsburg ambassador to Suleiman the Magnificent, wrote in 1633: 'I have envied the Turks this system of theirs. It is always the way of the Turks whenever they come into possession of a man of uncommonly good parts, to rejoice and be exceedingly glad, as though they had found a pearl of great price. And, in bringing out all that there is in him, they leave nothing undone that labour and thought can do – especially where they recognize military aptitude. Our Western way is different indeed! In the West, if we come into possession of a good dog or hawk or horse, we are delighted, and we spare nothing in our efforts to bring the creature to the highest perfection of which its kind is capable. In the case of a man, however – supposing that we happen to come upon a man of signal endowments – we do not take anything like the same pains, and we do not consider that his education is particularly our business. So we Westerners obtain many sorts of pleasure and service from a well broken-in horse, dog and hawk, while the Turks obtain from a man whose character has been cultivated by education the vastly greater return that is afforded by the vast superiority and pre-eminence of human nature over the rest of the animal kingdom.' Compare with this Plutarch's remarks on Spartan eugenics 1500 years earlier. 'They saw nothing but vulgarity and vanity in the sexual conventions of the rest of mankind, who take care to serve their bitches and their mares with the best sires that they can manage to borrow or hire, yet lock their women up and keep them under watch and ward in order to make sure that they shall bear children exclusively to their husbands – as though this were a husband's sacred right even if he happens to be feeble-minded or senile or diseased.'[9]

Up to the end of the seventh century Sparta followed the typical Greek development. The 'arrested' constitution shows elements of kingship, oligarchy and democracy, with the result that though it was in effect quite certainly oligarchic, the philosophers have some difficulty in classifying it precisely.

Aristotle calls it 'a happy mixture of democracy and oligarchy',[10] and Plato havers between terming it democracy and tyranny.[11] It was in fact arrested at the point where the oligarchic challenge to the kings had become effective, but democracy has made only limited advances. Spartan art tells the same story of normal development followed by a sudden halt. Work of unusual quality in the pre-classical period is followed by – nothing. The first half of the sixth century shows Sparta exporting pottery to all parts of the Mediterranean. By the end of the century the stream had dried up.[12] Any imports of luxury quality had ceased well before this. The new temple of Orthia did not contain the 'plentiful purple, speckled snake of gold and Lydian wimple' of which Alcman wrote so eloquently.[13] The broad historical reasons for the change are not difficult to see. Sparta was the only major Greek city not intimately associated with the sea. When in the crises of the eighth century the other states sent out maritime colonizing expeditions, Sparta appeased her land hunger by successful aggression against her land neighbours in Messenia. This alone did not divert her from her normal development, but a century later a Messenian independence movement tried to achieve freedom by force. They were crushed, but the danger to Sparta had been great, and fear of its recurrence gradually transformed her from a typically Greek extrovert to a pathological introvert.

The precise story of the change remains unsolved. It is by tradition associated with the name of a single statesman of genius, Lycurgus, but sceptics have been found to doubt his very existence and to pass him off as one of the gods of the country – not without reason.[14] As Plutarch justly says: 'There is so much uncertainty in the accounts which historians have left us of Lycurgus, the lawgiver of Sparta, that scarcely anything is asserted by one of them which is not called into question or contradicted by the rest. Their sentiments are quite different as to the family he came of, the voyages he undertook, the place and manner of his death, but most of all when they speak of the land he made and the commonwealth which he founded. They cannot by any means be brought to an agreement as to the very age in which he lived.'[15] There may have been a pioneering statesman called Lycurgus. The commonest of the traditional dates, early in the eighth century,[16] is quite impossible for the fully-fledged constitution attributed to him. Andrewes goes so far as to say that the perpetuation of his name is 'one of the most successful frauds of history'. For some time there was a tendency, based on the archaeological evidence of a continuance of culture well into the sixth century, to place the reforms late, and even to associate them with the name of Chilon. It is hard, however, to see, if they were truly his, why they did not remain associated with his name. More recent opinion fastens the essential transformation on to the reorganization of the Carneian Games in 676; this is as likely as any suggestion.[17] There may possibly have been a human of the name of Lycurgus who inaugurated the changes. The transformation was not sudden, immediate and absolute, but gradual.

The characteristics of the system as it impinged upon the imagination of the rest of Greece were political, economic, social and educational. At the head politically stood two kings. This dyarchy, though not unique, was unusual; it most probably arose from the fusion of two tribal groups into a single unity without either surrendering its sovereignty.[18] The kings' position was somewhere between that of a modern constitutional monarch and a modern prime minister. Their prestige was tremendous and the institution itself was never seriously attacked, and they enjoyed besides a certain mystical aura of sanctity. Their powers were however carefully circumscribed. They were field marshals in war, though the rule was eventually established that each should be in sole command of separate forces, not joint command of a single army.[19] In peace their power was less; they were *ex officio* members of the senate with normal powers of speaking and voting. They may also have had the right to propose legislation but Agis IV at least chose not to use it for his attempted revolution. They were sworn to uphold the constitution and liable to deposition by the ephors if they failed.

The senate was a typically aristocratic organ. It comprised the two kings and twenty-eight others who were elected by popular acclamation from among those who had attained the age of sixty.[20] The number twenty-eight has never been convincingly explained; it is enough to note that number-magic has its place among the later writers of Utopias, and that it is possible that the classical scheme was a modification of an earlier scheme associated with the numbers 3 and 27.[21] Aristotle seems to say that only καλοὶ κάγαθοί were elected to the senate.[22] This might be taken to indicate an aristocracy within the aristocracy, but there is no sign of any constitutional limitation on candidature, and he may only mean that in practice representatives of a small number of families tended to be elected (Rome suggests an immediate parallel); perhaps no more than that election was a reward for outstanding quality and service. They were responsible for legislation, though it did not become valid until it was ratified by the popular assembly; they also provided the court of criminal jurisdiction, and were in general the executive arm of government. In the classical period election to the senate was for life. Curiously, although the theorists treat the senate as the place of effective power,[23] it plays small part in the historical record.

The Assembly, except in its elective powers, was not markedly different from the Homeric assembly.[24] Membership was open to all citizens who had reached the age of twenty, except that they might be excluded if they were not of good standing; this no doubt includes a failure to match up to the rigorous training, and offences such as cowardice in battle. The people met in the open air. They 'had no right to propose any subject to debate, and were only authorised to ratify or reject what might be proposed to them by the senate or kings. But because in process of time the people, by additions or excisions, changed the terms and distorted the sense of the bills, the kings Polydorus and Theopompus inserted in the constitution this clause: "That if the people decide crookedly it shall be lawful to the authorities to prorogue the Assembly", that is to say refuse ratification of its will and dismiss the people as depravers and perverters of their counsel.'[25] Debates were normally initiated by the kings, ephors or senators. Plutarch's exact meaning has been much disputed; there are examples of individuals putting proposals without prior government support, but it is not clear that they were not senators.[26] The certain rights are well summarized by Michell. 'The *Ecclesia* decided on questions of peace or war and foreign policy. It appointed the generals and elected the gerontes, decided claims to the throne and voted on proposed laws. It also freed such helots as had displayed conspicuous valour in battle.'[27]

All this is fairly commonplace. Alongside these normal institutions, however, there was the ephorate, a committee of five in whom the real power of the state was vested. Their origin is wrapped in obscurity. They are not mentioned in the seventh-century poet Tyrtaeus:

> Phoebus Apollo's the mandate was which they brought from Pytho
>   Voicing the will of the god, nor were his words unfulfilled;
> Sway in the council and honours divine belong to the princes
>   Under whose care has been set Sparta's city of charm;
> Second to them are the elders, and next come the men of the people
>   Duly confirming by vote unperverted decrees.[28]

Nor, surprisingly, do they appear in Plutarch's *Lycurgus*. Broadly speaking, there have been three theories of the origin of the ephorate.[29] They have been supposed by some an ancient priestly college which came slowly to political power. Others have suggested, on the basis of a passage in Plutarch,[30] that they were originally a creation of the kings, chosen to perform civil and judicial functions when the kings were on military campaign, and that they later came to usurp and challenge the power of the kings. This is the least likely view, since it appears in a politically biased context. The third view associates them with the five divisions (*obes*) of Sparta, perhaps as divisional chiefs, perhaps as their deputies. We must frankly say that we have not the means of deciding; all the theories are speculative and the truth may be quite different. Certainly in historical times they acted as a check on the kings. In classical times the ephors were elected annually by the whole people and are in no sense tribal representatives. Their powers of oversight were considerable. They summoned and presided over both senate and assembly.[31] They were responsible for public finance.[32] They were responsible for education.[33] They had charge of the secret police.[34] They controlled the magistrates: 'they have power also to degrade magistrates, even while they are in office, to put them in prison and bring them to trial for their life.'[35] They do not seem to have normally exercised powers of punishment beyond fining, but these were fairly wide; they are recorded as fining a man for being unpopular.[36] Their initial injunction to the people at large upon entering office was to shave their moustaches and keep the laws;[37] the first part is no doubt a relic of some forgotten religious ritual. They could depose the kings for unconstitutional action, and any except the strongest-minded kings must have been tempted to a simple acceptance of the ephors' will. They had less direct authority in foreign policy, but in time of war they were responsible for mobilizing troops, and the military commanders were answerable to them.[38]

The apparent evidence is that Sparta enjoyed a 'mixed' constitution, and Cicero used the word.[39] In fact the admixture of democracy was somewhat illusory. In the first place the effective powers of the people were confined to elections and the right of rejecting unpalatable legislation. There is, so far as I can see, no evidence that the ephors represented a check on behalf of the commons upon the senatorial oligarchy; they are represented as challenging the power of the kings, not the aristocrats; they were themselves, so to speak, oligarchs not democrats. In this they differ *toto caelo* from the 'tyrants' whose rise we have already briefly noted. A curious reference in Xenophon, which has never been adequately explained, to a 'Little Assembly', may in fact mean that the real power lay with an inner 'cabinet' of kings, ephors, senators and a small number of influential citizens.[40] Secondly, even theoretically, political power did not extend beyond the citizenry. Residents without citizenship, whether slave or free, had no political rights. This was true of all Greek states; it has been well said that even the democracy at Athens was only an extended oligarchy. It was true in an exaggerated degree at Sparta, owing to the restricted number of citizens. How restricted this was remains a matter of some dispute. The evidence is, however, easily presented. Aristotle tells us, with some vagueness, that the number of citizens had declined from an original 10,000.[41] Plutarch attributes to Lycurgus the figure of 9,000 citizens.[42] Miss Chrimes tries to juggle with the figure 9 to reduce this to 6,561 or 9 to the fourth,[43] but it is unlikely that either figure is soundly enough based to allow deductions to be made from it. Our next clear evidence is from Herodotus, who gives the figure of 8,000 Spartan citizens at the time of Xerxes' invasion,[44] and 5,000 in the army at Plataea.[45] Herodotus, however admirable in other respects, is not notable for numerical accuracy, and the numbers may be exaggerated. At Mantinea in 418 and Corinth in 394 the numbers were nearer 3,000,[46] and by Leuctra in 371 the total number of Spartan citizens of military age seems to have dropped to under 1,200.[47] Isocrates in 342 suggests that even in early times the citizens did not exceed 2,000 and contrasts Sparta with cities of 10,000 population.[48] Finally, Aristotle gives the figure for his own day as under 1,000.[49] Various attempts to explain or adjust these figures have been made. For our purpose it is enough to observe two facts. First, whatever the original figure, in the classical period the citizen population of Sparta was small by comparison with other Greek states. Even the small community of Phlius could boast a citizenry of 5,000 at a time when exiled citizens numbered at least 1,000.[50] At Athens the figure of 43,000 for enfranchised citizens, of whom about a third lived in the city, has been suggested for the beginning of the Peloponnesian War. Whatever the precise figures, the discrepancy between Athens and Sparta is startling. Secondly, the whole tendency of the figures is to show a steady process of decline. This is natural. Apart from any other factor, recurrent wars must have exhausted the numbers of this military élite, and the indication is that they closed their ranks in pride rather than recruit from outside. The Spartan citizens were proud of their position as Peers or *Homoioi*. The qualifications were birth, successful passage through the educational and disciplinary system,[51] and continuing behaviour worthy of a Spartan and a gentleman. In addition he was expected to be a member of a common mess. In Xenophon's time financial difficulty did not debar from full citizen rights;[52] the closing of the ranks can be seen by the fact that in Aristotle's time it did, and failure to pay the mess subscription resulted in political disfranchisement.[53] Politically we are bound to conclude that Sparta was a narrow oligarchy in which the effective power rested with an even narrower oligarchy.

The economic regulations of Sparta raise no fewer problems. The picture given by Plutarch is a familiar one. Lycurgus finding 'a prodigious inequality, the city overcharged with many indigent persons, who had no land, and the wealth centred in the hands of a few' and 'determined to root out the evils of insolence, envy, avarice and luxury, and those distempers of a state which are still more inveterate and fatal, namely poverty and riches' made a completely new and equitable division of the land, so that each had enough and no one had excess. Alongside this he abolished gold and silver coinage, and substituted a coinage of iron bars. This cut at the roots of financial corruption and luxury; it also had the effect of cutting off trade with other countries. None of the alleged enactments of Lycurgus is as famous as this. Yet the evidence of archaeology shows that gold and silver coins of other states circulated freely in Sparta throughout the classical period, and literary evidence tells of Spartans of exceptional wealth[54] and even specifically alludes to the accumulation of gold and silver.[55] Plutarch tells us that Lysander deposited a talent and fifty-two minae, as well as eleven staters in the treasury of the Acanthians at Delphi, commenting that this is not easy to reconcile with the legend that he was a poor man.[56] It seems probable that the Spartans did retain a kind of exchange-medium in the form of iron bars or lumps, though none has for certain been found,[57] long after such methods had ceased to be used elsewhere. It also seems clear that though they permitted the accumulation of foreign coinage they did not mint their own coins until the third century. Finally there was some discouragement of foreign imports from the sixth century, whether by deliberate policy or as an indirect result of the archaic currency.

Socially, among much that is of interest we may single out three points for special mention. First there was a certain exclusiveness, represented by a policy of deportations (xenelasiai). The extent of this was exaggerated even in ancient times, as our own contemporaries exaggerate it in reference to some West African states. It remains true, as Müller put it, that 'the whole life of the Lacedaemonian community had a secluded, impenetrable, and secret character.' There are one or two examples, though not many, of foreigners being given Spartan citizenship, Tisamenus and Hegias of Elis, Tyrtaeus of Athens and Dion of Syracuse, while Hecataeus received messing rights.[58] We know of the appointment of consuls or proxenoi who looked after the interests of foreign visitors.[59] We have many references to the hospitality of the Spartans at festival times.[60] Despite all this it is clear that there was some restrictiveness. Pericles' celebrated words are directed against the Spartans: 'Our military training too is different from our opponents. The gates of our city are flung open to the world. We practise no periodical deportations, nor do we prevent our visitors from observing or discovering what an enemy might usefully apply to his own purposes. For our trust is not in the devices of material equipment, but in our own good spirits for battle.'[61] There are many references to these deportations which struck the imagination of the rest of the Greek world.[62] They were sometimes directed against individuals, sometimes general. Various reasons are given. The origin of the practice is of course attributed to Lycurgus, who opposed any novelty which might break the stability of the existing order; this is significant in later thought.[63] Xenophon upholds the view, and sees Lycurgus as seeking to avoid love of money and love of power which would ensue from foreign contacts.[64] At other times the justification was military security, and once even famine. Whatever the motive, the fact remains. It was combined with an attempt to prevent the citizenry from travel abroad. It contributed to the general stability, and to the appalling corruption which took place when temptation occurred. It contributed to the doctrine of the closed society which afflicted most of the later Utopian writers.

Secondly, internal unity was fostered, as has already been indicated, by a policy of communal messes. These were military in organization, and each contained about fifteen members.[65] Juniors, after a period in what we may call youth clubs, became eligible at the age of twenty. The fellowship of each mess or club was carefully preserved, and one 'blackball' was enough to prevent election.[66] Members paid a subscription of ten Aeginetan obols each month towards the cost of the food, as well as a contribution in kind. Attendance was compulsory, more rigidly than in any Rotary Club. Dicaearchus gives a vivid account of the meal: 'The dinner is at first served separately to each member, and there is no sharing of any kind with one's neighbour. Afterwards there is a barley-cake as large as each desires, and for drinking, again, a cup is set beside him to use whenever he is thirsty. The same meat dish is given to all on every occasion, a piece of boiled pork; sometimes, however, not even so much as that is served, beyond a small bit of meat weighing not over a quarter of a pound. Besides this there is nothing whatsoever, except, of course, the broth made from this meat, enough to go round among the entire company throughout the whole dinner; there may possibly be an olive or a cheese or a fig, or they may even get something especially added, a fish or a hare or a ring-dove or something similar. Afterwards, when they have finished their dinner in haste, there are passed round these so-called *epaikla*.'[67] These last are home-made dishes contributed by the members. We can recapture something of the atmosphere, merriment without insobriety, fluent conversation despite the laconic reputation of the Spartans,[68] friendly banter.[69] The motive behind it was partly to preserve at all times the sense of the citizens being an army, partly to develop fellowship through the basic sacrament of a common meal, partly to establish a norm of diet which should be adequate but not luxurious.

Thirdly, we must examine the position of women. 'At no time in the world's history,' wrote Seltman 'can women have been so contented, so healthy, and so happy as they were in ancient Sparta.'[70] They had much more freedom than over most of the Greek world, and Sparta was unusual in that marriage originated in love instead of being a family arrangement. The girls lived at home, but their lives were not centred on the home. They did not learn the traditional home arts of spinning and weaving. 'Instead of wool-work the girls participate in mental and physical training, completing the weaving of a life of discipline, difficulty and worth. They do not actually take part in military service, but they come half way along the path of domestic science and maternal and child welfare.'[71] Instead they were directed to the outdoor life and organized in packs like the boys.[72] They were full of free and lively banter, both of themselves[73] and of the boys.[74] The girls too were trained in athletics, and Seltman, following Simone de Beauvoir, has suggested that this delayed the attainment of puberty, and explains the fact that Spartan brides were nearer twenty than ten.[75] They were at all times loosely and lightly clad, and exercised naked.[76] This shocked the Athenians,[77] but, as Plutarch hastily adds, 'there was nothing disgraceful in it, because everything was conducted with modesty and without one indecent word or action.' Their beauty was proverbial.[78] So was their toughness.

> Lampito, my sweet! Delighted to see you, darling,
> How pretty you look! How healthy you Spartans are!
> And my, what biceps! I believe you could throttle a bull.[79]

Marriage, with relics of a ritual of violence, was in fact by consent and began in clandestine intercourse, perhaps as a sort of trial marriage.[80] The ties of marriage were firm but not possessive; indeed the Lycurgan laws were designed to banish such jealousy and possessiveness. Consequently there was developed a practice of wife-sharing by mutual consent of the three individuals,[81] and there is some evidence of polyandry;[82] the one recorded case of polygamy is explicitly said to be exceptional.[83] There is no doubt that the general effect of the Spartan attitude to women was to give them much more power, to create a type of strong beauty of rare quality, and to encourage confidence and companionship between man and woman to a degree rare in Greece.

Finally we turn to Spartan education. 'In a Doric state,' said Müller, 'education was, on the whole, a matter of more importance than government.' If we may accept Plutarch, the children at birth were inspected by a committee of senior citizens, and if they showed signs of unhealthiness or deformity, were left to die.[84] From the first they were intelligently brought up, without mollycoddling, and Spartan nurses were in some demand in the rest of Greece. For six years the boy grew up in the home. Then he was sent to a preparatory boarding school for six years. Education in a serious sense did not begin till he was ten; for the rest he was no doubt under a physical discipline that was half play and engaged in the rudiments of elementary learning. He then had six years of what we might call secondary education, and six years as an *eiren* or cadet, at the end of which he was regarded as qualified, and was accepted as a full soldier and held under military discipline until the age of sixty. The content of this education is not wholly clear. Despite the evidence of Isocrates to the contrary, they learned enough reading and writing for practical purposes.[85] They did not, beyond this, engage in book-learning, despite an interest in history, and mathematics had no appeal for them.[86] Music and dancing were highly cultivated, and Pratinas suggests that of all the Greeks the Spartans had most faithfully preserved the art of music; they enjoyed it as a relaxation from the austerity of life.[87] Musical competitions begin at the age of ten, probably in the form of choral singing. But most of the education was directed to training for military service. Apart from the normal athletics (the Spartans, curiously, refused to take part in boxing), they had two famous games, one an annual fight for the possession of an island, the other a ball-game in which the side in possession of the ball when time was called won. It is interesting to note that very similar methods were used for training Commandos in toughness. The celebrated flogging-matches at the altar of Artemis Orthia date in their most sadistic form from Roman times.[88] But flogging of the boys in classical times was a recognized punishment for quite trivial offences, though it was kept within bounds. Part of the training was under what we would today call 'Outward Bound' conditions; the boy was sent far into the country to forage for himself. Michell has reasonably suggested that this is the origin of the training in stealing which shocked the rest of the Greeks.[89] Alongside this training in physical toughness went a training in general discipline. When quite young the boys were admitted to the senior messes in order to listen and learn from the way their elders conversed.[90] In their own messes conversation was disciplined and they were punished for failure to converse properly. Each boy was under the supervision of a slightly older tutor, a system which inevitably led to homosexual attachments, though these too were under discipline and any manifestation of sensuality was severely punished.[91] Throughout, a demure behaviour in the presence of elders was expected and respect for seniority was as rigidly inculcated as in any West African tribe. The whole system is well summed up by Michell. 'The system was a hard one, in some ways an extraordinary one, and if carried out to its logical extremity an impossible one in which the wastage must have been high. If a boy went through it he emerged into manhood mentally and physically tough and hardened, an automaton trained to obey orders, taciturn with a "laconic" brevity of speech, a first-class fighting man but nothing more.'[92]

In summary we may quote Pater's words. They are steeped in romanticism, but we are apt to forget that the Greeks themselves viewed Sparta with romancing eyes:

'What, it has been asked, what was there to occupy persons of the privileged class in Lacedaemon from morning to night, thus cut off as they were from politics and business, and many of the common interests of men's lives? Our Platonic visitor would have asked rather, why this strenuous task-work, day after day; why this loyalty to a system, so costly to you individually, though it may be thought to have survived its original purpose; this laborious, endless, education which does not propose to give you anything very useful or enjoyable in itself? An intelligent young Spartan might have replied: "To the end that I

myself may be a perfect work of art, issuing thus into the eyes of all Greece."
He might have observed – we may safely observe for him – that the institutions
of his country, whose he was, had a beauty in themselves, as we may observe
also of some at least of our own institutions, educational or religious: that they
bring out, for instance, the lights and shadows of human character, and relieve
the present by maintaining in it an ideal sense of the past. He might have added
that he had friendships to solace him; and to encourage him, the sense of
honour.

'Honour, friendship, loyalty to the ideal of the past, himself as a work of art!
There was much of course in his answer. Yet still, after all, to understand, to be
capable of such motives, was itself but the result of that exacting discipline of
character we are trying to account for; and the question still recurs, *to what purpose*? Why, with no prospect of Israel's reward, are you as scrupulous, minute,
self-taxing as he? A tincture of asceticism in the Lacedaemonian rule may
remind us again of the monasticism of the Middle Ages. But then, monastic
severity was for the purging of a troubled conscience, or for the hope of an
immense prize, neither of which conditions is to be supposed here. In fact the
surprise of Saint Paul, as a practical man, at the slightness of the reward for
which a Greek spent himself, natural as it is about all pagan perfection, is
especially applicable about these Lacedaemonians, who indeed had actually
invented that so "corruptible" and essentially worthless parsley crown in place
of the more tangible prizes of an earlier age. Strange people! Where, precisely,
may be the spring of action in you, who are so severe to yourselves; you who,
in the words of Plato's supposed objector that the rulers of the ideal state are not
to be envied, have nothing you can really call your own, but are like hired
servants in your own houses, – *qui manducatis panem doloris*?

'Another day-dream, you may say, about those obscure ancient people, it
was ever so difficult really to know, who had hidden their actual life with so
much success; but certainly a quite natural dream upon the paradoxical things
we are told of them, on good authority. It is because they make us ask that
question; puzzle us by a paradoxical idealism in life; are thus distinguished from
their neighbours; that, like some of our old English places of education, though
we might not care to live always at school there, it is good to visit them on
occasion; as some philosophic Athenians, as we have now seen, loved to do, at
least in thought.'[93]

CHAPTER V

FROM PHILOSOPHIC POLITICIANS TO POLITICAL PHILOSOPHERS

LEADING POLITICIANS who have made a reputation in fields of more abstract thought and achievement are not unknown in the hurly-burly of modern existence. Paderewski was a musical genius who became the first prime minister of his country. In England various names come to mind – Gladstone, whose contributions to Homeric studies were favourably reassessed by Sir John Myres in his posthumous book, Balfour whose *Defence of Philosophic Doubt* was written at the beginning of his political career, *Foundations of Belief* in the middle, and *Theism and Thought* toward the end, Samuel who succeeded Balfour as president of the Institute of Philosophy and whom Einstein once described as 'a doctor of the soul'. In an age when politics was far less professionalized than during the last century, and philosophy as an abstract study was still embryonic, it is natural to find politics and philosophy going hand in hand.

Later Greeks spoke of their Seven traditional Sages, though exactly who they were is another matter. That uncritical gossiping chronicler Diogenes Laertius writes: 'The following were generally regarded as sages: Thales, Solon, Periander, Cleobulus, Chilon, Bias, Pittacus. To these are added the names of Anacharsis from Scythia, Myson from Chen, Pherecydes from Syrus and Epimenides from Crete. There are those who would also add the dictator Pisistratus. So much on the Sages.'[1] The Christian philosopher Clement of Alexandria gives a similar list. He does not mention Pisistratus but includes Acusilaus of Argos.[2] Our earliest example of these lists is a passage in Plato. Socrates is speaking, somewhat whimsically: 'Now there are some, both at the present day and in the past, who have tumbled to this fact, namely that to be Spartan implies a taste for intellectual rather than physical exercise, for they realize that to frame such utterances is a mark of the highest culture. Of these were Thales of Miletus, Pittacus of Mytilene, Bias of Priene, our own Solon, Cleobulus of Lindus and Myson of Chen, and the seventh of their company, we are told, was a Spartan, Chilon. All these were emulators, admirers and disciples of Spartan culture, and their wisdom may be recognized as belonging to the same category, consisting of pithy and memorable dicta uttered by each. Moreover they met together and dedicated the first fruits of their wisdom to Apollo in his temple at Delphi, inscribing those words which are on everyone's lips: "Know thyself" and "Nothing too much".'[3] The most interesting thing in this passage is the omission of Periander, who must have appeared in the tradition. Plato refuses to attribute sagacity to a dictator;[4] Cleobulus may also have been a dictator, but Plato does not mention him again and perhaps knows little about him.[5]

Three things strike us in these traditions about the Seven Sages.[6] First, so far as we can tell they all lived in the period round about 600 BC and the years immediately following. That is to say, they belonged to the period which has been called the Ionian Enlightenment. They stand at the beginning of the period in which philosophers on the one hand and statesmen on the other become known to us as definite personalities with definite, if disputed, policies. Secondly, the majority of them are known to us principally as politicians: this is obvious with Solon, Pittacus, Periander and Pisistratus. But even Thales, who is the only one of the whole list who has much place in the histories of philosophy, and who despite modern scepticism about the origins of Greek philosophical thought in general and the testimony of Aristotle in particular is still recognized as giving a new direction to man's thinking,[7] even Thales is said to have advocated a federal union of Greek states in Ionia, with their parliament at Teos.[8] Thirdly, the wisdom of these sages was gnomic-epigrammatical – not systematic. An epigram of Ausonius illustrates this conveniently:

Septenis patriam sapientum nomina voces
versibus expediam; sua quemque monosticha dicent.
Chilo cui patria est Lacedaemon, *Noscere se ipsum.*
Periander *trepidam moderare* Corinthius *iram.*
Ex Mytilenaeis *Nimium nil* Pittacus oris.
Mensuram optimam ait Cleobulus Lindius *in re.*
Exspectare Solon *finem* docet, ortus Athenis.
Plures esse Bias *pravos* quem clara Priene.
Mileti *fugisse* Thales *vadimonia* alumnus.[9]

In seven verses I shall tell the sages'
homes, names, sentiments – a line for each.
Chilon, a Spartan, 'Know yourself'.
Periander, from Corinth, 'Keep your anger under control'.
From the shores of Mytilene, 'Avoid excess', Pittacus.
'The mean is best', Cleobulus, from Lindos.
'Look to the end', a lesson from Solon, Athenian-born.
Bias, 'Bad men are in the majority', from great Priene.
From Miletus, Thales, 'Avoid debts'.

These men were not political philosophers in any real sense. They did not evolve ideal theories of human society and try to apply them. They looked at the actual political situation, proposed what they deemed best, and – we may suppose, for many of the dicta ascribed to them are patently apocryphal – distilled their practical experience in pithy sayings. Hicks described them as 'shrewd men of affairs . . . about whom a web of romance had been woven'.[10]

Here, then, we have practical attempts by thoughtful men to influence the course of politics without too many *a priori* assumptions about what that course should be. Solon is the most familiar and most studied of them all.[11] He is of

particular interest for the record of his work which we have in the fragments of
his own poetry. He may be taken as typical of this period. In so far as he had a
general philosophy it is expressed in a long elegiac poem which is perhaps worth
quoting in full.

Shining daughters of Memory and Zeus on Olympus,
    Muses, Pierides, listen to me in my prayers.
Grant me, at the hands of the blessed immortals, prosperity,
    and always a high degree in the opinion of men.
So shall I bring pleasure to friends and pain to my enemies,
    and my friends look on me in admiration, the others in fear.
My desire is to have riches; but win them unjustly
    I will not, for retribution must then come my way.
When it is gods who are giving it, wealth befalls a man as some
    solid plant, firm set from base of stock to the crest;
but cultivated with violence, it comes against nature,
    dragged and obedient under direction of crimes,
all unwilling it follows, and ruin is there in a moment.
    The beginning of disaster is not much, as when a fire
burns small in its first stages and ends in catastrophe. As fire's
    course is, such is the course taken by human misdeeds.
But Zeus forever is watching the end, and strikes of a sudden,
    as when a storm in spring abruptly scatters the clouds
and dredges up from the depth the open and heaving water
    where waves roll, and sweeping on across the generous land,
leaves in wreckage fair work men have done, till it hits the headlong
    sky, the gods' home, and the air is shining on every side
you look, and the blaze of the sun breaks out on the fertile acres
    in all its splendor and there are no more clouds to be seen.
Such is the punishment Zeus gives, he does not, like a mortal,
    fall in a rage over each particular thing, and yet
it never escapes him all the way when a man has a sinful
    spirit; and always, in the end, his judgment is plain.
One man has to pay at once, one later, while others
    altogether escape overtaking by the gods' doom;
but then it always comes in aftertime, and the innocent
    pay, the sons of sinners or those born long afterward.
But here is how we men, be we good, be we evil,
    think. Each keeps his own personal notion within
until he suffers. Then he cries out, but all until such time
    we take our idiot beguilement in light-weight hopes,
and one who is stricken and worn out in lingering sickness
    has taken measures and thinks he will grow healthy, and one
who is a coward expects to turn into a warlike hero.
    Another, ugly, thinks of the days when his looks will charm.
If one be penniless and sunk in the struggle of poverty,
    he, too, dreams upon the possession of huge estates.
They all rush off on their various business. One goes seafaring

across the wide sea, in ships, where the fish swarm, trying to bring
a little money home, at the mercy of brutal hurricanes
no hard bargainer for his own life. While another, one
of those whose living is won by the bent plowshare and hard labor,
furrows, year in year out, the tilth of his orchard ground.
One, who has learned Hephaistos' arts and the arts of Athene
and all their skills, by work of his hands assembles a wage.
Yet another, dowered by the grace of Olympian Muses,
has learned control of liveliness in the wisdom of verse.
One the lord far-ranging, Apollo, has made a soothsayer.
He sees the evil coming from far away to a man
when the gods grant such knowledge; yet there is no way for bird sign
nor sacrifice to ward off that which is fated to be.
Others, who understand the works of Paion with all his
drugs, are healers. But neither are these complete in their craft,
seeing that often from a small pain grows a big affliction
and no one, by giving mild remedies, can take it away,
while another, who is in agony from wasting afflictions,
can suddenly be healed by a simple touch of the hand.
Fate brings humanity her good; she brings him her evil;
and what the gods give us for gifts no man can refuse.
Danger, for all, lies in all action, and there is no telling
which way the end will be after a thing is begun.
One may be trying to do well and, through failure of foresight,
may fall into the curse of great disaster, while one
who acts badly may find God gives him all that he asked for,
sheer good luck, that sets him free from the fault of his mind.
But money; there is no end of its making in human endeavor.
Those among us who have already the biggest estates
try to get twice as much as they have. Who can satisfy all of them?
Money, when a man makes it, is the gift of the gods,
but disaster can grow out of money, and when retribution
comes at the sending of Zeus, none can tell where it will light.[12]

In this difficult poem three points must be singled out for special mention. First
Solon believes the world to be under divine government; he holds to a doctrine
of *hybris* and *ate*, that is, approximately, that pride comes, however distantly,
before a fall. But this divine government is not immediately obvious; it has no
obvious place in the ordering of society; it stands as a warning to us not to
forget the remoter consequences of our acts. Secondly, man advances by his
own efforts; Solon has as sturdy a sense of the laboriousness of life as Vergil in
The Georgics. His thinking is rooted in the actuality of the society he saw; he
cannot and does not envisage an effortless Utopia. Thirdly, in his list of pro-
fessions – merchant, farmer, craftsman, poet, prophet and doctor – he shows
some sense of the division of labour which was to form a fundamental principle
of Plato's idealism, and shows also his consciousness of the contemporary needs
of Athens. It is not without interest that he is himself the first Athenian poet of
whom we know.

The political situation in which he intervened is clearly summarized by Aristotle: 'The majority were enslaved to the minority and the commons were in opposition to the aristocracy. Civil strife became violent and for a long time they remained in a state of mutual antagonism, until both sides agreed to put Solon into political office as arbitrator.'[13] Solon gives his own account of the situation:

> The citizens seek to overthrow the State by love of money, by following indulgent and self-seeking demagogues, who neglect religion and pervert the riches of the temples. Yet justice, silent but all-seeing, will in time bring vengeance on them for these things. War, want, civil discord, slavery, are at our gates; and all these evils threaten Athens because of her lawlessness. Whereas good laws and government set all the State in order, chain the hands of evil-doers, make rough places plain, subdue insolence, and blast the budding flowers of Ate, set straight the crooked ways of tortuous law, root out sedition, quell the rage of strife; under their good influence all things are fair and wise with men.[14]

And his remedy?

> My purpose was to bring my scattered people back
> together. Where did I fall short of my design?
> I call to witness at the judgement seat of time
> one who is noblest, mother of Olympian
> divinities, and greatest of them all, Black Earth.
> I took away the mortgage stones stuck in her breast,
> and she, who went a slave before, is now set free.
> Into this sacred land, our Athens, I brought back
> a throng of those who had been sold, some by due law,
> though others wrongly; some by hardship pressed to escape
> the debts they owed; and some of these no longer spoke
> Attic, since they had drifted wide around the world,
> while those in the country had the shame of slavery
> upon them, and they served their masters' moods in fear.
> These I set free; and I did this by strength of hand,
> welding right law with violence to a single whole.
> So have I done, and carried through all that I pledged.
> I have made laws, for the good man and the bad alike,
> and shaped a rule to suit each case, and set it down.
> Had someone else not like myself taken the reins,
> some ill-advised or greedy person, he would not
> have held the people in. Had I agreed to do
> what pleased their adversaries at that time, or what
> they themselves planned to do against their enemies,
> our city could have been widowed of her men. Therefore,
> I put myself on guard at every side, and turned
> among them like a wolf inside a pack of dogs.[15]

In summary Solon cancelled outstanding debts and mortgages – the famous *Seisachtheia* or shaking off burdens – and abolished borrowing on the security of the person, and thus with one stroke ended serfdom in Attica. He produced a series of economic measures directed to the encouragement of trade and industry. He modified the archaic severity of the legal code. He produced constitutional reforms based on property qualifications, which left the power in the hands of the rich, but diffused beyond the old aristocracy and limited, and gave the commoners rights which were to prove the source and origin of the later democracy. He was not himself an extreme democrat – indeed he was not himself an extreme of any sort:

> I gave the commons their sufficient meed
> of strength, nor let them lack, nor yet exceed.
> Those who were mighty and magnificent,
> I bade them have their due and be content.
> My strong shield guarded both sides equally
> and gave to neither unjust victory.[16]

Solon then was not a radical reformer and those who later saw him as the founder of Athenian democracy have made him seem more radical than he really was.[17] Hignett indeed is sceptical about the whole business, and calls the economic reforms bogus.[18] This is overstated. Solon's solution was not permanent, but, as Adcock says, 'the greatest positive immediate achievements of Solon were a solution of the economic problem of Attica in his day, the equipment of Athens for commercial progress, and the establishment of an up-to-date and even-handed justice.'[19]

This is *ad hoc* policy, and when we come to set Solon alongside the other Sages in politics there is no common pattern discernible. Pittacus stood closest to him in general outlook, a moderate democrat, about whose legislation we know little, except that he appears as a temperance reformer who doubled the penalty for offences committed under the influence of liquor.[20] Periander was a very different person.[21] 'Far the most notable of the Greek Tyrants of the Renaissance, he is for better or for worse the type of them – ruthless to the old aristocracy, his enemies, but powerful and fortunate, and momentous for the civilization of Greece.'[22] He was an opportunist, who struck hard when he chose to strike, with widespread contacts overseas, an imperialist in his policy of expansion, enterprising enough to produce the first scheme for the Corinthian canal, patron of the arts, actively aware that a vigorous economic policy is a safeguard against revolution. One of the oddest aspects of the tradition is the attribution to him of the gnomic aphorism 'Democracy is better than dictatorship'.[23] Chilon again appears to us in a quite different political light. He is one of the more nebulous of these figures: Periander leaps to meet us from the pages of Herodotus, but Chilon remains a shadow in the background of history, associated with the extirpation of the dictatorship at Sparta's neighbour Sicyon,[24] responsible for establishing the ephorate as a real force in Spartan politics.[25] He is of particular interest for a possibly authentic saying that the highest quality a man can have is a quality of foresight enabling him to grasp by the use of reason what is likely to happen.[26]

Thales was much more of a professional philosopher than the rest of the Seven, but those whose names follow his in the histories of philosophy were not aloof from politics. Thus Xenophanes is associated in anecdote with the court of Hiero.[27] Heraclitus appears from the fragments as a soured aristocrat with what Burnet called 'a sovereign contempt for the mass of mankind.'[28] He belonged to the hereditary royal house of Ephesus; the rights of the house were probably in his day largely religious and he resigned them to his brother. He remained an oligarch. We see him interfering in politics in the story of how he persuaded a usurper named Melancomas to abdicate. More telling, because more certain, are his own words: 'The grown-up Ephesians ought to hang themselves, every manjack of them, and hand the city over to the kids. They deported the best man of them all, Hermodorus, with the words, "No single person is going to be best among us. If anyone wants to be, he can go somewhere else with some other people".'[29] Empedocles was perhaps an anarchist, but prominent enough in politics to be offered and to refuse the monarchy and to be at some point for some reason deported from his home town. A wealthy man, his sympathies were always on the democratic side.[30] Anaxagoras, again, was the object of one of those politically-inspired attacks which mar the general picture of Athenian tolerance.

No more than with the Seven is there any systematic pattern to be discerned here. The thinkers were expected to play their part in politics, as university men are in the younger countries today, but that part was unpredictable and *ad hoc*, and later critics found it hard to reconcile Empedocles' philosophy with his politics.[31] With the Pythagoreans, the 'so-called Pythagoreans' as Aristotle puts it,[32] the case is different.[33] Pythagoras is a mysterious figure whose very name is mentioned only five times in our records between 500 and 300 BC, though we have two full lives of him written in the third century AD. There is no reason to doubt the general tradition of a transcendent genius (who had moulded his thought to that of India) born in the island of Samos, and emigrating, perhaps with some associates, to Magna Graecia because he chafed under the rule of the dictator Polycrates.[34] Amidst all the welter of uncertainty about what followed we can be fairly certain about three things. First, the form of philosophy practised by Pythagoras (the reputed inventor of the word) was idealist. It linked mathematics, morals, music and matter in a single comprehensive harmonious structure. Mathematical proportion was at the root of the universe, and the structure of the material world and the world of human behaviour were alike to be thought of in terms of number. This means that we shall expect to find Pythagoras applying to human society an abstract and absolute standard, unlike those who took society as they found it and sought the next step in a given situation. Secondly, Pythagoras himself did not seek political office in the normal public sense; this is quite clear from a passage in Plato.[35] What he did was to form a religious fraternity which lived together as a society of friends, communistically,[36] and sought the perfection of religious holiness,[37] intellectual attainment and human fellowship. Thirdly, this fraternity was a constant object of political attack. Pythagoras himself was compelled to leave Croton, and died at Metapontum,[38] and the middle of the fifth century, possibly about the year 454, saw bitter attacks on the society.[39]

Just what the political contribution and influence of the Pythagoreans was is exceedingly difficult to disentangle. Our authorities are mostly late, unreliable and confused, and the story has plainly been worked over many times before reaching them. We may discount the view that Pythagoreanism was a primarily political movement,[40] a theory of respectable antiquity, as it can be traced back to Dicaearchus,[41] but untenable in the face of the evidence that its motivation was religious. But this is not, of course, to deny political implications. The analogy with Calvinism[42] or Freemasonry[43] is not preposterous, religious movements which were politically active. It is not likely that its political alignment was with the democrats, though Burnet made desperate efforts to prove it.[44] The dictatorships generally arose from the discontent of the poorer sections of the population and bore most heavily upon the aristocrats, and the fact that Pythagoras left Samos because of Polycrates suggests that his sympathies lay to the right. Diogenes' description of his influence at Croton comes near to being explicit. 'He sailed away to Croton in Italy, and there he laid down a constitution for the Italian Greeks, and he and his followers were held in great estimation; for, being nearly three hundred in number, so well did they govern the state that its constitution was in effect a true aristocracy.'[45] What we know of the general philosophy of the Pythagoreans confirms this. There is nothing which would lead them in incline to the left wing. On the contrary, as Thomson says, though his words are overcharged with dogmatic Marxism, 'the *symphronasis* or *homonoia* of the Pythagoreans expressed the subjective attitude characteristic of the class which claimed to have resolved the old class-struggle in democracy. The doctrine of the fusion of opposites in the mean was generated by the rise of the middle class intermediate between the landowners and the serfs.'[46] I have argued elsewhere that the parallels between the class-structure of Plato's *Republic* and Hindu thought and practice are too close to be accidental, and that the Pythagoreans must be the mediating power[47]. The Pythagorean doctrine of harmony may well lead to a system with a place for each and each to keep in his place. The Pythagoreans indeed, in the position which they seem to have attained formally or informally, appear to us not unlike the Brahmin priest-rulers. Certainly by the disturbances of which Polybius speaks the Pythagoreans appear as reactionaries.[48] The evidence of Aristoxenus supports this; he cites the Pythagorean view that 'there was no greater evil than anarchy; the secret of safety for man is to have somebody over him' and that 'it was right to adhere to the ancestral laws of the state, even if they were a little inferior to others.'[49] We may then suppose that the Pythagoreans belonged to the Upper Middle Class, that in politics they held to an organic structure of society with a ruling class, an executive, a working class and slaves, corresponding to the Indian Brahmanas, Kshattryas, Vaishyas and Sudras, and that they applied these principles to the society around them, they themselves appearing as the ruling class, though the inner fraternity no doubt acted as *éminences grises* rather than taking office themselves. It is just, however, to remark that it seems likely that

Pythagoras found Croton a corrupt and decaying oligarchy; he made no attempt to alter the system, but rather he gave 'a new lease of life to the oligarchical constitution by breathing a new and more ethical spirit into the rule of the Few'.[50] There is also an important story which tells how Pythagoras persuaded Simichus, dictator of Centuripe, to abdicate and to establish a government based on Pythagorean principles, though not involving actual Pythagoreans; the former dictator distributed his wealth to his sister and his fellow citizens.[51] Later we find clearly committed Pythagoreans in political office, and Archytas at Tarentum long held office, being freely elected, and, according to Aristoxenus, was never defeated in battle.[52] The Pythagoreans of Tarentum were the spearhead of the opposition to the dictatorship of Dionysius at Syracuse. It was this group which affected the thinking of Plato so deeply on his visit to Magna Graecia in 387, and Burnet says of Archytas that he 'was the friend of Plato, and almost realized the ideal of the philosopher-king'.[53] Epaminondas was another Pythagorean politician of a later generation, but we know him principally as a military commander, with a leaning to federalism, and a vaguely defined policy of Theban hegemony, modified, says Diodorus, by his *philanthropia*, which led him not to interfere in the internal constitution of other states.[54] Aristotle suggests that the rule of the 'philosophers' brought prosperity to Thebes.[55] The whole story of the incursion of the Pythagoreans into politics is a fascinating one, and directly relevant to our purpose, for it seems to represent the first attempt to work out ideal political principles in a practical social context. But it is no use pretending that we know more than we do, and we must leave our knowledge in this fragmentary and frustrating state.

An important landmark is the founding of Thurii.[56] Here we find two remarkable men coming together. Thurii was founded in 433 BC at the initiative of Pericles; it was to replace the earlier Sybaris. Pericles conceived the project not in terms of Athenian imperialism but as a Panhellenic venture, and in the outcome only two-fifths of the settlers came from Athens and her dominions. In accordance with the Panhellenic policy, he invited Hippodamus of Miletus to undertake the town-planning and Protagoras of Abdera to draw up the constitution. Hippodamus invented town-planning, according to Aristotle;[57] that is to say that he introduced to Europe the 'grid-system' of laying out streets at right angles to each other, which was practised in his home town of Miletus early in the fifth century and perhaps derived ultimately from Babylon, and which is so notable a feature of Hellenistic cities, and which is more familiar to Americans than to British or Nigerians. But beyond this Hippodamus is significant because he was also a political theorist, and Aristotle again says that he was the first person not actively engaged in practical politics to investigate the best form of government.[58] There are one or two traits in his personality which suggests Pythagorean leanings; the number three has a peculiar fascination for him, though this may be no more than a fashion of the period,[59] and he has a horror of perjury.[60] He apparently composed the first Utopia we know. He advocated a state of 10,000 citizens, divided into three classes, industrial and professional workers, agricultural workers, and soldiers; slaves are presumably

taken for granted. His political system implicitly criticizes the extreme democracy of Athens; he maintained that all public office should be elective. A high
practical idealism may be seen in his insistence that the ministers in addition to
looking after the common interest ought to see to the welfare of orphans and
foreign visitors. He also sensed the weakness of the Athenian legal system and
proposed to institute a court of appeal composed of elders. Economically he
thought that the land should be divided into three. One section would be used
for religious purposes, one would be publicly held for the support of the army,
and the remainder was to be privately owned by the farmers. There is no trace
of a professional ruling class in Hippodamus' thinking. Sparta may have contributed the separation of the military from the rest of the community, and he is
obviously not a left-wing democrat, but all citizens have equal rights in politics
and at law, and a further proposal to welcome and reward beneficial suggestions
from all sections of the community is democratic.[61] Aristotle is scornful of the
whole scheme. He points out (rightly) that the other two classes would be at
the mercy of the military, who would alone possess arms, and that it was difficult to see how any except the military could hold political office, and points
to other aspects which Hippodamus had not thought out in sufficient detail,
such as the question who is to cultivate the public land. Hippodamus' suggestions are clearly open to these and other criticisms, but his words mark something of a turning-point. We have left the age of the statesman who contributes
his conclusions to philosophy and come to the age of the philosopher who
offers his theories to politics.

We do not know what part, if any, Hippodamus played in moulding the
constitution of Thurii.[62] That task was entrusted to Protagoras, incomparably
the greatest of the sophists. No doubt Protagoras taught political theory – the
sophists claimed to train people for a political career – and a book on the subject
appears in the record of his published works,[63] but we have no idea of the content of either teaching or writing. At Thurii Protagoras followed a middle-of-
the-road policy. He evidently drew on a wide historical knowledge, rather as
Aristotle was to show later, and his thinking, perhaps inevitably in the circumstances of the case, was eclectic; parallels have been determined with Pericles,
Solon, Charondas and others.[64] His scheme was a modified democracy or
moderate oligarchy, with property qualifications for citizen rights and the
responsible offices of government confined to the upper class. Office was however limited to a period of five years, and there were other more democratic
practices. There was, for example, free education for all, and there is no reason
to doubt that the original constitution-maker intended an equitable distribution
of land, though the upper class tried to gain economic control. All constitu-
tionalists try to make change difficult, but it is doubtful if anything as drastic as
Protagoras' method has ever been essayed. We are told that anyone proposing
to alter the constitution had to speak with his head in a noose. If his proposal
was effective he was released; if he failed to persuade his audience the noose was
drawn tight. Even this terrifying treatment did not prevent change at Thurii.
There were changes in the direction of democracy, a division of the population

into ten tribes on a racial basis, and a curious combination of Spartan discipline, common messes and athletic exercise, with Ionian or even oriental luxury, for which their Sybaritic predecessors had been notorious, and which won for them from the comic dramatist Metagenes the title of the Thuriopersians. Thus this first experiment in practical idealism cannot be accounted an unqualified success.

Finally we must mention Phaleas of Chalcedon.[65] We know nothing about him, not even the date when he lived. We may however put him with some probability between Hippodamus (the first amateur in this field) and Plato.[66] Phaleas is important for his assertion that economic motives are the chief cause of revolution. He seems to have started from the assumption that it is above all important to ensure political stability and was, we are told, the first person to suggest that equalization of property would be the best means to this end. This, he thought, could be readily achieved in setting up a completely new state (such as was possible in an age of colonization). In an established community it was more difficult, though he made a practical suggestion that the rich should give dowries and not receive them and the poor should receive but not give them; he seems little aware of the meanness of some rich and the pride of some poor. We may note a further proposal that the professional and industrial workers should be recruited from the slaves and not the citizens; Baldry described this as 'a form of nationalization of industry hardly likely to have a popular appeal'. It has sometimes been argued, without overmuch justification, that Phaleas was a practical reformer rather than a political theorist, aiming to restore the ancient landholding aristocracy.[67] There is little to support this. Phaleas seems quite indifferent to the militarism which was the normal accompaniment of a Dorian oligarchy, and his views include a levelling of property between rich and poor. He appears rather as a moderate democrat. Aristotle has a characteristically sensible discussion of Phaleas' views. He agrees that some control over the amount of private property probably makes on the whole for harmony. But there are other factors in the situation. The stability of a state may be threatened from outside as well as from in; yet Phaleas has nothing to say about this. Crimes do not arise only from poverty. In making this point Aristotle produces two sentences of profound lucidity. 'It is not the possessions but the desires of mankind which need to be equalized.'[68] 'The greatest crimes are caused by excess and not by necessitude.'[69] Even in his own terms Phaleas' reasoning is faulty. He thinks it enough to equalize landholdings, but there are many more forms of property than that – money for instance. Aristotle is seen at his best in these criticisms. They are based on a sound knowledge of Greek history, as is plain from his illustrations. Elsewhere his commonsensical approach leaves him out of sympathy with the uncommon sense which can sometimes be produced by people starting from very different premisses. Here he combines his normal down-to-earthness with an ability to combat Phaleas on his own ground. None the less Phaleas has some claim on our attention as the first advocate of an Utopia which is based on economic theory.

CHAPTER VI

ANTISTHENES[1]

THE GREAT CATALYST OF GREECE was Socrates. He described himself as an intellectual midwife, helping others to give birth to the thoughts which were in them;[2] in this respect he must be ranked among the great educationalists of history. The diversity of his associates is remarkable. Plato was a metaphysician. Aristippus was a hedonist; Antisthenes was an ascetic. Euclides and Phaedo fostered the study of logic and dialectic. The later philosophic schools sought to establish an 'apostolic succession' reaching back to him, often falsifying history and sadly confusing modern historians in the process. Stoics took him as their ideal sage; sceptics linked their tenets with his refusal to dogmatize. A delightful story tells of his remarking to a silent young man 'Say something, so that I may see you.'[3] He was continually asking questions. 'He was for ever conversing with people, asking what is piety, what is impiety, what is beauty, what is ugliness, what is justice, what is injustice, what is temperance, what is intemperance, what is courage, what is cowardice, what is a city, what is citizenship, what is the ruling principle in man, what is the quality of a ruler, and so on, and so forth'[4] 'ceaselessly dragging somebody round and round in argument.'[5]

These questions included political questions: Socrates was executed by the democracy in 399. It is fairly certain that the real charges were political, but they could not be publicly pressed owing to the existence of an amnesty. Grote long ago saw that the respectable Meletus was only a façade for the politicians Anytus and Lycon. There is no doubt about Socrates' political concern. His peculiar vocation, and a mystical voice within, prevented him from playing much part in the formal political life of Athens, but he accepted the normal obligations of citizenship, military service and executive duties on the Council. Later, in prison, he refused to escape, on the grounds that he had accepted the protection of the laws of Athens, and must accept their verdict when it was unfavourable. Informally he was politically active, for his concern was men, and politics is the life of men in community. Indeed he justified his formal inactivity by asking 'Should I do more for politics if I merely practised as a politician than by taking care that as many people as possible should be qualified to be politicians?'[6] In his speech in his own defence he suggested that God has attached him to Athens to be a sort of insect stinging her into wakefulness.[7] He showed high courage in resisting immorality and illegality whether from democrats or oligarchs; in this he was not partisan. But his sympathies were not in doubt. When his country was at war with Sparta he fought patriotically. But he preferred the Spartan way of life to the Athenian. 'Everyone was Sparta-mad' as the character says in Aristophanes, 'long hair, empty bellies, grubby, Socratizing, staff in hand.'[8] He was vocal in opposition to the demagogues' aggression against Sicily.[9] Furthermore, he believed that politics was as skilled a profession as any other, and should thus be the province of the technical expert. No one would ask the man in the street to pilot a ship into harbour; it is illogical to invite him to pilot the ship of state through the troubled waters of life, a far more difficult and responsible task. Such a view ran counter to the whole theory of Athenian democracy. Worse, it was absorbed by men like Critias, Char-mides and Alcibiades, who fancied themselves the technical experts, but who lacked the moral integrity which Socrates insisted on as the first qualification of the truly successful statesman. It was because of his supposed influence on these that he was executed.[10] But he left a legacy of political zeal which is to be seen in three at least of his associates, Antisthenes, Xenophon and Plato.[11]

Our capacity to estimate Antisthenes is severely hampered by the absence of any writing of his own, and our uncertainty whether the anecdotes preserved by later gossip-writers or sermonizers are authentic. We have to rely upon such aphorisms to guide us as to the contents of his lost works. We cannot even be sure that the writings of which we know are truly his, for one anecdote shows him attacking reading and writing.[12] But this is contradicted by his general enthusiasm for education, and we lack the context of the remark. The list of his writings proffered by Diogenes Laertius shows a clear interest in politics.[13] They include two books *On Law*, one bearing the alternative title *On the State* (the same title as Plato's so-called *Republic*), one work on economics (possibly the same as that entitled *On Victory*), four books entitled *Cyrus*, one of which, like those called *Archelaus* and *Menelaus*, was a treatise on Sovereignty, and works entitled *Aspasia* and *Alcibiades*. We know something of the contents of these from Athenaeus.[14] In the second *Cyrus* he abused Alcibiades personally, in his discussion of politics – presumably the book *On the State* – he attacked the demagogues, in *Archelaus* his teacher Gorgias, and in *Aspasia* Pericles' sons. It is tempting to guess at his further ideas from his relations with his contem-poraries, but that path, though entertaining, is a dangerous one. He seems to have been a pupil of Gorgias, and to have been acquainted with some of the other sophists.[15] Certainly Socrates was the greatest influence on his life.[16] But beyond that all is controversy. Athenaeus declares that his *Satho* was an attack on Plato, and there are stories showing the rivalry between the two followers of Socrates.[17] References to Antisthenes have been alleged in the *Phaedrus*, *Clitophon*, *Protagoras*, *Republic*, *Hippias Major*, *Hippias Minor*, *Ion*, *Gorgias*, *Euthydemus*, *Cratylus*, *Theaetetus*, *Sophist* and *Politicus*, so that Dummler remarked that he must have been as versatile as Proteus,[18] and de Strycker that if these conclusions are correct 'we must admit that the polemic against Antis-thenes formed one of the chief aims of Plato's literary activity.'[19] On the other hand Wilamowitz protested against this idea of a feud between Plato and Antisthenes,[20] and A. E. Taylor said that he could find no certain allusions to

Antisthenes in Plato.[21] So too with Isocrates. H. von Arnim finds a similar feud between him and Antisthenes.[22] But Sayre points to Theopompus' praise of Isocrates as convincing against this, and if there was a controversy it is unlikely to have been ill-humoured.[23] Finally Dudley speaks of the contemptuous tone of Aristotle's references to Antisthenes, whereas to Sayre they are commendatory and respectful.[24]

We know that Antisthenes' chief interests were logical and ethical, and most of our records of him fall into one or other of these two categories. But we can deduce something of the views on politics which he must have expressed in the book *On the State* and elsewhere, and this is our present concern. Our traditions represent certain clear distinctions between Antisthenes and the Cynics, which is a point in favour of their authenticity. It is fairly certain that *On the State* presented some sort of ideal commonwealth; we are specifically told that Antisthenes laid the foundations for the political practices of Diogenes, Crates and Zeno.[25]

There is not very much that we can be certain about its contents. It must have been based upon the city-state. It is so unlikely that he would have transcended his age that this would hardly be worth mentioning, were it not that he has been claimed as a cosmopolitan, partly from his supposed association with Diogenes, partly from his mixed parentage, partly because his biographer writes, 'That toil is a good thing he established by instancing Heracles the Great and Cyrus, taking one example from the Greek, the other from the non-Greek world.'[26] The last passage is not to be pressed. Cyrus, as Dudley points out, is a hero not only in Xenophon but even in the Old Testament.[27] More near to genuine cosmopolitanism is his moral aphorism that to him nothing was alien. Evil alone was foreign.[28] It is probable that in his city-state he looked to Sparta rather than Athens. His words after the battle of Leuctra when he declared that the Thebans were like schoolboys boasting of having beaten their master show some admiration of Sparta.[29] The use of the Spartan *tribon*, common only to the lower orders in Athens, may not be genuinely attributed to him.[30] But Theopompus' innuendo about Plato borrowing from Aristippus, Antisthenes and Bryson, must be based on some resemblances, and may indicate a similarity of approach at this point.[31] Certainly his attack on democracy was sharp and clear. We have already noticed his abuse of the demagogues in this particular treatise, and of Alcibiades and Pericles' sons, elsewhere. This draws the comment, 'To these fellows no statesman is any good, no general has any brains, no professor is worth mention, no poet is any use, no democracy is commendable – except Socrates alone.'[32] Aristotle quotes him as using the familiar proverb of the hares claiming equality in the face of the lions.[33] To elect a man who had no qualifications to office was like voting horses to be asses.[34] It is possible that the condemnation of Socrates may have turned him, like Plato, against the democracy. Legend later recorded his attacks on Anytus. On the other hand the critique of democracy is closely similar to that of Socrates in his lifetime. Whatever the reason for it, his belief is tolerably certain. But even democracy was one stage better than tyranny, for under democracy wrongdoers were condemned, under tyrannies innocent men.[35] This last is a strange saying for a friend of Socrates, but it may indicate that in democracy there was at least adherence to law, and Socrates was legally though not morally guilty.

The ideal of government was kingship. This is seen from his exhaustive treatment of the topic in writing, and his most famous aphorism, 'It is a king's part, Cyrus, to do well and be evil spoken of.' This is quoted with approbation by Epictetus and Marcus Aurelius, applied by Alexander to himself, and even attributed to the author in face of abuse from Plato; the last story is almost certainly apocryphal.[36] This king will be the wise man, the philosopher himself. In this present world he does not get too near political life, nor too far away, for fear of burning himself or freezing.[37] But nothing is alien or unmanageable to him, and he alone has the powers of wisdom and leadership needed for the task.[38] At the other end of society those who are unfitted will have no share in government. 'It is strange that we should weed out darnels from corn, and the weak in time of war, and yet in our political life should not exclude the unworthy.'[39] States are destroyed when they fail to distinguish the good citizens from the bad.[40] In the light of this it is at least possible that in *The Statesman* and *The Republic* Plato is referring to Antisthenes' theories.[41] In the former he rejects the analogy between statesmanship and the superintendence of a flock; in the latter he develops beyond a city of 'simple-lifers' calling it a city of pigs. From Plutarch's account of Zeno we know that he reduced the state to a herd of men,[42] and even if we reject the apostolic succession from Socrates to Zeno via Antisthenes we have noted a specific reference to influence in the field of political thought.[43] If Plato is referring to current ideas it is difficult to see to whose they could refer but those of Antisthenes.

It is unlikely that Antisthenes introduced any revolutionary economic ideas. Ascetic he was, but he did not, like the Cynics, completely scorn wealth, and was deeply aware of the evils of poverty. He rather inclined to regard material goods as an irrelevance.[44] True wealth lay in the heart. When Callias argued that to give men riches was to save them from crime, he responded that poverty led to covetousness and possession to greed for more; unless the heart were healthy, both produced strife.[45] Wealth without virtue he compared to drinking on your own – it brings no pleasure.[46] A man who loves money for its own sake is evil, a subject and a slave.[47] This is simply moralizing. An aphorism of his about war is of greater interest. Someone remarked that war would destroy the poor. Antisthenes replied that it would create many.[48] This shows more insight and compassion than other allusions, which reveal a tendency to exalt war.[49] It is of particular significance because the inhabitants of the city of pigs in Plato's *Republic* guard against the two specific evils, poverty and war;[50] the reference to Antisthenes is strengthened. The emphasis elsewhere on the wise man as a reconciler shows that it was an aim of Antisthenes that his commonwealth should live at peace with its neighbours; in this there is a contrast with Plato. Aristotle tells us specifically that 'the community of women and children and property and public tables for women are peculiar to Plato',[51] and this is decisive against any radical economic proposals on the part of Antisthenes.

Antisthenes was a moralist, not a political thinker, and his approach to politics was that of the moralist.[52] He had an intense interest in ethics and was, like Socrates, concerned over the unity of the virtues. He used parables to convey ethical theories; he said that the walls of cities might fall to the traitor within, the walls of the soul were secure. Stronger than any wall is a community of like-minded brethren. He maintained that courage and wisdom might harm communities, as individuals, but righteousness could not. Hence the sage would play his part as citizen by the laws of God, not those of men, and follow the laws of virtue, not those of the state.[53] (We must suppose his commonwealth to have been an attempt to portray the two coinciding.) Like many moralists he laid great stress on education, and it must have played a considerable rôle in his commonwealth. It is told of him that he saw a drawing of Chiron the centaur teaching Achilles, and remarked, 'For the sake of education it is a good thing to submit even to a beast.'[54] He even rebuked Socrates for his failure to educate Xanthippe, and criticized Alcibiades for being uneducated.[55] He had few pupils himself, but was personally responsible for introducing students to some of the sophists.[56] When asked which was the noblest crown, he replied, 'That from education'. We get a small glimpse of the system he advocated, a combination of physical exercise for the body and education for the soul – *mens sana in corpore sano*. Philosophy was the study for those who were to consort with the gods, rhetoric for those who would live among men. The result of this system of education would be the inculcation of nobility.[57] Virtue can be taught, as Socrates showed him in the case of courage, and nobility is the only virtue.[58] The sort of character resulting, if Antisthenes followed Socrates' words to him, would be one helpful to others and making the most of the opportunities of society, and in consequence diplomatic in arranging treaties (and marriages!) and a valuable friend and ally to states and individuals.[59] It is likely that this educational system was to be shared between men and women. It appears that Socrates first brought the status of women to Antisthenes' notice, in declaring that women's nature was no worse than that of man except intellectually and physically. He drew at the time a lively retort from Antisthenes.[60] But Antisthenes himself later declared 'Virtue (*arete*) is the same for women as for men.'[61] In its context in the biography this clearly refers to moral virtue, but if it is a verbal citation it may originally have referred to function in society. It seems likely that Antisthenes' feminism came out in giving women and men identical educational opportunities, and identical openings in public life, within his commonwealth.

Antisthenes' ideal commonwealth had no practical results. But it is important to see that Plato, by far the greatest of the Utopians, was not an Athene sprung fully armed from the head of Zeus. He was writing in a mood of speculation current in his day. There is some reason to believe that Antisthenes was in the field before him. He rejected much that Antisthenes stood for, but we need not doubt that he was at points influenced. Antisthenes' influence permeated further. We may not say that Diogenes was his pupil, but we may accept that his writing formed a starting point for Diogenes and Zeno. He is in this field the precursor.

CHAPTER VII

XENOPHON

XENOPHON WAS BORN somewhere about 430, and must have fought for Athens in the last stages of the Peloponnesian War. At some point he came in contact with Socrates. It is hard to say what attracted him. Both had some sympathy for Spartan institutions, and Xenophon's simple moral piety obviously responded to Socrates' search for ethical truth. In 401, against the advice of Socrates, he joined the younger Cyrus in his bid to seize the Persian throne, and when the expedition failed, according to his own account was instrumental in saving the Greek mercenaries and enabling them to return to Greece. His chief associate in this was a Spartan named Chirisophus. He then served under a Thracian prince named Seuthes, and a succession of Spartan commanders, including King Agesilaus, for whom he conceived a warm friendship and admiration. At some point the Athenians banished him, no doubt for his pro-Spartan sympathies and his support for Cyrus. For twenty years he settled down to the life of a country-gentleman, farming and hunting and writing, near Olympia, and then was forced to move to Corinth. In 369 Athens concluded an alliance with Sparta, and the decree of exile was rescinded. Xenophon's sons, educated in Sparta, were now able to serve in the Athenian cavalry, and he no doubt visited Athens from time to time. But he probably did not move, and it was at Corinth that he died some time in the 350s.

Xenophon thus brought to the tasks of political philosophy an interesting and unusual background. In the first place he was a man of the world. He had travelled. He knew and understood the Persians. He had lived for extended periods in four Greek states: Athens, Sparta, Elis (for though Scillus was under Sparta while he was living there, it could hardly be said that it was Sparta), and Corinth. Secondly, he was a professional soldier, a practical man, and he saw politics from the standpoint of the practical man, not that of the philosopher or the political theorist. Thirdly, there were three great influences upon his life, Socrates, Cyrus and Agesilaus. From Socrates he had absorbed a sense of ethical values, a functional approach to political and other problems, and with that the need for appropriate training for the job in hand. From Cyrus he had acquired a sympathy for values other than those acknowledged in the traditions of Greece, and a respect for individual leadership. Agesilaus had reinforced his admiration for Sparta. From all this we shall expect to find in him an advocacy of monarchy, militarism, moralism, and education. This we do.

Of his writings three call for our brief note here. First *The Constitution of the Spartans*. The attribution of this to Xenophon has been challenged, though stylistic evidence favours its authenticity.[1] There are some relatively minor divagations from other works of Xenophon, but not so great as to be incompatible either with a change of view or with sheer inconsistency. Elsewhere, for example, Xenophon takes the view that the woman's place is in the home;[2] here he approves of their public education. Elsewhere he approves of good eating for children;[3] here of an ascetic regimen. The fact is that *The Constitution of the Spartans* is an almost completely idealized view of the 'Lycurgan' system. The author admires the education system, the military training, the discipline it produces, and the single-minded direction of everything to the creation of an ordered, healthy and successful state. One can well see Xenophon writing in these terms at a time when he was very close to Agesilaus. Here Sparta appears almost as an ideal commonwealth. And in fact the final chapter strikes a note of disillusion. It may have been added somewhere about 378. Even Sparta did not live up to her own ideal.

The second work which concerns us is *Hiero*. It is a dialogue between Hiero, dictator of Syracuse in the early fifth century, and the poet Simonides, and in the end it is a defence of autocracy. It expresses the one thing which was lacking to Sparta as an ideal state in Xenophon's mind, the absence of an effective military autocracy. The king at Sparta was hedged round with checks and balances. It is interesting to ask what called out this treatise. There is a tradition that Xenophon visited Syracuse,[4] though whether in the time of Dionysius I or II is not clear. If the former, then *Hiero* might have been written to greet the accession of Dionysius II, which would create a piquant cross-link with Plato. Or perhaps it was the meteoric career of Jason of Pherae which he was watching with interest.

Hiero is a short work, but it is constructed with considerable skill.[5] It starts from the apparent advantages enjoyed by the autocratic ruler, and the way in which they turn to dust in face of the fear and hatred in which he lives. No one has portrayed the loneliness of the absolute monarch more eloquently and imaginatively than Xenophon in these pages; he is a man without friends and cannot trust even his own family; he cannot eat or drink without thinking of poison; he is afraid of crowds, afraid of being alone, afraid of being unprotected, afraid of his own guards.[6] Even abdication is not open to him without danger.[7] Three-quarters of the work is thus taken up with the deflation of the autocrat. But then the whole mood of the dialogue changes and in the last sections Simonides shows than an autocrat who uses his power wisely for the service of others has unlimited powers of well-doing and so of arousing affection. Xenophon thus in the end takes up the position which Plato is to reach, that monarchy can rise higher or fall lower than any other form of government. *Hiero* is not of course in any way an examination of the ideal polity. But it is a necessary preliminary to *The Education of Cyrus*.

The Education of Cyrus is a work of much wider scope than its title might imply.[8] It is in fact our first historical novel – Plato was right to call it a fiction-

and it affected the fictional form of many subsequent Utopias. It has a flawless hero in the elder Cyrus; there is not much doubt that Xenophon is fusing a historical romance with his hopeful vision of what his own idolized leader, Cyrus the younger, might have become. There is military adventure,[9] and exotic pictures of life at an oriental court.[10] There is romantic love-interest, carefully interspersed with the narrative of the central books. There is a philosophical exposition of the immortality of the soul.[11] There is everything that a historical novel ought to have, and much that it ought not to have. For this is a vast sprawling growth, which needed the pruning-knife.

Xenophon begins from the instability of the political order. Democracies are overthrown by those who do not like living under them, monarchies and oligarchies by the democrats. Dictators are promptly deposed, or their survival seems a miracle. Very few people know how to exercise authority. By contrast a shepherd has little trouble with his flock, a cowherd with his cattle, or a groom with his horses. The scarcity of those with real authority and the analogy of the herdsman leads Xenophon to the practical conclusion that the only constitution which can hope for stability is a monarchy based on intelligence. As an example of this he produces his idealized portrait of Cyrus, who maintained his authority because his subjects viewed him with mingled awe and admiration.

Xenophon was a soldier, and it is this which makes the central section of this work so tedious. He is fascinated by the details of military administration. Not everyone shares that enthusiasm. But just as Plato applies to politics the analogy of craftsmanship, so Xenophon applies the analogy of soldiering. The army is a community organized to achieve its goal as efficiently as possible. Xenophon's ideal is to apply this to the peace-time organization of the state. It involves a pyramidal command-structure, with the ultimate authority resting with the commander-in-chief. It means a chain of command with a proper respect for the authority of seniors at all levels. It means specialization of function and division of labour.[12]

Everything depends on the commander-in-chief. We have seen that he must evoke awe and affection.[13] He will evoke awe as others come to respect his moral integrity and the thoroughness of his expertise.[14] These two themes recur continually through the book. There is the absolute need for probity and self-discipline, and an equal need for attention to detail.[15] Failure in either can lose a war or a kingdom. Cyrus' kingdom is seen to some extent under the image of a Welfare State. He is said to have inaugurated something of a National Health Service,[16] not to mention a Postal Service.[17] Affection arises largely from generosity and benefactions. But these are part of a wider skill in concern for, understanding of, and appropriate action towards human beings of different kinds. Xenophon presents this as a surprising amalgam of convention, shrewdness, and startling originality. Thus one important factor in handling people is the reward of merit.[18] Another is the devisal of unobtrusive tests to check who is fitted to take particular responsibilities.[19] He was not averse from playing potential rivals off against one another.[20] More unexpected is his recognition that to take a meal with another is to do something to create a bond of friendship;[21] it was, of course, the theory behind the Spartan messes, and has its place later in the story of Christianity. Even more astonishing is his attitude to women, and the concept of marriage as a partnership,[22] and to slaves, who are kept in their places, but treated as human beings with personal care and concern.[23]

To produce this paragon and those others who will support him, the key is education, and the first book is an idealized account of the Persian system of education. Xenophon is very modern in his discussion of the relationship between education and the social order. There will be problems unless the system of education and the social order are alike directed to producing a healthy community.[24] Society is divided into four age-groups, boys (up to sixteen), youths (up to twenty-six), adults (up to fifty-one) and elders (past military age). The ages are approximate, and passage into one of the higher groups depends upon successful completion of the previous training. The distinctive quality of the education is that it is exclusively moral and military.[25] The boys are there to learn not reading and writing, but justice and self-control, not (we might say) the three 'R's but the four cardinal virtues. On graduation from the boys' class they are involved in military training, hunting as part of this, and guard-duty. Then come administrative duties, while they remain in military reserve. Finally the elders have the responsibility for moral leadership and judicial decisions. It is clear that Xenophon is speaking, even ideally, of only a small ruling class, whom he numbers at 120,000 – small, that is, by Persian standards, though a large citizenry for any Greek polis. The interaction between education and the social order is very important; we can say, if we like, that education continues through life, or that it is part only of a wider social order, which is contained in moral traditions and the rule of law. It is this total attitude which Cyrus absorbs through his education and which he seeks to establish in the state he rules under the gods.[26]

Xenophon had a simple piety, and he endows his hero with the same attitude. At the outset his father steeps him in the importance of divine omens, and of constancy in prayer, especially in thanksgiving for success, and also in the pragmatic maxim that the gods help those who help themselves.[27] After his final success, Cyrus vows to set his subjects an example, first in religion,[28] and then in morality.

It is important to see that though Xenophon's ideal state is fictionally cast in the pattern of Persia, and we may note the courage and broadmindedness which it took to overleap normal Hellenic prejudices, the state is not, and is not intended to be, pure Persia. Persia it is because Persia offered the example of a traditional monarchy and not an irresponsible dictatorship. Xenophon's ideal society, for the reasons already discussed, was the rule of the single best man. But if he had been content to draw a picture of Oriental society, his Greek readers would have found it at worst repulsive, and at best quaint, but irrelevant. He therefore incorporates a good deal which is borrowed from Sparta, and the education, and the emphasis on common messes, and the way of life generally are a fusion of Sparta idealized and Persia idealized. But Xenophon, even in exile, remained an Athenian patriot, and he will not suggest that his ideal scheme is irrelevant to his own country. This is the point of a very odd allusion to Socrates in the context of Armenia, put to death unjustly and proclaiming that men who act unjustly do so from ignorance.[29] The implication is that there is no essential difference between injustice on the part of a *demos* and injustice on the part of an autocratic monarch, and that the just rule of a Cyrus would be as valid in Europe as in Asia. But Xenophon goes beyond this, and in Cyrus' army organization he gives a place to the democratic assembly of the common soldiers;[30] he does so in confidence that the majority will stand for justice, not in the sense of equality but of rewards appropriate to merit, and will in any case follow a wise lead given by wise leaders. Xenophon's ideal polity in this way has elements of democracy, at least in the need to obtain the consent of the governed, though he does not expect political initiative from that quarter, and of oligarchy, since no individual can govern without effective and trustworthy subordinates. But it remains basically monarchy, the rule of the best individual. And where Plato looks for a philosopher-king, Xenophon looks for a soldier.

The sad chapter which concludes the work, whether by Xenophon or another, is in fact a pragmatic criticism of his Utopia. It tells how things fell apart after Cyrus' death. Morals declined; a Persian's word was no longer his bond; there was financial corruption, and terrorism. Men became physically flabby and out of condition. Traditions were lost. Educational principles were forgotten. Effeminacy in civilian life went with military inefficiency. The Persians became dependent on Greek mercenaries.[31] If this appendix is by Xenophon it is an affirmation that the initiative has passed from Persia to Greece, and that if the Greeks will follow the pattern of life and order laid down by Xenophon they too will lead the world. But a Utopia which depends on the will and personality of a single individual is in the end precarious.

CHAPTER VIII

PLATO

TO UNDERSTAND PLATO'S POLITICAL PHILOSOPHY it is necessary to establish some facts about his upbringing and life. His father Ariston was proud to trace his lineage back to the old kings of Athens and beyond that to the god Poseidon. His mother Perictione belonged to the same family as Solon.[1] Her uncle Critias and her brother Charmides were prominent members of the Thirty who for a brief period exercised ruthlessly dictatorial rule after the collapse of Athens in 404. Plato came from a family of great distinction, with strong political traditions of an aristocratic kind. He was plainly expected to make his mark in politics.[2] Secondly, he lived for over a quarter of his life under the shadow of war, hot or cold. He saw some of the more irresponsible actions of the Assembly, the illegal mass execution of the generals after Arginusae,[3] the rejection of a negotiated peace through the demagogy of Cleophon.[4] Thirdly, he became associated with Socrates, and Socrates, as we have seen, was critical of the whole theory of Athenian democracy, believing that politics required as much specialist expertise as any other serious endeavour, and had sympathies with the Spartan system.

Plato in the seventh *Letter*[5] gives a retrospective account of his feelings at this time. There was, he says, widespread discontent with the democracy, and great things were expected from the Thirty. With Critias and Charmides among them, this seemed an auspicious moment for Plato's entry into public life. But they quickly made the previous government seem an age of gold: Plato seems slightly more upset by their attempt to implicate Socrates in their crimes than by the crimes themselves: in any event he was repelled and withdrew. The democracy was restored by Thrasybulus, and behaved with exemplary moderation. Only they elected to make an example of Socrates. It is clear enough, though Plato does not say so, that the real motive behind the prosecution was political and that Socrates was seen as a corrupting influence on Alcibiades, Critias and Charmides.[6] The amnesty did not permit such a charge, and the accusation was one of impiety. Socrates was executed and Plato once again withdrew in disillusion. He seems to have travelled, certainly to Megara, possibly to Cyrene and Egypt.[7] He watched developments in Athenian politics, and compared them with what he saw elsewhere. The more he saw, the more difficult it seemed to secure good government. Reliable people were not forthcoming; the rule of law was undermined. 'I had once been full of enthusiasm for public service. Now when I concentrated on the political scene and observed its general chaos I ended by feeling dizzy. I continued to look for a way of improving these particular situations and the general political system, waiting on the right moment for action, till in the end I came to realize that every single state suffers from bad government. Their political systems would require a combination of miraculous organization and good luck to rescue them. I was forced to say in a eulogy of true philosophy, that it offered an observation point for the identification of justice among communities and individuals. I added that mankind will not be free from disaster until either those who have a real love for wisdom take political office, or those in political power come by some divine dispensation to the truths of philosophy. It was in this frame of mind that I paid my first visit to Italy and Sicily.'[8]

In Magna Graecia he encountered Archytas and other Pythagoreans. He also encountered and befriended Dion, son-in-law of the dictator of Syracuse, Dionysius I.[9] The second encounter was to have a major impact on his life, the first on his thought[10]. Plato had been exercised by a number of problems. Suddenly, with the contact with the Pythagoreans, the pieces of the jigsaw fell into place. Socrates had shown a cool agnosticism about life beyond death.[11] The Pythagoreans offered the certainty of immortality, and with it the redress of earthly injustice. Socrates had sought for ethical definitions. He had not been content with examples; he asked for the common quality which is present, say, in all courageous acts, and is called 'courage'.[12] Furthermore, Hermogenes had taught Plato that true reality cannot change, and Cratylus that the material world is always changing.[13] Pythagorean mathematical philosophy offered the key. For it revealed an ideal world of truths which are only imperfectly realized in material objects. It is eternally true that in a right-angled triangle the square on the hypotenuse is equal to the sum of the squares on the other two sides, but it is never more than approximately true of a triangle you draw in the sand. So Plato came to his Theory of Forms. There is a perfect world of Forms, real and unchanging, where true courage and piety and justice are to be found, and discerned with the mind; the manifestations of the Forms in the material world are imperfect and impermanent. Finally, Plato received from the Pythagoreans the vision of a community, devoted to philosophy and concerned about politics.

He returned to Athens, wrote *Phaedo* as the first fruits of his intellectual excitement, and at some point, probably in the 380s, founded his university in the Academy. It was a school for statesmen, and it had a political reputation. Athenaeus records Plato as sending Euphraeus as adviser to Perdiccas of Macedon; Euphraeus was later involved in the politics of his own city of Oreus.[14] Plutarch has a long list of Academics who were prominent in public life: Aristonymus in Arcadia, Menedemus at Pyrrha, Phormio at Elis, Eudoxus at Cnidus, Aristotle in Stagira. Xenocrates and Delius, as well as Aristotle, were involved with Alexander. Pytho and Heracleides were leaders of a liberation movement in Thrace.[15] Hermeias of Atarneus certainly had some connections with the Academy. Plato's sixth letter commends Erastus and Coriscus to him, and Aristotle was his friend. Aristotle also tried to influence Themison of Cyprus by his *Protrepticus*. Timonides and Eudemus were at Dion's side in Syracuse; so were Philostratus and Callippus, who assassinated Dion for betraying his principles. There must have been many students from the Academy prominent in Athenian life: Chabrias and Phocion and others like them,[16] Lycurgus,[17] perhaps even Demosthenes.[18] Plato himself was invited to help at Cyrene[19] and Megalopolis,[20] but only accepted the invitations from Syracuse in 367 and 361. If the third letter is genuine he may have been responsible for the constitutional organization of Phoebia and Tauromenium. It is important that the work of the Academy is seen as having its outcome in practical politics.[21]

The Republic (the familiar English title is notoriously maladroit but inescapable; better *The State*) must be the product of those same years in which Plato was building up the Academy. It is the theoretical working out of the practice, perhaps a kind of manifesto.[22] We cannot here concern ourselves with the wider philosophical implications of this magisterial work; simply with it as an account of the ideal commonwealth. But it is important to remember that the ideal commonwealth is drawn in a wider context.

The first book may well have been written independently, before the journey to Sicily.[23] On its own it is a characteristically inconclusive 'Socratic' dialogue on the subject of justice. It is brilliantly and dramatically written: examples give place to definitions, definitions are offered and rejected, and the dialogue ends in *aporia*. There is no hint of the construction to come. It is important to see that, although Plato has been accused of subordinating the individual to the state, in fact he subordinates the state to the individual. The theme of *The Republic* is the search for justice in the individual, and the examination of the state is undertaken to throw light upon this.[24]

Glaucon and Adeimantus restate the case for immoralism made (in the literal sense) incoherently by Thrasymachus. Socrates in reply turns to see if they can discern justice 'in larger letters' in the community. One of the interesting features of *The Republic* is the unobtrusive, not clearly identified interaction between the logic of politics, historical actuality, and ethical norms. Socrates starts from the logical basis for community. No individual is self-sufficing. The principle of specialism of function, essential to the ideal political community which Plato will proceed to sketch, is the logical basis for the existence of a political community at all. A farmer, a builder, a weaver and one or two others are needed. The basic 'state' consists in this way of four or five people. But in practice it would have to be larger. The farmer depends on tools, and therefore on a blacksmith, the weaver on wool and therefore on a shepherd. Unless the state is self-sufficient (and Plato's thinking is confined to the ancient city-state), it will depend on imports, and therefore traders. Shopkeepers facilitate the exchange of goods. Manual labourers support the economy. It will be noticed that in one respect at least Plato and Marx are at one. The roots of politics lie in economics.

Even with this degree of elaboration, the standard of life remains rustic and elementary and it is possible that Plato is satirizing some contemporary 'simple-lifers', perhaps indeed Antisthenes. Glaucon described it as a merely animal existence ('a community of pigs') with none of the refinements associated with civilization. It is ironical that Socrates (2, 372 E) calls the simple state the genuine and healthy one, whereas the state we associate with Plato's ideal is described as in a state of unhealthy inflammation through the pursuit of luxury. Ironical too that the Guardians, Plato's philosopher-rulers, appear first as a military class, isolated by the specialized function of soldiery, existing for aggressive war to provide more land to minister to luxury. But Plato is making a shrewd analysis in identifying the economic causes of war, and in recognizing the militarism of any state organized beyond the unsophistication of the Arapesh. The League of Nations was reduced to defining the nation-state as 'a community organized for war'.

The principle of specialism implies that political rule is exercised by a special group selected with a view to that purpose and trained for it. Plato's formula for an ideal commonwealth is to have the right people in the ruling class, the right education and the right way of life for them. We hear little or nothing about the 'third' class, the great mass of the people who attend to the economic and general life of the community; the slaves, who were almost certainly there as a substratum, are not mentioned at all.[25] Even the 'second' class, the Guardians in their military and executive function, the 'Auxiliaries', the drop-outs from the highest test of all, are largely incidental to Plato's thinking. Everything else in his thought is subordinated to the philosopher-rulers.

Plato picks out four virtuous qualities. We call them, with Ambrose, the cardinal virtues, but there was no standard identification of them at this period and it is largely because of Plato's analysis that they became canonized.[26] Wisdom is the virtue appropriate to the ruling class, courage to the auxiliaries, self-control belongs to all classes, and justice exists where each group performs its own function and does not meddle with the specialism of others. Thus the rulers correspond in function to intelligence in the individual, the soldiers to temper, and the third class to desire. The whole structure is so close to Hindu thought that it is hard to think that it is not derived from it, no doubt through the Pythagoreans, who surely derived their theories of transmigration from India.[27] There the Brahmins are the philosopher-rulers, and their quality is Sattva, intellectual and moral virtue, the Kshattryas are the soldier auxiliaries and their quality is Rajas, emotional energy and passion, the Vaishyas are the producers and traders, and represent Tamas, desire for physical satisfaction, the Sudras, the fourth caste, are set off from the others as 'once-born' only. The last correspond to the unmentioned slaves. We are not to impose too rigid a tripartite structure on Plato. His thinking is really dualistic, as his dialectic insists. There is a basic division between rational and irrational, rulers and ruled.

But though Plato envisages a relatively small ruling class who hold all power, and in this sense his thinking is oligarchical, in other ways it is radical and revolutionary. In the first place he provides quite explicitly for mobility between classes. He certainly believes in eugenics and expects the rulers, under careful eugenic selection, to produce children of the right physical and intellectual quality to carry on the work. But he knows that outstanding children are produced by unexpected parents and that brilliant parents can produce very ordinary children. So the allocation of children to one class rather than another is on the basis of their own capacity not their parents' attainments. Secondly, he holds to the equality of the sexes, a proposition almost unthinkable except for purposes of comic fantasy at Athens, and not remotely practised politically anywhere in the Greek world. Thirdly he cuts at the root of the abuse of power by separating political power from economic power. The Guardians have to lead a life of the highest economic – and sexual – self-abnegation.

Perhaps I may here be permitted to obtrude a personal reminiscence. In 1966 I experienced the most exciting seminar I have ever conducted, with a group of final honours classicists in Ibadan, Nigeria. We were discussing how Plato would react to present-day Nigerian politics. It was in the period after the first assassinations and the military takeover. We agreed that he would not necessarily object to seeing the soldiers in power, but that he would be highly critical of the Sandhurst curriculum. Then we looked more seriously at the way of life he prescribed for his Guardians in the light of our experience of the first republic of Nigeria. We saw that the two points on which Plato was insisting in mapping the way of life for his Guardians were that they should be removed from the temptations provided by wealth and family. And we saw that he had precisely identified the two rocks on which the first republic had been shipwrecked – corruption and nepotism (especially in its extended form of tribalism). We thought his solution fantastic, but his diagnosis of the problem unerring. And we observed the profound insight which realized that a system of education cannot operate successfully if the general mores of society are pulling in the opposite direction.

But is the solution so fantastic? Plato is too well aware of human nature to think that more than a small proportion of people have the personal qualities necessary to persist in the life of the Guardians. He does not advocate universal communism. Communism operates solely among the Guardians. Among the rest of the community there is private property, though the Guardians take care to avoid extreme inequalities. He does not advocate universal sexual self-discipline. The majority of the people live normal sexual lives. The Guardians must abstain except at definite festivals where they mate with a partner allocated to them by a lot rigged in accordance with the best eugenic principles. Plato thus expects abnormal self-control from only a small proportion of his citizens. He demands less of them than the mediaeval church demanded of its monks, whom they in many ways resemble.

Plato has also been criticized for his system of education as a means for the production of political wisdom, though Rousseau called this section 'the best treatise on education in the world'. Plato accepts, because it is a part of himself, the basic system of education familiar to him, an education in the liberal arts lasting up to the age of eighteen. He does however propose to censor the material studied in accordance with ethical principles of his own. In particular, he proposes to eliminate all theologically and morally improper stories of the gods (he would have had a good time with the Old Testament!). He censors all dramatic recitation (it should be remembered that there was no silent reading) on the grounds that it was not in line with the formation of a consistent character. (Shelley centuries later defended poetry precisely on the grounds that it made us sensitive to the character and experience of others.) And he banned all debilitating musical modes or rhythms; one cannot think that he would approve of *L'Après-midi d'un faune*. We may deduce that the whole community engages in this basic education; otherwise upward mobility between the classes would be impossible. In any case basic education is a necessity for any form of social living.

The next two years would be spent on physical training. This would also be military training. This is partly that the Guardians start as a soldier class anyway, and partly that Plato is killing two birds with one stone. But he starts from the need for physical fitness, and regards military training as the best means to that end. Then follow ten years of mathematics. The analysis of the different branches, arithmetic, geometry, astronomy and music, is taken from Archytas, with the addition of solid geometry. Mathematics is important for its practical applications in agriculture, navigation and military tactics. But it is more important because it helps to lift the mind above the relativities of day-to-day life up to the eternal verities. Even this is not enough. Mathematics did not in Plato's mind deal with fundamentals, partly because it made use of limited hypotheses, partly because it never freed itself completely from the use of diagrams and visible figures. Ultimately Plato wanted his philosopher-rulers to have ascended to a self-evident, non-hypothetical first principle. He wanted them to have what he called a synoptic view. It was the function of dialectic to help them to this. Plato's metaphysics, expounded in *Phaedo* and here taken for granted, saw reality in what he called the Forms, eternal, unchanging, perfect, and known only to the intellect; the material world is impermanent, imperfect and unreal, and such existence as it has is due to its relationship with the Forms. Thus with our senses we never discern perfect 'treeness', perfect equality or perfect justice; we perceive particular trees, more or less equal objects, relatively just acts, which 'imitate' the perfect form, or perhaps participate in it. Five years of training in dialectic enable the philosopher-ruler to distinguish the world of timeless being from the objects which come to be and pass away, to identify the essence, and to gaze with his mind's eye upon the Form of the Good which exists even beyond the other Forms, beyond reality, and is the source of all reality, all knowledge.

It is precisely this which is so strongly attacked by Plato's present-day critics. Politics, it is said, is the art of the possible. Men of principle are dangerous in politics because they are unrealistic. Aristotle asked what was the use of the Form of the Good to a weaver at his work,[28] and the modern critic asks the same question about the statesman. Politics, it is said, must be pragmatic. The criticism is unjust. No doubt Plato is unfashionable in having a metaphysic at all. None the less the politician must have some kind of end in view. There are choices before us; more than one course is possible; and we have to choose in accordance with our vision of the good society. Plato is saying that we should first get that vision clear. Until we know our direction, if not our destination, we cannot find the best means for the next stage of the journey. But, over and beyond that, it is totally false to say that Plato was not concerned about the pragmatic in politics. On the contrary, the next fifteen years of his training, from thirty-five to fifty, is spent by the embryonic statesman in obtaining administrative experience in a subordinate capacity. One would have thought that fifteen years of practical training was enough to satisfy the most exacting pragmatist.

So Plato reinforces his conclusion, that political troubles will persist until philosophers become rulers or rulers take seriously to the study of philosophy, that is until political authority and the pursuit of wisdom coincide (*Rep.* 5, 473 C-D).

Aristotle, as we shall see, criticizes Plato's scheme in the second book of *Politics*. His criticisms are to some extent wide of the mark, because they are directed against the way of life of the Guardians as if this applied to the whole community. He attacks the community of family relationships on the general ground that Plato 'waters down' affection;[29] he thinks that it would only lead to quarrels and suggests that it would be more appropriate for the subjects, to prevent them uniting, than for the rulers; he is offended by the danger of incest, though horror of incest depends on the commitment to the family in the first place. He is equally critical of communism of property, and claims that common property is no one's property; to eliminate private property is to destroy that kind of carefulness, not to diffuse it. In general he holds that Plato has confused unity with uniformity (an odd criticism of a Utopia based on specialization of function), and that the real problem lies not in institutions but in human nature: 'you can't make men good by Act of Parliament'.

Plato sets great store by two factors: his system of eugenics and his system of education. We do not, and probably cannot, know enough about eugenics, and Plato admits as much in suggesting that degeneration from the perfect polity would arise out of a miscalculation in this field.[30] It is, however, just to say that he allows for this in making provision for interchange between classes. Nor do we know enough about education. Even intellectually, some people of high ability have blind spots, and mathematics is a blind spot for many. Even if we allow for argument Plato's premiss that the education of the ruler must lift him above the relativities of the material world to the eternal truths, Plato himself asserts that mathematics is a second-best way to this end,[31] and there must be many relatively innumerate people who would be admirable Guardians by his own standards. On moral education we know still less. We do not know what it is which causes two people confronted with the same influence, one to accept it, and the other to react against it. We can make generalizations, but there are always exceptions. Plato again allows for this both in the interchange between classes, and the subdivision of the Guardians. But his criteria for this last are confused. Supreme courage is not necessarily associated with a narrow failure to achieve a first-class honours degree.

This apart, Plato's scheme offers itself to three major criticisms. Firstly he does not believe in 'grassroots' democracy. Indeed he is reacting against the muddle achieved by 'grassroots' democracy in national politics at Athens. Plato believes that politics is a profession for the expert. He believes that the majority of human beings are not expert in this field, are not qualified to be expert in this field, and will be genuinely happier, as well as better governed, if they stick to their own last and do not 'interfere in matters which they do not understand' (like Gilbert's House of Peers). It is foolish sentimentalism not to accept the fact that there is such professional expertise in politics. It is exercised in the complexities of the modern nation-state by the Civil Service, and by some (but not all) politicians. It is at least arguable that in matters concerning the community as a whole every member of the community should be entitled to a say, and that his expertise consists precisely in the fact that he is a member of the community; furthermore, that if we think of his fulfilment as an individual it is to be found in the exercise of choice, and if he is not exercising choice in the matters which affect the community of which he is a member he is not really finding his full stature as an individual. The right, or need, to choose must include the right, or possibility, of choosing wrongly; it is incompatible with a static perfection. But, wrong choices apart, choices which have a validity of their own may conflict; in this sense politics is the science of compromise. It is important to see that this criticism of Plato's scheme is equally valid against our modern elective aristocracies (which is how a Greek would view what we call Parliamentary democracy). The vast majority of citizens do not have any say in decisions affecting the community at large; and representative government, while not incompatible with grassroots democracy, does not entail it.

The second defect in Plato's scheme is that though he takes pains to separate his ruling class from two of the main temptations associated with power, wealth and family, he forgets the corruption of power itself. Acton's much misquoted aphorism – 'Power tends to corrupt, and absolute power corrupts absolutely. Great men are almost always bad men'[32] – is the judgement of a sensitive and learned historian, and is borne out by history. It is strange that Plato, who in *Gorgias* showed himself so bitterly aware of the corrupting effect of power, should have been blind to it in *The Republic*. The ascetic dictator is the most dangerous of all dictators.

The third objection to Plato is that he envisages the ideal of a static perfection. This is a dead ideal, not a living one, as he found later when he was forced by criticism to admit life, and therefore movement, into the world of the Forms.[33] It will be noticed that this is not the same criticism as that offered by those who claim that politics is entirely pragmatic. A decision or policy can be said to 'work' only in relation to some end or goal. But that goal itself need not be a static perfection.

Plato does not intend his ideal city to be thought of as an actuality or even as a practical possibility, though he no doubt wishes that it might be.[34] But as surely as Paul declares the Christians to be a colony of heaven,[35] living out their citizenship of heaven in their earthly state, so Plato calls anyone who shares his vision to live out his citizenship of the ideal commonwealth.[36] The one place where the pattern may be seen in its perfection is 'in heaven'.[37] Plato's meaning is controversial, but probably it is to be taken literally of the ordered perfection of the stars, which were for him, it should not be forgotten, living creatures endowed with souls.

In 367 Dionysius I died, and was succeeded by his son, Dionysius II, now aged thirty. The court was divided. Dion, the new ruler's uncle, wanted Dionysius to become a constitutional monarch, guided by philosophical principle. Philistus favoured the continuance of autocracy. No doubt both, however they rationalized it, valued their own position. Dion invited Plato to educate the young king in statesmanship. Plato was sixty. His pupil had been bred to power, and lacked discipline. It was not a promising commission, but it was one which could not be refused. Plato 'followed reason and justice as far as humanly possible'[38] and went to Syracuse. He would have no second-class solutions. The science of politics required detachment of the mind from the relative to the eternal. The means to this was mathematics. It is remarkable that Dionysius submitted to the discipline. He was no boy; he was of the age when Napoleon became first consul, when Pitt had been prime minister for six years, when Mozart was composing *Figaro*. His courtiers followed him. The palace was a whirl of dust as geometrical figures were sketched in the sand and erased. The ultimate aim was moral harmony. But Dionysius would not touch philosophy.[39] Further, he was jealous of Dion, and exiled him. Dion removed, the dictator seemed closer than ever to his tutor. But Plato would not accept the political role which Dion had been playing. The most he did was to establish some kind of friendly relations between Dionysius and Archytas. In 366 he returned to Athens, the dictator's promise to reinstate Dion unfulfilled.

Dionysius was in fact at war. He may have been genuinely afraid that Dion would form a fifth column. For four years Dion remained with Plato in Athens. Then the long war drew to its conclusion. Dionysius asked Plato to return to Syracuse. It is hard to discern his motives. He may have been seeking security against Dion. He may have felt the need of Plato to balance the court factions. But he seems also to have had a genuine respect and affection for Plato as a man. Plato refused. Dionysius brought pressure to bear. There were favourable reports from Archytas and other mutual friends. There were threats against Dion and his family. There was even the carrot of philosophy, for Dionysius, sincerely or subtly or both, started studying philosophy and asking questions which demanded a personal answer from Plato. In 362 Plato reluctantly went. He spent a long period with Dionysius in which he went through the plan of the philosophic education necessary to the statesman.[40] He regarded this both as a test of Dionysius' sincerity and as a necessary preliminary should he prove sincere. He exemplifies the sort of point he was making. Take a circle. We have the word *circle*, which is accidental and impermanent; it could be something quite different. We have the verbal description or definition of a circle. We have the visible circle, always imperfect. We have the knowledge of the circle in our minds. But none of these is the true circle. We are in fact back to the

Theory of Forms, approached through mathematics, as the basis for statesmanship. Dionysius listened with apparent attention; and this was their last philosophic conversation. Dionysius began to interfere with Dion's property. Plato remonstrated. Dionysius' mercenaries struck against a pay-reduction. The dictator suspected the hand of Dion. Plato was a virtual prisoner, and was rescued only by the intervention of Archytas.

Plato's Sicilian adventure could scarcely have succeeded. If he had had control of Dionysius' education from birth, something might have been made of the man. If Dionysius had not had the double handicap of his father's example and his own exclusion from any apprenticeship in government, something might have been done. Dion brought Plato in, but Dion himself is an ambiguous figure, who was as much a liability as an asset. The important fact is that Plato's whole philosophy was that true reality can only be imperfectly imbedded in human life. Syracuse at its best could offer no more than a distorted reflection of the Form of Good Government. Plato was not trying to set up his Republic in Syracuse. He was trying to live as far as humanly possible himself as a citizen of the city of his vision, and he was trying to reduce the distortion. And, marginally, he succeeded.

We must add a postscript to the attempt to translate principle into practice at Syracuse by a note on Dion's brief period of rule.[41] In 357 Dion led a mercenary army against Dionysius. He was welcomed as a liberator, and Syracuse came over to him, leaving the dictator's faction on the fortified island of Ortygia. The presence of the dictator's troops is an important factor. Dion did not have a really free hand. Dion and his brother Megacles were elected 'generals with full powers': this acknowledged the continuance of crisis. Dion insisted on twenty 'colleagues', but he was virtually a new dictator, and it was with him that Dionysius negotiated. The situation was complicated by the arrival of an exiled democrat named Heracleides. There was personal friction between him and Dion, but behind that lay differences of political commitment. Heracleides carried measures for the redistribution of land, and secured a more constitutional government in the summer of 356, and indeed the withdrawal of Dion and his troops. But a military setback caused the recall of Dion, and he was once more appointed general with full powers, this time with no colleagues. He held office from early 355 till mid-354; the period is obscure. He succeeded in reducing Ortygia, but did not dismantle the fortifications, did not resign his extraordinary office, and was extravagant in rewards to his own party. He now began to press for a new constitution, calling in professional advisers from oligarchical Corinth. The detailed proposals are not known, and for an associate of the Academy Dion seems to have been singularly ill-prepared, but plainly they would be hard for the democrats to stomach. Heracleides opposed them forcefully and Dion was now reduced to political assassination. But violence breeds violence, and Dion was himself assassinated by a conspiracy led by his associate Callippus, who was perhaps disillusioned by Dion's fall from grace, though our sources portray him as an unscrupulous adventurer.

Dion has been variously identified as a frustrated idealist and as a self-seeker who gulled Plato into believing in his sincerity. We are coming increasingly to see that African history offers startling light on classical times. The story of Kwame Nkrumah is the story of a genuine idealist, who was swept to power as a liberator, found democracy disturbing and unstable, imprisoned some of his former associates, held on to power because he genuinely thought that the country could not do without him, but was corrupted by that power into an extravagance on behalf of himself and his party. Such was Dion.

We must now see what effect practical experience in Syracuse had upon Plato's vision of the ideal city. The primary result was to transfer his hope from people to institutions, and particularly laws. 'Do not let Sicily, or any state anywhere, be subject to the authority of human beings, but to laws.'[42]

Plato's thought besides had by now, as we shall see from *The Statesman*, moved from any belief in the practical possibility of a class of Guardians to the realization that even a single philosopher-king was a mirage. He recommended a team of lawgivers from Greece to arrange a settlement which would bring both factions in Syracuse under the rule of law.[43] A little later he showed the ambiguities his thinking had reached.[44] He recommended a commission as before, but outlined the constitution they should initiate: three kings (Dionysius, his half-brother, and Dion's son),[45] as constitutional rulers; thirty-five Guardians of the Law, a Council and an Assembly. This is a compromise between the Guardians and the Philosopher-King; it is a compromise between monarchy, oligarchy and democracy. But the basic point is that it is all submitted to law. The *nomophylakes* are a pointer from *The Republic* to *The Laws*. It is possible that this new stress on the rule of law was due to Archytas. Stobaeus preserves six fragments of a treatise *On Law and Justice*.[46] Their authenticity is controversial, but there are strong reasons for accepting them.[47] They offer a mathematical theory of law and harmony and balance in the state. They too approve a mixed constitution, and insist that law must conform with nature, be politically authoritative, and advantageous to the whole community. This accords well with what Archytas actually achieved at Tarentum through a reasoned redistribution of economic resources.[48]

The Statesman need not detain us long.[49] It must have been written at much the time that Plato was engaged at Syracuse. It is one of a group of dialogues, *Theaetetus* (surely datable to the early 360s), *The Sophist, The Statesman* and (projected but never written) *The Philosopher*. Instead Plato turned to *Philebus* (early 350s). It is at least possible that it was the débâcle of 362 which broke the sequence. In *The Statesman* we have no carefully constructed ideal constitution. Nor do we have the belief in a moral and intellectual aristocracy, or (as it is today called) a meritocracy. We have instead a consistent statement that the ideal state would be under the absolute rule of the philosopher-king, the one truly wise ruler, to whom statesmanship is a science, as professional as medicine to the doctor. Such scientific mastery will be the possession of very very few. Plato has given up the hope of a class of Guardians. The only hope is for a single individual, whether he holds the position of power or is the figure behind the throne. Such an individual will not need laws. Laws can give only generalized solutions; the wise statesman will give individual answers according to individual need, which he will perfectly understand. In this reliance on the single individual we see disillusion with the court at Syracuse, and no doubt also with the state of Athenian politics, in neither of which could he see the hope of an aristocracy in the real sense. There may be a touch of admiration for what the Pythagorean Epaminondas had achieved in the revival of Thebes. But Syracuse is in his mind. He did not believe in Dionysius. He did not believe in Dion. He did not even believe in himself. For though lying in the background to this discussion is the pathetic question, 'Could Syracuse have a philosophic ruler? And if not, could I be the truly philosophic statesman behind the throne?', in the end he has to answer that the philosopher-king is not born naturally as the 'monarch' in a hive of bees, and that human beings have to make do with a second best.[50] The rest of the analysis offers the traditional Greek division of monarchy, oligarchy and democracy but makes more fundamental the distinction between constitutions operating under the rule of law and constitutions operating without law. Plato then arranges the six systems of government in order of merit: monarchy under law, oligarchy under law, democracy under law, democracy without law, oligarchy without law, monarchy without law. *Corruptio optimi pessima!*

Plato has not, however, completely abandoned the ideal composition of the state in *The Republic*. There the Guardians *pur sang* were backed by the administrative and military skill of the Auxiliaries. Here this is elaborated. The true statesman will need a sub-ruling class to support him. These will have specialist functions – oratory, military strategy, the judicature. This is a refinement on the earlier work where he had not identified specialisms among the Guardians. And, although he does not put them quite on a par with these three, there are other subsidiary functions also, of educators[51] and magistrates.[52] The earlier discussion has distinguished the statesman from other functionaries found in actual communities, and no doubt in Plato's. Some of these are of some seniority, like the priests and diviners.[53] Then there are the subordinate civil servants, the 'administration'.[54] These are the primary producers;[55] the merchants and slaves are classified together as serving their needs.[56] We have here no impression of a sharp division between the Guardians and the rest. Rather there is a sense of the isolation of the true statesman from anyone else, and a steady progression of function down through the community.

There is one other question of importance in *The Statesman*. This relates to the myth.[57] The myth identifies the Age of Cronos as one when God takes personal care for the governance of the universe, sets his subordinate deities as shepherds of different groups of living creatures, who need no sex for life nor labour for survival. It was the peaceable kingdom. But we live in the Age of Zeus, when God and his subordinates have withdrawn, and must fend for ourselves. The point of this is surely threefold. First, it makes clear Plato's rejection of the physical world as it is: his ideal world is an aristocratic and puritan world without work or sex. Secondly, it reinforces his belief that the only real statesmanship is that of the single ruler. Grube is surely wrong in seeing the myth as a rejection of the philosopher-king as irrelevant to 'the Age of Zeus'.[58] He may be hard to find, but he is not irrelevant. The Age of Cronos is, so to speak, the Platonic Form of the political community. The ideal state is one in which no one engages in politics except God's vicegerent; there is not much doubt that Plato wistfully casts himself for the rôle. Thirdly, the power of the myth is, as Skemp says, surely, that it 'places the whole political life of man within a Universe which has moral meaning within itself, which in the terms of the myth is "an ensouled creature". Human societies live and move within a "cosmos" and their relation to it cannot be one of indifference. The Universe may at one time aid the good life and at another time (the time we are now living in) it may be inimical to it; and in either case the state of the Universe affects the state of politics at the time.'[59] Politics is, for Plato, always to be seen *sub specie aeternitatis*.

We must here pause to mention briefly the curious and fragmentary *Critias*, because it incorporates a Utopia of a rather different kind. At the beginning of *Timaeus*,[60] which, whatever its date,[61] is written dramatically as a sequel to *The Republic*, Socrates expresses the wish to see the citizens of his ideal community in action. It looks as if it was some time before Plato felt able to essay this, for *Critias* is assuredly one of the later dialogues, and when he did essay it, he left it incomplete: the reason was no doubt political disillusion. The story of *Critias* is encapsulated in *Timaeus*.[62] The ideal commonwealth is identified with primaeval, antediluvian Athens, and she showed her greatness in conflict with the powerful island-continent of Atlantis out beyond the Straits of Gibraltar, an island which sank below the surface of the sea in a violent earthquake.

The fragment of *Critias* contrasts the geography and social order of Athens in its perfection and Atlantis. Hephaestus and Athene, the powers of practical and theoretical skill, were in charge of Athens. The land was rich in soil, well irrigated, with an abundance of timber in the mountains, and with crops and pasturage superb alike in quality and quantity: it was thus able to sustain Plato's inflamed state without aggression. He does, however, have a whimsical reference to a current political controversy with Boeotia when he suggests that in those days the mountain-conformation placed Oropus firmly in Attica.[63] The inhabitants were handsome and virtuous. They were divided into three classes. There were 'godlike men' who evidently took the decisions;[64] the soldiers, living apart from the others on the Acropolis, with equality of the sexes, no discomfort; and the craftsmen and farmers. It will be noticed that Plato has here added perfection of nature to perfection of human organization, but he has not carried it into the realm of fantasy.

The description of Atlantis is vigorous and vivid, but contains little of philosophical or political importance. It was under the guidance of Poseidon, whose mate Clito produced five pairs of twins. There were thus ten political units under ten kings, one of whom was overlord. Plato depicts this occidental kingdom in terms of oriental luxury. Its natural resources were superabundant and exotic: basic foods and luxuries, spices and aromatics, obscure and prized minerals, and pasture enough even to support elephants. There were cold and hot springs, quarries of different coloured stones, luxurious temples, palaces, houses, baths, gardens, sports fields, docks and harbours. The planning was scientifically carried out, and the city-system was based on concentric circles and is indebted to the Greek picture of Babylon and Ecbatana.[65] Their forces numbered 120,000 cavalry, 120,000 heavy infantry, 120,000 archers, 120,000 slingers, 360,000 light infantry, 240,000 marines, 1,200 ships. The kings had the absolute right of life and death. They met in conclave to compare policies at intervals of four or five years, 'honouring the odd and even equally'. Then suddenly, just as the story breaks off, Plato moves away from his anti-Utopia and speaks of them as fallen from a high estate.[66]

'They are at the close of the dialogue called "Critias", in which he describes, partly from real tradition, partly in ideal dream, the early state of Athens; and the genesis, and order, and religion, of the fabled isle of Atlantis; in which genesis he conceives the same first perfection and final degeneracy of man, which in our Scriptural tradition is expressed by saying that the Sons of God inter-married with the daughters of men, for he supposes the earliest race to have been indeed the children of God; and to have corrupted themselves, until "their spot was not the spot of his children". And this, he says, was the end; that indeed "through many generations, so long as the God's nature in them yet was full, they were submissive to the sacred laws, and carried themselves lovingly to all that had kindred with them in divineness; for their uttermost spirit was faithful and true, and in every wise great; so that, in *all meekness of wisdom, they dealt with each other*, and took all the chances of life; and despising all things except virtue, they cared little what happened day by day, and *bore lightly the burden* of gold and of possessions; for they saw that, if *only their common love and virtue increased, all these things would be increased together with them*; but to set their esteem and ardent pursuit upon material possession would be to lose that first, and their virtue and affection together with it. And by such reasoning, and what of the divine nature remained in them, they gained all this greatness of which we have already told; but when the God's part of them faded and became extinct, being mixed again and again, and effaced by the prevalent mortality; and the human nature at last exceeded, they then became unable to endure the courses of fortune; and fell into shapelessness of life, and baseness in the sight of him who could see, having lost everything that was fairest of their honour; while to the blind hearts which could not discern the true life, tending to happiness, it seemed that they were then chiefly noble and happy, being filled with all iniquity of inordinate possession and power. Whereupon, the God of Gods, whose Kinghood is in laws, beholding a once just nation thus cast into misery, and desiring to lay such punishment upon them as might make them repent into restraining, gathered together all the gods into his dwelling place, which from heaven's centre overlooks whatever has part in creation; and having assembled them, he said"—'

Plato's Atlantis has fascinated generations. More than a thousand books have been written about it. In the end it is his own invention. But it incorporates features drawn from many sources, Herodotus's account of the Persian forces, and general pictures of Persian luxury certainly; oral tradition about Minoan Crete equally certainly; a folk memory of the Santorini eruptions certainly; and perhaps some dim notion of a continent far to the west. It remains a tantalizing fragment. Enough to note the reassertion of the ideal scheme of *The Republic*, though he has little real belief by now in his philosophic rulers; the idealization of nature; the portrayal of Atlantis as the really 'inflamed' state; and the insistence that imperfection arises as a result of degeneration from something better.

The work of Plato's last years which really matters is *The Laws*.[67] Here we have a revised version of *The Republic*, coming to terms with practical experience, but still an attempt to sketch an ideal commonwealth. Three men, an unnamed Athenian who is the mouthpiece of Plato, a Spartan named Megillus and a Cretan named Cleinias are walking in the north of Crete. The conversation is supposed to take place over a long, a very long, summer's day, but apart from a reference to the fields and the shade of the trees,[68] the scene is scarcely envisaged. Crete and Sparta offered constitutions admired in antiquity, and this explains the choice of interlocutors. The ideal constitution is thus to be seen in the context of existing constitutions. These are criticized by Plato. In fact the first three books provide an introduction in terms of ethical and historical analysis. The institutions of Sparta and Crete are successfully orientated to producing courage; but more important is self-control, and this is not achieved by total repression. The Athenian enjoys scandalizing his audience by advocating the educational value of moderate intoxication. This leads to a discussion of the importance of education, conceived not as literacy and numeracy, still less as vocational training, but as moral discipline. Where Plato's analysis is so excellent is that he sees that education is no mere matter of schooling. It continues through life, reinforced or weakened by the institutions of society.[69]

Plato now passes from the education of the individual to the constitution of the state and offers a philosophy of politics on the basis of an analysis of history. There is some idealization of primitive man, pertinent to our theme. They were endowed with adequate resources for a life of simple comfort. Plato has no doubt that vice, crime, violence and war arise from the corruptions of wealth. Once more complex societies emerge Plato stresses the dangers of autocracy, the advantages of a diversified constitution with elements of monarchy, oligarchy and democracy, and the absolute necessity of the rule of law. There are in nature different claims to authority: parents over children, upper class over lower class, elders over youth, owners over slaves, stronger over weaker, wise over ignorant, and those blessed by fortune over the rest. These may conflict. The conflict must be resolved by compromise and the rule of law. Extreme political positions are illustrated by Persian autocracy and Athenian democracy, both in their different ways irresponsible. At this point Cleinias says that he is currently engaged in drawing up a code for a new colony in an abandoned part of Crete. We learn later that the inhabitants are called Magnesians.[70] Magnesia-on-the-Maeander was traditionally settled from a mother-city in the Messara,[71] and it looks as if Plato is drawing on local knowledge.[72] In this sense Plato's final ideal is not a Utopia; it has a local habitation and a name.

To establish a constitution requires a legislator working with a dictator, if a benevolent dictator can be found,[73] but it will also require the consent of the governed. So Plato still casts himself for the rôle of *éminence grise*, but cannot see how he can exercise that rôle save through an individual – despite Dionysius. The point that Plato is making, however, is that it matters less for healthy government whether the power is exercised by one individual, by a small group or by the direct voice of all the citizens than whether those in power are themselves under the rule of law.[74]

After a worthy and wordy preamble on the duties of religion, morality, physical fitness and social responsibility we pass to the organization of the state. The absolute ideal remains communism in relation to property and to family life. The practical ideal is to have a limited number of families with inalienable holdings. The number will be 5040.[75] This is $2 \times 3 \times 4 \times 5 \times 6 \times 7$: it is divisible by all the numbers from 2 to 10, as well as by 12, 14, 15, 16, 18, 20, 21, 24, 28, 30 and others. Plato would not approve of decimalization: 5040 = the number of old pennies in a pound $\times$ the number of shillings in a guinea. The number is the number of families, not the number of citizens; the children are also citizens.[76] Money is to be kept to a minimum; there are to be no loans at interest, and no extremes of wealth or poverty. In our language, all acquisition above four times the value of the basic holding will be subject to 100 per cent tax. In the avoidance of economic class conflict rests the foundation of national security.[77] The lots of land will be varied; each will include one area close to the city and one more distant.[78] But there will be inequalities, within strictly controlled limits, and Plato divides his state into four property classes.

The choice of officials is the subject of complex legislation. Most important are the thirty-seven Guardians of the Laws, nineteen from the settlers and eighteen from the mother-city, to be elected by majority vote after a careful weeding out of nominations. They must be not less than fifty years old and not more than seventy thus having a maximum tenure of twenty years. The military High Command are also elected. There will be a Council of 360, ninety from each of the four property classes, chosen by a process which includes both election and, as a concession to democratic opinion, lot. The Council will operate in groups of thirty for a month at a time. Other officials will be chosen by a similar combination of election and lot. That there is an Assembly of all citizens is taken for granted, and alluded to incidentally but not spelt out.[79] There is thus, as Aristotle says,[80] the blend of oligarchy and democracy. The monarchical element is represented by a strong executive.

The production of healthy children and their right upbringing are essential to the continuing well-being of the state. The proud equality of men and women in *The Republic* has fallen away. Plato now says that women have much less natural potential for excellence.[81] All the more reason to bring them into open society, where they may be influenced for good. More remarkable is the demand that the Minister of Education shall be regarded as the most important minister of state, and elected from among the Guardians of the Laws as the outstanding citizen all round.[82] There is much of interest in his provisions for education. Some of them, such as the censorship of the liberal arts,[83] strike us as reactionary; others, such as the training for ambidexterity,[84] or the equal opportunities for the sexes,[85] seem astonishingly radical. Basic mathematics is needed for all – and higher mathematics for some.[86] And there will be physical education directed to military training.

It would not be appropriate here to examine in detail all the various legislation. For all Plato's critical attitude to Athenian practice his proposals are in fact closely based on Attic law, with significant modifications.[87] The important fact is his belief in regulation by means of laws. Alongside this is his theory of punishment. He adheres to the Socratic paradox that no man is willingly unjust. How then is it ethical to punish an involuntary act? Plato's answer is to distinguish between the act and the state of mind. The state of mind requires remedial treatment, but an act which damages others must be atoned by compensation. That done, the object of law is to restore relationships between offender and offended.[88] Retributive punishment is ruled out – that is the act of a wild beast. It is all remarkably enlightened.

In the middle of this complex legislation comes the famous tenth book, which is in large part a treatise on natural theology.[89] It is perhaps the first systematic treatise on the subject, and it remains one of the more remarkable. Its importance for us rests in Plato's insistence that a healthy politic depends upon a sound religion, or in other words that in the end our particular concerns arise out of our *Weltanschauung*. These pages in fact introduce and justify legislation against three heresies, that gods do not exist at all, that they exist but are indifferent to human affairs, and that they exist and are concerned about human affairs but can be deflected from their purposes by prayer and sacrifice.[90] The first of these was the normal ground for charges of impiety; the second was the position later made famous by Epicurus, who drew on his predecessors more than he chose to admit; the third was the current orthodoxy, and had such a law prevailed at Athens few of Plato's contemporaries would not have been indictable. The punishment for impiety is up to five years' imprisonment, with a process of re-education. We are inclined to regard this as illiberal, as Plato is indeed the first political thinker to propose such penalties on opinion. But prison was not used normally in Greek penology except for criminals awaiting execution, and in its way it is a remarkable innovation. By contrast, a second offence is to be punished with death, and those who claim powers of raising the dead or influencing the gods are to suffer life imprisonment.

At the end of *The Laws* Plato introduces a topic he has touched on before,[91] the introduction of a supreme synod, exercising a general review function of the workings and moral fibre of the state. Its members will improve on the concepts of the original founder: so Plato at the last admits the possible imperfections of his judgement. They will keep contact with what is going on overseas, and learn from others – another notable change. They will presumably avert the degeneration which Plato saw as endangering his earlier Republic. The basic constituency of the synod is the ten eldest guardians of the laws, the priests who have won high distinction, the Minister of Education and his predecessors, and senior citizens selected for travel and study abroad[92] – broadly speaking, the Guardians proper of *The Republic* – with an equal number of younger men between the ages of thirty and forty to gain experience. The synod is sometimes called the Nocturnal Council, but that with its sinister overtones of secret meetings at dead of night is entirely misleading. They do not meet at night, but in the early morning before the normal working day. It may be taken for granted that their education will be that of the Guardians in *The Republic*. The practical implication is perhaps that the Academy's function was to train such men. Some interpreters have treated the synod as a sinister and illiberal institution. On the contrary it seems that Plato has put his finger on a very practical reform. Any organization, from a state down to a school or firm or church, could well do with a small group who are involved, but free from day-to-day routine, who are set aside because of their good judgement, and can take what Plato would call a 'synoptic' view, who are free from concentration on the individual trees and can look at the development of the forest as a whole. In the grim realities of life, such men are usually up to their necks in immediate activities. In Plato's ideal commonwealth the ablest and wisest will always be freed for the ultimately more important task.

The first thing that strikes us about Magnesia is the elementary nature of its economic organization. It is a simple agricultural community in which each family lives self-sufficiently from its own plot. Property is strictly limited. No citizen is to engage in gainful employment other than farming – no industry or craft, no trade or commerce, no banking or money lending. There is to be no accumulation of money in the form of gold or silver. It sounds fantastic, but the Spartans achieved something very similar, and only in the great trading centres of Athens and Corinth was it unthinkable – Plato showed what he thought of those in his determination that a healthy city was detached from the sea.

Secondly Magnesia is a religious state. Just as we must free our minds from economic sophistication so we must free them from religious indifference. There is a lot about religious festivals in Plato's ordinances. This is not an attempt to dope the people with opium. It is entirely natural for a simple agricultural society. Atheism and agnosticism were still rare; Plato no doubt regarded them as arising from a lack of roots. No doubt Plato tends to the authoritarian in politics because he believes in a static metaphysical reality; three times he calls human beings – approvingly – God's marionettes.[93] But his fostering of religion is far more complex; this is one element only.

The third notable feature of *The Laws* is the support for a mixed constitution, though Plato does not use the actual term. The important fact here is that Plato is coming to terms with the realities of human nature. On the one hand he no longer believes in the possibility of an infallible individual or group at the top. On the other he has come to see the need to secure the active consent of all the members of society if the state is to be stable.

Fourthly, Plato stands by the emphasis on education familiar from *The Republic*. He has some strikingly wise things to say about education. For example, 'Complete ignorance of a whole area of study is nothing to worry about, nothing disastrous. Far more damaging is a wide range of miscellaneous information without real education.'[94] For Plato, education is education for life. It contains a proper vocational element, and this is the first thing Plato stresses. The prospective farmer will play at farming, the prospective builder should be given toy bricks, the prospective cavalryman will have a hobby-horse, and learn to sit on his teacher's shoulders, and be trained on a pony.[95] But alongside this is moral education. 'It's a sense of moral responsibility, not money that ought to be your children's inheritance from you.'[96] The same passage goes on to present the main objects of choice and avoidance. The primary good is truth;[97] the most dangerous vice is self-love.[98] The object of the educator is to encourage the growing child to admire things which are healthy for the personality, and to shy away from those which are not. It is, in fact, to educate the attitude to pleasure and pain.[99] It is the function of the arts to reinforce these attitudes, partly because they inculcate a sense of rhythm and harmony, partly because they buttress reason with emotion.[100]

Fifthly he has not renounced at all the part to be played by the philosopher. He is there as the legislator; he is there in the *nomophylakes*; he is there above all in the so-called Nocturnal Council; and he is there no doubt in offering to guide the education of those who will bear responsibility. There is to be the rule of law. But even laws will need modification and someone must have the wisdom to modify them rightly. In the end the individual man of wisdom remains indispensable. In separating those of supreme insight in the Nocturnal Council Plato is endeavouring to see that they are used to the full. And their capacity is advisory rather than dictatorial. Cornford in his Samuel Dill lecture offered a poignant parallel to the Grand Inquisitor story in *The Brothers Karamazov*. He imagined Socrates arraigned before the Nocturnal Council with Plato in the President's chair, commenting: 'Socrates had held out the same gift of unlimited freedom and self-rule; and Plato had foreseen that mankind would not be able to bear it. So he devised this commonwealth, that the few who are wise might keep the consciences of the many who will never be wise.'[101]

But the most important thing about *The Laws* is the insistence on the rule of law.[102] The principle is laid down early. 'I can see that the state in which law is subject and without authority is on the brink of destruction. I see clearly that a state in which law is master of those in office, and those in office are slaves of law, enjoys security and all the other blessings which states receive from the gods.'[103] Clearly Plato believes that there are absolute moral standards; he has not abandoned the Theory of Forms. A system of law will encapsulate these, less perfectly than the man of real wisdom, but better than a Dionysius or even a Dion. And it will be a protection against a Dionysius. It is important to see that though Plato's laws would greatly circumscribe the individual's freedom of choice, particularly economically, Plato regards economic derestriction as fostering the licence of the few, the oppression of the many, and the genuine freedom of none. It is powerful individuals, not laws, who constitute the main danger to freedom, and Plato intends his laws to maximize real freedom.[104]

CHAPTER IX

ARISTOTLE

ARISTOTLE WAS NOT A UTOPIAN; there is a sense in which he was an anti-Utopian. But he had decided views on the necessary conditions of a healthy politic. It is important to see him against his background. He was a product of the fourth century, being born in 384 BC and dying in 322. He came from the small town of Stagira in the north of the Greek world, but this did not justify Méautis in his contemptuous characterization of him as a semi-barbarian. For better or worse he was Greek to the core, arrogantly and emphatically Greek; all his political presuppositions were Greek. His horizons were wider than most: his father was court physician to the king of Macedon. But Aristotle never favoured the large kingdom or the centralized autocracy. He came to Athens, proud, exclusive Athens, in 367 to study with Plato. Plato was an aristocrat and an indigene: he claimed descent from the ancient royal house of Attica. Aristotle belonged to the middle class and was an alien. At no point in his life was he directly involved in Athenian politics, for aliens could not become citizens. For twenty years he studied with Plato, who found him disturbingly brilliant, nicknamed him 'the Brain' and said that where others needed the spur he needed the curb. When he arrived Plato was absent on the ill-fated attempt to make a philosophic ruler out of Dionysius II; his first impression of Plato will have been the disillusioned return, and this, combined with the final débacle of 361, and the subsequent career of Dion, would be enough to make him critical of Utopianism. One wonders what seminar discussions accompanied the writing of the often bitter realism of *The Laws*; it was a work which influenced Aristotle's thought.

About 347 two decisive events affected Aristotle. One was the destruction of Stagira by Philip of Macedon, the other the death of Plato. Aristotle was an alien, and could not inherit the property of the Academy, and Speusippus succeeded to the headship of the University. Aristotle, an altogether abler man, left. We need not assume pique. We might assume courtesy, for his continued presence would be an embarrassment to Speusippus. But he had been twenty years in the Academy; loyalty to Plato had kept him; it was time for a move. He went to Assos, where two former colleagues, Erastus and Coriscus, were established. This too was a formative period politically. Erastus and Coriscus were involved with the political education, along Platonic lines, of Hermeias, dictator of Atarneus. Aristotle engaged in political discussions: some strands of his *Politics* seem to date from this period. He developed his knowledge of practical politics, especially in the fields of economics and foreign relations. He also came to a close affection and admiration for Hermeias; he married Hermeias' ward, wrote his epitaph, and commemorated him as a poet. It is noteworthy that this did not cause him to play down his condemnation of dictatorship as a system of government.

A period at Lesbos was of fundamental importance to his development as a scientist; there can have been few major scientists whose key observations have been made so late in life. From this he was pulled out to be tutor to Alexander, prince of Macedon. Except that they read *The Iliad* together we do not know what form the instruction took. Aristotle wrote two political monographs for the prince, one on *Kingship*, and one on *Colonial Foundations*; the latter may have had some practical effect on Alexander's policies. But there were other influences on Alexander. Tarn in reference to his mother alluded to the curious conjunction of 'a philosopher who taught that moderation alone could hold a state together' and 'a woman to whom any sort of moderation was unknown'.[1] There is a certain idealization of kingship in some passages of *Politics*, which may be affected by admiration for Alexander. But whatever political instruction the philosopher tendered, the prince outgrew it. It is an ironical picture this – the theorist whose horizon was the city-state training the practitioner who was to fling his empire halfway across Asia, the theorist to whom the barbarian or non-Greek was by nature a slave training the practitioner who was to admit Greeks and Persians as joint partners in his rule.

When Alexander succeeded to power, Aristotle returned to Athens to found his own university, the Lyceum, engaging in scientific research and the comprehensive interpretation of the universe. The dominant political figure at Athens was Lycurgus, and once more we are made aware of the curious interaction between practical politics and the search for the ideal.[2] Lycurgus had been a student at the Academy with Aristotle and Xenocrates (who succeeded Speusippus), and had absorbed some of the teaching which Plato propounded in *The Laws*; for example his scheme for a two-year period of compulsory military training is evidently based on Plato's proposals.[3] Lycurgus was a democrat who was tolerant of the propertied class, an Athenian patriot with half an eye on Sparta, 'a financier with a moral mission' (as Tarn put it).[4] Alongside the military reform, itself more than half moralistic, there were religious reforms, and a remarkable piece of legislation which forbade the enslavement of free men captured in war. Financial prosperity showed itself in a building programme. Some of this was military: the repair and improvement of the city defences and modernization of the fleet. Other measures were educational: the restoration of a gymnasium, and construction of a new stadium. In all we have the impression of a shrewd and constructive statesman, with a vision of the good society always before his imagination, yet practical, and content if things move a little forward. The amusing thing is to find his actions incorporated into Aristotle's blueprint for the ideal state. Thus Aristotle denies that the prisoner-of-war may automatically become a slave.[5] In his sketch of the ideal state he includes a brief survey of building schemes, including defensive fortifications and places for physical training.[6] An almost casual reference to guard-houses in the countryside shows that Aristotle has completely absorbed Lycurgus' period of military conscription and training.[7] It is amusing to see how this has passed from Plato's theory through Lycurgus' practice back into Aristotle's theory.

During Aristotle's last year political opposition to Macedon was mounting in Athens, and with the news of Alexander's death it exploded. Aristotle had had close associations with Alexander and with the military governor of Greece, Antipater. He withdrew to Euboea remarking wryly, with Socrates in mind, that he wanted to save the Athenians from sinning a second time against philosophy. In exile he was the target of political attacks, which he did not long survive, dying in 322.

This is not the place to attempt a comprehensive evaluation of Aristotle's political thought, but some things must be said as a background to his ideal society. First, Aristotle writes neither as an armchair philosopher nor as a practising politician, but as a detached and concerned spectator whose thought is shaped by experiences; he is never a mere theorist. If he vilifies dictatorship, it is because he has seen what Dionysius did to Plato. If he makes an apparent exception of the noble monarch, it is because he has known Alexander, and seen that monarchy can be noble. Secondly, Aristotle is a scientist. He works by accumulating evidence, surveying it and generalizing from it. One of the major research projects in the Lyceum was the collection of 158 constitutions of Greek states, treated historically and empirically. The evaluation of actual evidence, not *a priori* theory, is the groundwork of Aristotle's thought. Thirdly, Aristotle's thought was not static. The eight books we call *Politics* are something of an amalgam. Aristotle was a teacher, and kept his lecture courses under continual revision. The exact chronology is uncertain, and the reconstruction which follows, though plausible, is not to be pressed dogmatically. Aristotle seems to have begun with a course of lectures on the nature of the state (Book III). Next he added a course on the search for an ideal state (II). Then he decided that he ought to elaborate his whole syllabus in political science. He therefore rearranged his courses, beginning with the evolution of the state from its natural basis in the family (I), passing on to the ideal constitutions propounded in the past (II), and to a more thorough introduction to political science (III); to this he added his own formula for the ideal society (VII–VIII). But he had not put this last in its final form when he realized that his treatment was in danger of becoming insufferably theoretical, and inserted a course of lectures on practical politics (IV–VI); even here the order is uncertain, and some scholars think that the treatment of the pathology of the state in the fifth book should be postponed till after the constitutional examination in the sixth is completed. The important thing is that Aristotle did not expose his students to his own prescription for political salvation until after they had made a detailed examination of the nature of the state and the practicalities of politics, and had studied and criticized other ideal commonwealths.

Some points in his general thinking must be remembered. Ethics and Politics are for Aristotle separate aspects of the same subject. Man is for Aristotle man in society. At the beginning of his *Ethics* he affirms 'Every science and every subject, every action and every choice appear to aim at some good; so the Good has been well defined as "the object at which all things aim".'[8] He begins his *Politics* by repeating this assertion and coupling it with the statement that every *polis* (city-state, independent municipality) is a kind of association.[9] It is indeed the supreme kind of association, and must aim at the supreme good. The fundamental natural unit is the family. Related households join to form a village in order to satisfy their physical needs; villages join in a city-state, the ultimate form of association, because it reaches the goal of self-sufficiency. This is a natural process, and Aristotle declared man to be not a political animal (which is a mistranslation) but a living creature whose nature it is to live in city-states.[10] The city-state, which comes into being for the sake of life, exists in its fullness for the sake of the good life. The family is chronologically prior; the city-state is logically prior. This is the background to all his thinking.

The second book, in which he discusses earlier essays in Utopia, is of considerable interest, and we have already drawn upon it for our examination of Phaleas and Hippodamus. Particular interest naturally attaches to his criticisms of Plato. Aristotle passes straight to the community of wives and children. This he rejects out of hand, but his arguments seem more emotional than rational. Plato is aiming at unity, but a city-state is an aggregation not a unit, and an aggregation of men different from one another; it is hard to see how this is valid as a criticism of Plato, who founds his state on differentiation of function, or what it has to do with the particular proposal for community of wives and families. He is on seemingly sounder pragmatic ground when he suggests that 'Men pay most attention to what is their very own: they care less for what is common, and only when they feel themselves personally concerned.'[11] This is a typical conservative assault on socialism or communism. Aristotle suggests that it is better to be a cousin in real life than a brother in Plato's state; Plato's family communism waters down affection.[12] Aristotle does not really come to grips with Plato. He shows a residual horror of brother-sister incest, but such horror depends on the acceptance of the family system. He seems more concerned with the general concept of *meum* and *tuum* than the relevant question whether the parent-child relationship is necessary and important for parents, child or both. It is interesting that in some of the Israeli *kibbutzim* where the relationship of parent and child is maintained, but children grow up in their own age-groups, there is a real extension of fraternal relations without any watering-down; the familial feeling is so intense that the girls and boys as they grow up prefer to marry outside the *kibbutz*.

Next he turns to communism in property. It is important to see that Aristotle puts right out of court a system in which property is privately owned and used for private advantage; he is, it should be remembered, thinking largely of agricultural land. Of three alternatives, public ownership and public use, public ownership and private use, and private ownership and public use, he prefers the last, though he does not make clear the legal enactions and social conventions which will induce private owners to use their property in the public interest; Aristotle exposes himself to the charge of unrealism which he levels at Plato. He suggests further that Plato is depriving his ruling class of natural happiness. Aristotle's contention is that common property is no one's property. To extend the ownership of property through the community is not to extend that type of carefulness but to eradicate it. The source of evil, he asserts, lies not in institutions but in human nature.[13] This however is an over-simplification. Institutions do matter; at the very least a competitive society encourages competition and a co-operative society co-operation. There are two particularly interesting aspects of Aristotle's critique of *The Republic*. One is that it is confined to the communism of families and of property. The other is that he does not offer any alternative remedies to the abuses of nepotism and corruption which Plato is seeking to eliminate.

Aristotle has a brief discussion of Plato's revised scheme in *The Laws*. He regards *The Laws* as not differing essentially from *The Republic*, but being more thorough in its treatment. But we learn little significant from his critique about his own views, except to reinforce the fact that he is thinking in terms of a severely limited municipality, and that he has his feet well grounded in practicality.

We may now turn to Aristotle's own construction in the last two books of *Politics*. He returns to a point which he has established in *Ethics*: happiness lies in the life of virtue, and if this is true of the individual it must also be true of the community. But will the virtuous activity be found in immersion in politics or in the contemplative life divorced from politics? Aristotle does not really answer this. There is in fact a paradox. He has already argued to the contemplative life. He says now clearly that the best constitution must enable all sorts of men to achieve happiness.[14] The best constitution then leaves room for the contemplative life, but it is the very constitution which will tempt contemplatives into active politics, and it is the result of good political activity to leave place for contemplative activity. By analogy with the contemplative life Aristotle holds that the happiest state will not be engaged in busybody intervention but will be self-contained.

Characteristically, he turns promptly to practical details. First population. It is not numbers which determine political greatness. There is an optimum size for a city-state; a ship six inches long or a quarter of a mile long would cease to be a ship; and a city-state of ten citizens or 100,000 ceases to be a city-state; the former is insufficient, the latter too many to meet in assembly.[15] We laugh at this parochialism but he is of course right; we have found that there is indeed an optimum size for businesses, universities, airports, and our urban agglomerations and vast states have ceased to be anything that Aristotle would regard as a genuine political unit, and have lost all sense of community. Second, territory. This should be large enough for a comfortable but not luxurious standard of living for the citizens: Aristotle is closely aware, in the actualities of Athenian history, of the advantages and disadvantages of proximity to the sea. Third, race. Aristotle suggests that the people of Europe (he means the more northerly Balkans) have drive without intelligence, the people of Asia intelligence without drive, and the Greeks the best of both worlds. Beyond this jingoistic judgement lies a serious attempt to relate climate to culture, which was fostered by the medical schools; it is strongly reminiscent of Montesquieu.

He now moves on to details of organization. He restates his doctrine that the object for which the state exists is the best possible life. His attitude at this point is of considerable interest. In the first place his approach seems highly idealistic. But he reminds us in passing that he accepts slavery without question; a slave is an animate piece of property, not an integral part of the state, and is incapable of sharing in the highest life. Aristotle's middle-of-the-road driving here lets him down; enlightened Greek thought was already questioning such assumptions. Further he takes a pragmatic view of free men; they will not all be capable of full participation in the highest life; consequently there is no such thing as an ideal constitution in the abstract, since the best constitution will be relative to the particular citizens. This is refreshing, but it is odd to find it in a treatise on the ideal constitution.

There are six essential activities in a community: food-supply, industry, military service, the administration of property, religion and justice: lacking any of these activities a state would cease to be self-sufficient. It is interesting to compare this ideal analysis with the practical analysis of democratic structure in the fourth book: there the parts of the state are gentleman-farmers, industrial workers, traders, farm-labourers, and the military.[16] These differences of occupation form the basis for a class structure, which can however be simplified. The farm-workers, industrial workers and traders do not have the leisure for the full life of political bliss. Further, political, economic and military power cannot be separated, and Aristotle suggests that the same people should form the army in their youth, the administration in their prime, and the priesthood in their old age, and they should be invested with all landed property. There are thus effectively, as with Plato, two classes, rulers and ruled, and, as with Plato, the ruled carry on the business activities, but Aristotle does not go with Plato in demanding sexual and economic self-abnegation of his rulers. He allows for both a private and a public sector in the ownership of land. In the middle of this discussion comes a characteristic appeal to history; Aristotle continually co-ordinates his theories with factual evidence, and he now shows that a class structure, and especially the separation of the farmers from the military, is found in Crete and Egypt, and appeared even earlier in southern Italy; he does not mention India, which would be much to the point, because he does not know it; contacts between Greeks and Indians were very, very occasional before Alexander's conquests, and were easier in the sixth century than the fourth.

There follows an interesting discussion of town-planning. The determinative factors should be four. First health. Here Aristotle is following the most advanced medical opinion of the day which had begun a concern with environmental hygiene; the Hippocratic treatise *Airs, Waters, Places* isolates three topics which he too treats. Second, political appropriateness. We expect this to mean convenient public buildings, but he merely says that a level plain is appropriate to a democracy, not to an aristocracy. This is not quite as jejune as it sounds. At Haifa or Entebbe the houses become more and more wildly expensive as they mount the hill; Aristotle is making a shrewd observation about human nature. Third, beauty. Aristotle does not mean natural beauty, like the siting of Hong-Kong or Rio de Janeiro, or semi-natural beauty, like the cherry-trees of Washington or the London parks, or even artistic beauty, such as is provided by the palaces of Rome, but a satisfying orderliness, offered by Hippodamus' grid-system of streets. Fourth, defence. This suggests that streets should not be straight – it is said that the curving streets of Boston were a protection against the Indians – and Aristotle suggests a curious compromise by which the streets should cross obliquely rather than at right-angles; it is hard to see the military advantages of this. Military considerations also demand an acropolis and strong walls. Other details include communal restaurants, associated with military posts and temples, a city centre closed to the lower classes and containing recreation facilities for the senior citizens, a shopping centre which should be completely independent of the city centre and which should be sited conveniently for the transport of commodities – and then Aristotle's realism gets the better of him, and in curiously jingling Greek he says that in fact theory bows to practice and growth depends on chance not intelligent planning.[17]

The rest of *Politics* is devoted entirely to education. Here again we are conscious of Aristotle as Plato's follower, though he does not seem to have given quite as much fundamental thought to education as Plato. Happiness, as he has established in *Ethics*, is the realization and complete practice of virtue, unconditionally and absolutely. A state is good in respect of the goodness of its individual citizens (though Aristotle accepts that a community may be good without consisting entirely of saints). Virtue is the product of nature, habit and reason,[18] and habit and reason require education. Aristotle now embarks on an analysis of remarkable interest. Still keeping close to Plato, he divides the state into rulers and ruled, and the human psyche similarly into the intrinsically rational part, and the part whose *rationale* consists in obedience to reason; the former is further divided into theoretical and practical. In a free and healthy state government is in the interest of the governed. What education should the citizen of a free society enjoy? If he would learn to rule he must first learn to obey; in this way the education of rulers and ruled is the same, training in a rational obedience to reason. Beyond this, to be a good citizen is to be a good man; education will be directed to bringing to the highest pitch the highest excellences of the personality. Education cannot neglect practicalities; citizens must be trained for action and for war. But primarily education is a training for leisure. This is a lesson we have not yet learned, and in a world in which the five-day week is general, the four-day week surging forward, and the three-day week on the horizon. For Aristotle leisure is the opportunity for the highest work of man, distinct alike from business and amusement.

Education is concerned with the whole man, and the discipline of the body and of the emotions and of the will leads up to the training of the mind and of the psyche. Aristotle starts from eugenic provisions; he favours marriage at eighteen for the female and thirty-seven for the male, and in winter; parents should have a sound knowledge of sex, and keep fit without becoming athletic fanatics. Aristotle advocates abortion rather than the normal Greek practice of leaving unwanted children to die, which he confines to those born deformed. Adultery is to be discouraged by social opinion.

Education falls into three periods, roughly from 0–7, 8–14, 15–21. The first period itself falls into three. During the first two years, the important factors are a healthy diet (without too much wine!), physical movement, and an early habit of enduring cold (cold baths and light clothes). The next three years will be occupied with games and stories; Aristotle is not opposed to a few tears; they are good exercise. Then follow two years where the training is still predominantly in the home, but they can watch the more formal education they will later experience. It is important during this whole preliminary period that the children shall not be exposed to bad language or indecent spectacle. In the second period formal schooling starts. Aristotle insists that this is a matter of public responsibility; a citizen belongs to the community of which he is a citizen. Education should be state-regulated and controlled by law. Traditionally education embraced reading and writing; physical training; and music and literature; with drawing sometimes thrown in. The absence of mathematics and science, and of anything practical or vocational will be immediately noticed; also, by comparison with modern curricula, of historical studies and of foreign languages. Unfortunately Aristotle's discussion is incomplete and inconclusive. But he makes one very important point. If education is for leisure, it must be more than recreational. It should be worthwhile in its own right, and this is the real place of music and literature.[19]

After a brief discussion of physical training, in which Aristotle objects to over-athleticism and the Spartan cult of courage at the expense of all other virtues, advocates light exercise before puberty, and the separation of physical and intellectual discipline thereafter ('Hard work physically allows the mind no scope; hard work mentally allows the body no scope'[20]), he turns at some length to the place of music in education. It has three functions – innocent relaxation, the fostering of moral education, and intellectual pastime. The second probably touches us most; as we have observed with Plato the Greeks were interested in the capacity of music to evoke anger or calm, courage or control, and these are fostered partly by modality, partly by rhythm. Aristotle commendably favours a training in performance (from a rattle to divert young children onwards), but objects to flutes which produce a mood of religious ecstasy, and harps which require professional skill. Aristotle's ideal is that of the amateur; Thomas Jefferson is a good example of Aristotelian man. Aristotle now offers a slightly different analysis of the function of music – education, the purging of the emotions, and intellectual pastime.[21] The second point is new; it is the celebrated defence of tragedy in his *Poetics*. The 'modes' subserve these ends in different ways. Aristotle's lectures as we have them conclude with the proposition that education in music should conform to three standards – the mean, the possible and the becoming; for the first he has in mind the Dorian mode, for the third the Lydian; for the second he evidently thinks that some of the modes are out of range or control at different periods.

It is an odd ending. The lectures – or at least the manuscript notes – are of course unfinished. He has told us nothing of the third stage except that three years of academic work should be followed by much more intensive physical training. We would expect too an account of the life of the citizen after formal schooling ends. Yet for the sketch of an ideal society to tail away in the middle of a discussion of music is not wholly wrong. Aristotle is not building castles in clouds. His is no Utopia. It is a Greek city-state wrought to the highest pitch of perfection: a discussion of practical detail is wholly in place.

CHAPTER X

DIOGENES

IN CONSIDERING THE REPUBLIC OF DIOGENES (*c.* 395–320 BC) we are faced with a new set of problems. We have a far more certain knowledge of some at least of the contents of the book than of that ascribed to Antisthenes, it is true. But the whole account of Diogenes is so overwhelmed with the accretions of legend that it is uncertain in the first place whether he wrote *The Republic* or indeed anything at all, and in the second which, if any, of all the anecdotes and apophthegms attributed to him, may pass as genuine and be taken as evidence of his political thought. The evidence on the former point can be briefly and simply stated. Diogenes Laertius cites four accounts of him as an author.[1] The first is a list of his writings of unknown origin which includes *The Republic, The Democracy of Athens,* and books on *The Art of Ethics* and *Wealth.* A list taken from the seventh book of Sotion, an Alexandrian of the early second century, is short and includes none of these titles. Satyrus, a late third-century Alexandrian, in volume 4 of his *Biographies,* and Sosicrates, a second-century Rhodian, in the first volume of his *Successions,* say that he left nothing in writing. The catalogue of Theophrastus' writings includes a single volume compendium of the writings of Diogenes,[2] but there is no evidence to show which Diogenes is referred to, and it may be the physicist of Apollonia. More weighty evidence is that of Philodemus, who not merely accepts *The Republic* as authentic himself, from stylistic reasons among others, but attests its acceptance by Cleanthes and Chrysippus, and shows that its rejection was due, at least in part, to the discomfort which its doctrines caused to the later Stoics, some saying, '*The Republic* is not by Diogenes of Sinope, but another man of the same name. It is some mischief-maker, not Diogenes.'[3] Two or three stories are alleged to show that Diogenes regarded writing with disfavour.[4] For example, Hegesias asks to borrow one of Diogenes' books and receives the reply, 'You're a fool, Hegesias; you prefer real figs to painted ones, yet you pass over the true training, and seek to apply yourself to written rules.' But this story, far from showing that Diogenes wrote nothing, shows that he had writings in his possession, but realized that they were not the only nor the most fundamental method of teaching.

This is all the direct evidence. The indirect evidence depends largely upon personal impressions and arguments about the character of Diogenes which are dangerously circular. Sayre writes, 'A man as indolent and indifferent as

Diogenes would not be likely to undertake the effort of writing a book. The conditions under which he is said to have lived would have made it impossible for him to write books. If we accept the writings we must reject the numerous stories describing his way of life.'[5] And again, 'His criticisms were wholly destructive; he seems to have had no system of education or plan of government in view.'[6] These judgements would seem dangerously subjective and involve omitting the evidence of his written works from the estimate of his personality, and then rejecting them because they do not conform with that estimate. Furthermore, Sayre's ascription of *The Republic* to the Athenian tragic poet mentioned in *The Suda*[7] is made impossible by Aristotle's express statement that no constitution other than Plato's introduced the community of women and children, which means that this work must be dated after that passage of *The Politics* (about 330).[8] This, according to the current chronology, would make Diogenes in the seventies at the date of publication, which is not impossibly old for an author, and he may have been younger. No certainty is possible. The direct evidence shows that by the middle of the third century there were Stoics who accepted it as genuine and Peripatetics at Alexandria who did not. Tarn suggested that it was a forgery based on Zeno's *Republic*.[9] This will not do, for in the first place it differed materially from Zeno in certain particulars, and in the second Cleanthes would hardly have asserted its genuine ascription to Diogenes knowing, as he must have done, that it was a forgery based on the work of his own master. It is hard to ascribe a work of such influence to any other figure of the time, and hard to see on what such a forgery could be based, and in default of stronger evidence I am inclined to accept the evidence of Cleanthes as decisive.

As to the second question, von Fritz's careful analysis has shown that Epictetus, Dio Chrysostom and Julian can only be used with material reservations, and has effectively dissected the fundamental document, Diogenes Laertius' biography, into its composite parts.[10] Without doubt many of the stories about Diogenes are unhistorical, idealizing, tendency-stories and the like. But Glover has an aphorism that an anecdote, to pass currency, must be true to type, and the majority of the later stories, where they reflect political ideas, which is all that concerns us here, can be attached to the circle of ideas associated with Diogenes. Even if *The Republic* itself be not Diogenes', it must be nearly contemporary and a part of that same group of ideas.

Diogenes' aim was to put false coinage out of circulation.[11] To begin with, he approaches politics as did Antisthenes, from the side of ethics. Justice is the most useful and the most pleasant of all mankind's possessions.[12] The politicians around him make a fuss about justice but they do not practise it.[13] His approach to the origins of society is moralistic; men come together into cities to escape being wronged by those without.[14] He showed occasionally a deeply humanitarian outlook. He was a physician sent not to the whole but to the sick. Men flocked to dentists and doctors to heal the sickness in their bodies, but neglected the sickness in the soul.[15] 'Naturally Diogenes goes to Corinth,' wrote Wilamowitz, 'the Capuchin belongs in the city of sin.'[16] Communities had to realize that their strength lay in their men rather than their walls.[17] So he saw cities and individuals brought low by the immoralities of men[18] and declared that the insatiate and the folly-stricken should be purified and banished from the city.[19] It thus seems that like Antisthenes he planned the expulsion of those deemed unfit for citizenship, and so shelved without solving one of the fundamental problems of government. But one suspects that his identification of the worthless was shocking to the respectable.

Diogenes refused to associate himself with a single city. He divided his time between Sparta and Athens like the Great King moving from his summer to his winter residence.[20] He is often spoken of as residing in Corinth. We have records of his appearances all over the Greek world. He declared himself to be a citizen of the universe and in Lucian's skit when asked where he came from replied 'Everywhere'.[21] Himself from Sinope on the Euxine, he showed sympathy with the moral struggles of Greek and barbarian, Persians, Medes, Syrians, Macedonians, Athenians, Spartans.[22] He had praise alike for Agesilaus and Epaminondas.[23] Julian says that he refused initiation into the mysteries because it meant committing himself to Athenian citizenship, and would gladly have entered the temple had it not meant subjecting himself to a single set of laws and constitution.[24] This is an interesting contrast with Socrates. Socrates accepted the privileges of citizenship, and in so doing accepted its responsibilities as well. So he took pride in the part he had played in political affairs, and in military service in his country's defence, and refused to evade the judgement the community laid upon him.

This does not mean that Diogenes was a cosmopolitan in political theory. His famous declaration need mean only his refusal to commit himself to a single state. He was fond of quoting the lines beginning, 'Without city, home or fatherland'; that is to say that his approach was negative rather than positive.[25] Thus W. Windelband says, 'When Diogenes called himself a cosmopolitan, there was in this no trace of the ideal thought of a community of all men, but only the denial of his adherence to any civilized community.'[26] He was 'as free as a bird, unconstrained by law, undisturbed by politicians.'[27] So too his follower Crates claimed Obscurity and Poverty for his fatherland and described himself as a citizen of Diogenes.[28] That Diogenes' approach was thus negative becomes clear when we examine what we know of his political ideas; for we find that *The Republic* was almost certainly based upon the city-state, and there is no trace of the tension which the Stoics felt between loyalty to the organized community and to the world-wide community. The work of Alexander had not yet seeped into the consciousness of the Greeks, as we see in the history of the years which followed his death, and in any event Diogenes was no great admirer of that work. We have already seen that Diogenes probably envisaged the banishment of unworthy citizens which suggests, though inconclusively, a limited society. But the evidence of Plutarch is definite. Speaking of Lycurgus, he writes, 'His organization of the commonwealth was accepted by Plato, Diogenes, Zeno, and all who have won approval by their treatment of the subject.'[29] It is strange to find Diogenes, the apostle of individualism, taking as his model that city of

regimentation from which he is said to have been banned,[30] but there can be
little doubt of it. He must have found there three things which caught his
imagination. The first was the powers of endurance of the men, trained by
askesis (training, self-discipline) and *ponos* (toil, labour). To return from Sparta
to Athens was to pass from the men's apartments to the women's.[31] It was
from Sparta that he adopted the 'philosopher's' cloak, though the fact that it
was the garb of the poor in Athens was an additional factor. Then, secondly,
he admired the self-discipline of the Spartans. Diogenes, in all his excesses is
insistent that what he does is entirely within his control. In one of his few
certainly authentic aphorisms he calls the taverns 'the mess-rooms of Attica',[32]
contrasting the disorderly drunkenness there with the discipline and control of
the groups in the Spartan common messes. He remains in Athens while praising
Sparta because it is the Athenians who need his ministrations.[33] He is like a
Spartan dog, sturdy and independent, and the British bulldog will serve to
remind us of the traditional likeness between national types of dogs and men.[34]
Finally, in the greater freedom allowed to women in Sparta he, like most of the
Utopians of his age, found the nearest approach to the ideal partnership of men
and women for the good of the commonwealth. As a result of all this he re-
serves his rare words of praise principally for Sparta and Spartans. There are
good men nowhere in Greece, but good boys in Sparta.[35]

The type of education advocated by Diogenes has proved a very vexed
question. There is one tradition which would seem to show that the early
Cynics did not despise the conventional content and methods. Thus Diogenes
says, 'The most burdensome thing on earth is an ignorant man', and again,
'Education is a controlling grace to the young, a consolation to the old, riches
to the poor, an ornament to the rich.'[36] He is represented with a considerable
output of writings, including seven tragedies.[37] Crates is described as a man of
considerable education.[38] Hipparchia turns from the loom to education.[39] The
evil spirit of avarice is one which scoffs at letters except for commercial purposes.[40] Diogenes appears to have trained Xeniades' sons in the conventional
studies.[41] But though all this may in fact be true it certainly does not represent
the peculiar contribution of Diogenes to educational thought. To him academic
studies were irrelevant; lack of learning became indeed exalted among his
successors. He turned Hegesias from books to life.[42] He said that the noblest
men were those who scorned riches, learning, pleasure and life, and chose
rather poverty, ignorance, hardship and death.[43] He held that we should pass
by such studies as the arts, mathematics and science as useless superfluities.[44]
Paideia is *paidia*; education is a kind of children's game, if you suppose that he
who knows most literature or delves into most books is the wisest and best
educated of men.[45] So too Teles makes Crates deride the tyranny first of nurse,
then of tutor, trainer, schoolmaster, music teacher, art master, then of the
teachers of mathematics and horsemanship, then of his superior officers as an
ephebe.[46]

But there is a positive side to all this. Dio Chrysostom[47] represents Diogenes
as saying that there are two sorts of education, the divine and human, the former

great and strong and simple, the latter small and weak, full of dangers and
deceptions. Both are needed, but the latter depends on the former which might
be called manliness or great-mindedness. This reads as if the later sophist is
tacking his own ideas of culture (addressed rather apologetically to Trajan) on
to a genuine strand in the Diogenes tradition. That is to say that Diogenes'
contribution to educational theory lay in saying that the sole, or almost the sole
purpose of education was the training of character, not to serve the community
physically (like the Spartans), nor intellectually (like Plato's Guardians), but so
that the individual might stand on his own feet before God and man. His aim
was the self-sufficiency of the individual. This was a task which sound education
could accomplish. When he saw a boy eating greedily, he struck the tutor not
the boy, ascribing the fault to him.[48] This education consisted of two parts,
mental leading to self-knowledge, and physical leading to self-control.[49]
Either half of the training was incomplete without the other. On the one hand
it is no good using a thing if you do not know how; it would be folly to pro-
claim a man an expert in grammar, geometry or music if he were not versed
in the art; you do not know a man unless you know his mind; to change the
currency and to know yourself – on these two commandments hang all the
laws of life.[50] On the other he is represented as training Xeniades' sons in
horsemanship, archery, and the use of the sling and javelin (though the limits
he set upon the trainer at the palaestra do not accord with what else we know
of him) and he used to produce arguments to show how physical fitness led to
virtue.[51] The method of this education is two-fold; he practised it himself with
his few but distinguished pupils, and undoubtedly it was the system of which
he theoretically approved.[52] The first part consisted in the spoken homily,
which in his hands seemed like a magic spell. Dudley describes these as 'informal
lectures on ethical subjects, enlivened by analogies from the crafts and from the
habits of animals, and illustrated by quotations from Homer and the allegorical
interpretation of myths ... the spoken precursors of diatribe.'[53] The second
and more important part was the *askesis* he inflicted on himself, the inuring of
body and mind to hardships by continuous practice, as in manual crafts, music
and athletics, the experts achieve their surpassing skill by dint of incessant toil.
If men so labour in matters of no moment, how much more should we discipline ourselves for the struggle of life? By strenuous practice along the course of
nature instead of in these unprofitable fields, we can overcome pleasure and
pain alike, in short everything, and enjoy that liberty which Heracles won
through his Labours. So it was to *askesis* that he directed Hegesias, and he himself
would roll in his jar over the burning sand, embrace statues covered with snow,
walk on snowy ground barefoot, eat raw meat, beg alms of a statue to get
practice in being refused, and visit brothels, wrangle with the inmates, and
habituate himself to their abuse. It was to this training that Diogenes set his
followers. He said that boys ought to be educated by discipline, and, like a
chorus-master, used to pitch the note a little too high so that they would
strike the right one; the aim of all this discipline was to secure the right tension
in the soul.[54]

Diogenes' educational theories have come in for far less notice either than his own political ideas or than the educational theories of men like Plato and Aristotle, but he realized and expressed clearly three basic educational truths, that education should be directed to the formation of individual personal character, that its method should be practice not theory, and that the teacher must give the example of his life as well as the precept of his lips.

There can be no certainty about the system of government advocated by Diogenes. The one strand in the tradition which seems clear is his contempt for autocracy which he links with his contempt for riches.[55] There are innumerable anecdotes illustrating this. When a tyrant asked him the best bronze for a statue he replied, 'That from which Harmodius and Aristogeiton were moulded.' He said that Dionysius treated his friends like purses, hanging them up when full and throwing them away when empty. He told Philip that he had come 'as a spy on his insatiate greed'.[56] The Alexander stories are famous; it is told how Diogenes requested him to stand out of the sun, how he set the title Diogenes the Dog on a level with that of Alexander the Great King, how on hearing of Alexander's deification as Dionysus he growled, 'You'd better make me Sarapis', how he claimed that his staff was his sceptre, how he refused all the treasures of Macedon.[57] The sixth oration of Dio Chrysostom consists of an attack on tyranny, the misery, fear and suspicion of the tyrant, and the manner in which he can accept neither peace or war, for the one makes his subjects idle, and the other restive.

Many of these stories are anachronistic and apocryphal. Alexander did not return to Greece as Great King and world-conqueror; the cult of Sarapis was not introduced till later; the correspondence with Perdiccas has been shown by von Fritz to be a historical impossibility;[58] the letter to the king of Persia which Epictetus mentions represents the atmosphere of the fifth century, for in the fourth the Athenians did lose their liberty without dying.[59] But it is impossible to believe that if, as Gomperz conjectured of the early Cynics, 'the form of government which they proposed was doubtless an enlightened and provident despotism',[60] these stories could have been attached to the name of a man of such ideas or that with that belief the later Cynics could have stood out so strongly against even the benevolent emperors of Rome.

In turning to democracy we are on less certain ground but here too there are indications of his contempt. We have seen his preference for Spartans to Athenians, with their undisciplined messes and effeminate ways, and how he attacked the popular politicians who were for ever prating of justice and failing to practise it. He made coarse and abusive attacks on Demosthenes, and it does not seem likely that his work on the Athenian Democracy was an eulogy.[61] Dio Chrysostom represents him as saying that demagogues and sophists are mercenary leaders.[62] He has a scathing picture alike of the weak and impotent democrat and of the hardened and bold-faced ranter who ousts him.[63] Diogenes was fierce in his attacks both on riches and their power, and on the envy of the poor for the rich and their craving for wealth. For rank and birth he had no time at all. In so far as these political systems represented the power of rich or poor they were to Diogenes objectionable and utterly to be rejected. There are left two possibilities. The first is the opinion of von Fritz, that Diogenes' *Republic* attacked all law and government, that is to say that Diogenes was in political philosophy an anarchist.[64] This is plausible in view of the later history of the Cynics but it stands open to one great objection; if Diogenes had proposed anything so revolutionary in the field of government it is almost impossible that it should not have been mentioned together with the other extremist ideas in Philodemus and the other later attacks on *The Republic*. It is more reasonable to suppose that Diogenes followed Plato – despite their alleged rivalry – in putting the reins of government into the hands of the philosophers. There is some indication of this in his early desire to take the lead in politics, and in the words put into his mouth by Hermippus (or Menippus) when asked what he would do – 'Govern men'. When Xeniades bought him, Diogenes said, 'Obey me, though I am a slave, as you would obey the instructions of a doctor or pilot.' It is no profit to use anything if you do not know how. He himself was a teacher instructing his disciples and many of them became prominent in political life. The sage in this wicked world might pursue non-attachment, for here the practice of politics implies a desire for fame, but in the ideal commonwealth he would be the leader and governor, and the ordinary man, like Xeniades, is called upon to obey.[65]

'He maintained that wives should be held in common, recognizing no other marriage than union by mutual consent. For this reason he thought that sons should be held in common as well.'[66] 'It is the Stoic doctrine that amongst the wise wives should be held in common, with a free choice of partners, as Zeno says in his *Republic* and Chrysippus in his treatise *On Government*; so too Diogenes the Cynic and Plato.'[67] According to Philodemus women were to wear the same dress as men; to exercise naked in public; intercourse was to be permitted without restriction of place, person or sex.[68]

Diogenes' attitude to sex was remarkably free. But he approached it from a male vantage-point. Community of wives and children is part of the ideal of non-attachment, not a positive principle. There is no indication that he thought of women as equal to men; on the contrary, he appears somewhat anti-feminist. He had no premonition of Hipparchia!

Diogenes, unlike Antisthenes, was a pacifist, or near pacifist. He kept himself clear from wars and factions. He was as free as a bird, being completely untroubled by military service.[69] Socrates accepted military service as part of the responsibility of citizenship. Diogenes rejected citizenship of a single state and thus escaped military service. He knew that in festivals and crowds men show their true character, in wars and camps it lies concealed.[70] In one of the best anecdotes of antiquity the news reaches Corinth that Philip is on the march. And immediately there is a regular to-do. One man is polishing his armour, another is wheeling stores, another patching the wall, another strengthening the battlements. In the midst of this Diogenes is sitting unconcerned. Then suddenly he rises and rolls his tub with vigour along the street, and then rolls it back again, for he too must join in the general business.[71] But he did something more than attack the uselessness of war, he analysed its causes. These are physical lust (not a very important cause, but he is thinking of *The Iliad*), the insecurity of the autocrat, and the craving for riches. All these he seeks to banish from his commonwealth, and so remove the causes of war. It is thus probable that his Republic was without military organization. As to attacks from without, he would have sought so to develop non-attachment in his people that there was nothing of which a conqueror could rob them, though his ultimate answer was that the only true citizenship was the freedom of the whole universe.[72]

Diogenes said that the love of money is the mother-city of all evils.[73] Where there are riches, whether in home or country, there can dwell no virtue.[74] 'If poverty is not with you as a foundation, neither will virtue be.'[75] To Diogenes the accumulation of wealth meant the decay of man.[76] He condemned the spirit which scoffs at education and letters except when they have to deal with estimates and contracts. He saw the troubled lives of men, plotting against one another, planning alike the power of the rich and the craving of the poor for that power and those riches.[77] Men must be freed from the power of wealth. For the individual the way led through abrogation. This was with him a philosophical principle. Hence in theory he had no respect for property, and shocked his contemporaries by declaring that he saw nothing immoral in temple-stealing.[78] In an interesting passage Julian[79] examines the views of a late Cynic named Oenomaus, who 'discarded that second law, sanctified by nature and God, which bids us keep our hands from the property of others and permits us neither by word nor act to treat these matters indiscriminately' – the word is significant conveying the notions both of confounding the law and holding the property in common. Thus Cynics 'pour all the commonly accepted conventions higgledy-piggledy into the common pool and trample on them by introducing a system of society which inclines to the hateful and evil instead of the pure and good'. The indictment is followed by a passage critical of Diogenes himself, rare in Julian, which makes it probable that he had Diogenes in mind in penning it. It follows that Diogenes' Republic was a communistic Utopia, as we know from other sources. Yet there was despite all a form of currency, it being prescribed that knucklebones should be legal tender.[80] How these two ideas were reconciled is uncertain. There would seem to be three possibilities. (a) The Republic was a class state, like Plato's, in which the philosopher-rulers lived communistically, and the rest of the community had the use of property and money. This might seem supported by the syllogism above, but we have no evidence of any such division or maintenance of property. (b) The communism was not complete but had the practical system of exchange included in it. This does not seem probable. Diogenes was an extremist. If, however, it be the true explanation, it is based on an ordinance of Plato who in *The Laws* advocates a coinage which is suitable for exchange within the community but valueless outside.[81] A similar system was practised in Sparta, where the currency consisted of heavy iron bars. (c) It is most probable that Diogenes, like Samuel Butler in *Erewhon*, is parodying the system he knew, with a side-glance at Plato. He is saying in effect that all this fuss about gold might as well be made about knucklebones, which are in reality just as valuable. This accords best with what we know of him, and would not have to fit into the structure with too precise a logic.

There is a strange passage in Diogenes Laertius which runs, 'As to law, he said that it was impossible for society to exist without law. Without society there is no benefit from civilization. Society is civilized, and there is no benefit from law without society. Therefore law is civilized.'[82] This would seem to defend the institutions of conventional society. But to Diogenes neither law, society nor civilization were of any consequence. Hence the importance of law was only relative to existing society, and probably in the ideal commonwealth the judicial system went the same way as the military system, save only for the right of banishing undesirables. This is in accord with von Fritz's ideas.[83]

We have a few other indications of unconventional views: a questioning of slavery, but from the search for non-attachment to possessions, rather than concern for humanity;[84] an acceptance of cannibalism, even to the suggestion that it might be used as a form of capital punishment.[85] The ambiguities of his position are here plain. Whatever is, is by nature, and is therefore right, and being right must have its place in the body politic. But slavery also is. Property also is. There is a sense in which Diogenes is concerned to do no more than stand the Greek world on its head, rejecting its practices and introducing the practices which it rejected. He might have approved of Rousseau's formula for a healthy society: to decide what society is at present doing, and do the exact opposite.

Diogenes was not in general offering a Utopia in the way that others were. He was asking what a community would look like if people lived according to nature. His answer was not systematic. The cardinal point was the abolition of property; most of the rest flows from that. To this should be added the saving grace of education.

CHAPTER XI

THE IMPACT OF ALEXANDER

ALEXANDER IS BY ANY STANDARDS A WATERSHED. Behind him lay the craggy terrain of quarrelling city-states; in front of him stretch the vast plains of world empires. For the Greeks he flung back the horizons, at least into Asia. Peoples of whom they had never heard, the Aspasii and the Assaceni, the Oxydracae and the Gandaridae, swam within their ken. Places like Sogdiana and Arachosia and Gedrosia suddenly found their places on the map. He had absorbed Asia Minor and Palestine and Egypt; he had swept through Mesopotamia and Iran; he had penetrated to the neighbourhood of Tashkent to the north-east, and then into India as far as the Beas before turning back and down to the mouth of the Indus. The world could not be the same again.[1]

It was not merely an expansion of administration or of geography. It meant a total readjustment of thought. Alexander had had as his tutor Aristotle, to whom the alien, the non-Greek, the 'barbarian' was by nature a slave, a tool endowed with life; only the Greeks had full and true humanity.[2] He had been encouraged by Isocrates, who saw no hope for the Greeks unless they would unite, and when they refused to unite freely, looked for some strong man to unite them, and took as a focal point for unity opposition to Persia.[3] Here were perhaps the two outstanding intellectuals alive in, say, 340, neither able to see beyond the diocese of Greece, but appearing liberal beyond bounds when compared with the self-seeking ambitions and narrow parochialism of Demosthenes. Few Greeks before Alexander seem to have had a wider vision. Herodotus, of course, with his vast sympathies and insatiable curiosity; the sophist Hippias perhaps;[4] Antiphon, whose work *On Truth* contained a remarkable declaration of the unity of mankind;[5] the Hippocratic writer of *Airs, Waters and Places*, who sees mankind as a single species for detached and objective study; the early Cynics such as Diogenes and Crates, who claimed to be 'citizens of the universe',[6] but meant by it a detachment from narrower loyalties rather than an attachment to wider ones. It is wrong to deny with Tarn the vision of these men; it is equally wrong with Baldry to see the belief in the unity of mankind almost as a steady stream and to play down the fact of the suddenly widened horizons.[7]

The controversial question is not, or should not be, whether Alexander marks a historical watershed, but how far the changes he worked were an accidental by-product of personal ambition and military genius, and how far a consequence of deliberate policy. With all the resources of modern scholarship, we have no agreed picture of what Alexander was like. Indeed G. Walser in 1956 took the view that across more than a century no scholar had really looked at the evidence with an open mind, and that all subsequent Alexanders were variants on Gustav Droysen's world-shaking Hellenic nationalist of 1833, a depressing but not wholly unjustified thought.[8] The most influential of these portraits was Tarn's; it made of Droysen's figure an intellectual visionary, fostering the unity of mankind by deliberate policy.[9] Tarn's picture was followed in broad outline by Kolbe and Robinson.[10] A rather differently idealized Alexander as a mystic seeking apotheosis was offered by Georges Radet.[11] Ulrich Wilcken's portrait, painted at much the same time, is also in the line of descent from Droysen, but is a much more pragmatic, though highly rational, controller of events.[12] In reaction against Tarn we may mention three interpretations: A. R. Burn's anti-hero, a military genius and dominant personality without real vision or understanding; F. Schachermeyr's ruthlessly self-centred conqueror; Ernst Badian's lonely and ambitious pragmatist, who escaped from the narrow factions of Macedonia to be trapped in the image of an oriental despot.[13]

The case for Alexander as a visionary is based on five passages. First, Plutarch in his *Life of Alexander*[14] tells how Alexander went to the oracle of Zeus-Ammon at Siwa in the deserts of Libya, and was greeted as son of Zeus. The very fact that Alexander should go through some hardship and danger to consult this oracle is indicative of his frame of mind. The oracle was respected by the Greeks, but it was not Delphi or Dodona, and the god was not pan-hellenic only, but a deity of wider currency. It was in this context that Alexander heard and approved a philosophic assertion that God is the sovereign of all mankind, and went beyond it in adapting the Homeric tag that Zeus is 'father of gods and men', to say that God is the *common* father of *all* men, and his only distinction is to honour the 'best'. Alexander was in Egypt at the time. If the story is reliable it suggests an openness and readiness to judge man by his quality not by his race – no more, but no less.

Secondly, Tarn made an imaginative reconstruction of the banquet at Opis in 324 BC. The primary source is Arrian, and behind him Ptolemy;[15] the account therefore is basically reliable. The occasion is an occasion of reconciliation between Macedonians and Persians. Alexander sat at table; his Macedonians were next to him, then the Persians, and around them other peoples. The ritual was inaugurated by Greek and Persian religious officials jointly, and Alexander offered prayer for the other blessings, and for concord and partnership in rule between Macedonians and Persians. Tarn stressed the presence of other peoples at Alexander's table, the common libation, and the possibility that concord was an absolute term, and not just between Greeks and Persians. Badian has handled Tarn's reconstruction very roughly.[16] The scene was, he suggests, of no great importance to Arrian, and the common bowl was shared only between Alexander and the Macedonians nearest him; there is no evidence that anyone else was *at the same table*. (It is equally just to say that there is no evidence that they were not.) The words and purport of the prayer are not clear, but the partnership in rule is confined to Macedonians and Persians. This is the most that can be said. No doubt the prime object of the occasion was reconciliation between Greeks and Persians, and it is surely fantastic to see here an inauguration of a world union. Still, Alexander was no fool. There were other peoples there, and if his words did not necessarily include them, they did not necessarily exclude them either. I see Alexander as a pragmatist, leaving his options open.

Thirdly, a passage in Plutarch,[17] which may or may not come from Eratosthenes,[18] specifically says that Alexander believed that he had a mission from God to harmonize men generally, and to be the reconciler of the world, bringing men from everywhere into a unity and mixing their lives and customs, their marriages and social ways as in a loving-cup. Tarn linked this passage with the common bowl at Opis, but, as we have seen, Tarn's view of the banquet cannot be sustained, and therefore cannot bear this interpretation. Badian well suggested that if an actual common bowl was in mind it may have been the appearance of Darius' great bowl (which Alexander took over) at the marriage feast at Susa (to which we shall come in a minute) rather than the reconciling feast at Opis. The phrase 'reconciler of the world' is a very striking one; it may be early Empire rhetoric and due to Plutarch, but there is no real reason to doubt that he found it in Eratosthenes or one of his other sources. This is in many ways the most impressive of the 'theoretical' passages. It may be a Hellenistic reflection on the changes produced in practice by Alexander. But it could represent something he suddenly said: there is no sign of it as a settled policy.

The fourth passage is fairly certainly from Eratosthenes, and states that Alexander ignored the advice to treat Greeks as friends and non-Greeks as enemies, and received and favoured all men of good repute.[19] The passage is a reflection on what he did, not a statement of what he said: it describes practice, not policy. Still it links well with the first passage; and it is likely that Alexander came to a deliberate, not just an unconscious, rejection of Aristotle.

Finally we should note a passage from Diodorus, in which it is stated that among Alexander's papers was found a proposal 'to combine cities and transfer populations from Asia to Europe and in the opposite direction from Europe to Asia, using intermarriages and family ties as the means of bringing the great continents into concord and friendship based on family unity.'[20] If this were authentic it would be decisive for Alexander's vision, but it seems to incorporate material from Theophrastus, and therefore it would be rash to build anything on it.

Modern scholars are rightly cautious in accepting Tarn's idealistic philosopher as the real Alexander. But Alexander certainly did break through some boundaries, and it may well be that frontiers had in practice simply become irrelevant to him. I do not think it wise to reject altogether the possibility that he may have said things about the unity of Europe and Asia or the irrelevance of the distinction between Greek and 'barbarian'. Even if none of the sayings is authentic, they still represent early reflections on the actual effect of his work and the personality which inspired it.

But, even if we reject Alexander as a visionary, and accept him as a pragmatist, the results of his pragmatism are clear enough. The Germans call it *Verschmelzungspolitik*, a policy of fusion or amalgamation. As he swept onwards he found Greeks whom he could not trust, Dymnus, or Demetrius, or Philotas, or Hermolaus, or Cleander and Sitalces, Heracon and Agathon.[21] At the same time he became aware of Asiatics whom he could respect as opponents, like Memnon, or rely on as administrators, like Ada of Caria.[22] Indeed, as he overran the Persian empire it became obvious that he would have to rely on Persian administrators. Furthermore, far in Bactria he encountered Roxane, daughter of the prince Oxyartes. It was the general opinion of the Greeks that she was one of the two most beautiful women in Asia. Alexander did not treat her as a spoil of war, but married her formally, and whether this was from policy to pacify the peoples in this distant land, or from love for the woman,[23] does not now matter: action may become policy, policy may become action. After his return to Susa the policy was clear. He formally married Darius' daughter Stateira or Barsine,[24] eighty of his leading officers married daughters of the Persian nobility, and the liaisons of some 10,000 of his soldiers with their Asiatic concubines were legalized. Regiments recruited from among the Persians which had served with distinction in India were given the title 'Companions'. A few Asiatic princes, including Roxane's brother, were enlisted in his personal regiment.[25] Resentment among the Greeks began to mount. At Opis they rioted; he dismissed them, and began to organize his forces from Persians alone. They were alarmed. 'What hurts us,' they said, 'is that you have made the Persians your kinsmen.' Alexander's answer is significant: 'I count you all as my kinsmen.'[26] Whatever else the banquet at Opis was or was not, it represented the seal on Alexander's *Verschmelzungspolitik*.

Alexander's was a complex personality. He was a Macedonian, with fewer racial prejudices than the Greeks from farther south. There is something Homeric about him, even if some of the identifications with Achilles were imposed by a later tradition.[27] His anger could be terrible; his generosity could be heart-warming. That he was ambitious in a very ordinary, human sense is not to be doubted; but he had also a strange, almost mystical 'yearning' (*pothos*).[28] He seems more like a man moved by impulse than by a transcendental and consistent vision. The picture of him as seeking to realize Utopia is not to be sustained. But he has an essential part to play in the story of Utopia. He changed a narrow vision to a broad one, partly because he expanded the Greek world geographically, partly because he came to ignore racial distinctions. Henceforth Utopia could not be the private property of one small people.

CHAPTER XII

EUHEMERUS

No one was prepared for Alexander's death; there were no plans for the future; the future was assumed to be in his care. But the future was bound to be different from the past. The horizons had receded, and those on whom the future depended were for the most part in Babylon; they were certainly not in Greece. What ensued was tempered scarcely at all by idealism, perhaps somewhat by the vision of Alexander, transmitted and transmuted, predominantly by ambition for power, and to some considerable extent by the pressures of practicality.[1]

It was half a century before the new pattern was clear, half a century of enormous historical complexity. For us here the details are less important than the kaleidoscopic quality of the history. Officially the army accepted the sovereignty of Alexander's half-brother, a mentally deficient, and his posthumous son by Roxane. In practice the power lay with Antipater, the last of Philip's generals, in Europe, and Perdiccas in Asia. But some of the governors were influential. Ptolemy, a skilled statesman, secured Egypt, Lysimachus Thrace and Antigonus Phrygia. It was an uneasy alliance. Alexander's personality had held them together, and men who had been puny at his side expanded and conflicted. First Perdiccas fell, accused of ambition. Antipater held the rest together till his death in 319. Then things really fell apart. There were jockeyings for power between Antipater's able, magnetic but conservative son Cassander, who was in and out of control in Greece; the ambitious and energetic Antigonus, together with his brilliant son Demetrius Poliorcetes ('the Besieger'); Polyperchon who succeeded Antipater in Macedonia; Eumenes, Alexander's former secretary, loyal to the house of Alexander; Seleucus, the governor of Babylon; and, of course, Lysimachus and Ptolemy. In the course of the struggles the princes were killed, as was Alexander's formidable mother Olympias. Antigonus was killed at Ipsus in 301; Cassander died in 298; Demetrius, after some startling successes, fell in 285 and drank himself to death two years later. Lysimachus was killed by Seleucus in 281, and the northern power ceased to count; Seleucus, with the world at his feet, was assassinated the following year. Of all the Successors only Ptolemy died a natural death. Fifty years from Alexander's death there were three great kingdoms – Ptolemaic Egypt under Ptolemy II, Seleucid Asia, under Seleucus' son Antiochus I (though these two were fighting for power in Palestine), and Macedon, under

Demetrius' son, the remarkable Antigonus Gonatas. Pergamum emerged to independent power at the expense of the Seleucids in the latter half of the third century; before the century was out, Rome was a force to be reckoned with in the eastern Mediterranean.

During these jockeyings for power Demetrius Poliorcetes drew up a remarkable constitution for a panhellenic league.[2] This dates from 303–2 BC, and might well have been a long-lasting means to Greek unity had it not been for Demetrius' defeat at Ipsus. The constitution made no provision for an Assembly. There was to be a Council or Congress meeting during the great athletic festivals, that is six times in four years, but with provision for special sessions. The Council's decisions were binding on the members, provided that there was a quorum of 50 per cent. Executive action was left to the individual states. One unusual feature of the constitution was that the presidency was different in peace-time and war-time. In peace-time the president was chosen by lot from a board of five, representative of different states, but in war-time the office was vested in Demetrius or his deputy. It is likely that the constitution contained a pious declaration of 'freedom and autonomy'; these were the catchphrases with which Demetrius sought to outbid Cassander's oligarchical policies. Demetrius, it has been said, knew how to conquer but not how to rule.

Cassander was to the right, though moderately so. His instrument in the government of Athens was the Aristotelian Demetrius of Phalerum (not to be confused with 'The Besieger').[3] He made a genuine attempt to put into practice his philosophy of politics; he held it by conviction, for his brother Himeraeus was anti-Macedonian and a democrat. The balance between idealism and pragmatism in Demetrius is a fascinating study. He believed that power should be in the hands of a small group of trained and skilled experts; he also believed that it needed a broad base. So he set the property qualification for citizenship at 1000 drachmas (half as high as the right-wing had set it in 321 BC), but replaced election by lot with voting procedure. He himself was charged with revising the laws, and his revision, based on the theories of Theophrastus, gave him in the eyes of future generations a standing in line with Dracon and Solon as the third of the great Athenian legislators.[4] This included sumptuary legislation, especially control of funerary expenditure, but also limitation on the number of guests at parties;[5] legislation directed at the public effects of private morality (for instance, controlling the dress and behaviour of women in public); and some kind of provision for standardized procedure in property contracts, though, curiously, not the public registration which Theophrastus had advocated. For the rest we do not know, but there is enough to see that the philosopher's law-giving was directed to three ends. First, there is a basic principle about law: if custom is offensive, law must mould society by prescribing something different. Secondly, Demetrius is concerned to preserve and protect the property of the wealthy. Aristocracy, government by the best, is for him the same as plutocracy, government by the rich. There is a double implication. Only the rich have the background, education and leisure necessary for good government; a good statesman will be ineffective unless he has financial resources.

Thirdly, Demetrius does believe that it is possible to direct morality by Act of Parliament. For enforcement Demetrius went to Plato and Aristotle[6] and established seven *nomophylakes*, Guardians of the Law, who 'compelled the magistrates to use the laws, and took their seats with the presiding officers at the meetings of the Assembly and Council, to prevent anything being done to the detriment of the state.'[7] This was clearly regarded as oligarchical, though he would have seen it as relating, so to speak, to the rule of philosophy rather than to the rule of philosophers. He also established a Board of Commissioners for Women (*gynaeconomi*), another concept taken from Aristotle, where it also is identified as oligarchical, to help to implement his moral legislation,[8] though this side was largely left to a much strengthened Areopagus.

Also in Cassander's circle was Euhemerus of Messenę.[9] Euhemerus wrote a romantic adventure story called *The Sacred Inscription*.[10] The object of the book was to establish his well-known theory about the origin of the gods in deified men. He decided to set this in the framework of a historical fiction.[11] According to this the narrator was instructed by Cassander to undertake a number of distant journeys. On one of these he travelled southwards as far as the Ocean, setting sail from Yemen. This is of itself somewhat odd. The Ocean was for the Greeks the river which surrounds the land mass of the earth. Alexander was in search of it when pressing east through India. The water south of Arabia between India and Africa was not thought of in this way: on the whole, despite Necho's Phoenicians,[12] the Arabian Sea was thought of as an inland lake with India and Africa joining together to the south. Euhemerus sailed for several days till he came to a group of islands, the largest of which was called Panchaïa or the Sacred Isle. It is not necessary to go into the several attempts, ancient and modern, to identify these islands.[13] The Greeks were aware that there were islands like Socotra, or the Laccadive and Maldive group or Ceylon or even the Indonesian archipelago, and this is enough for a peg for a traveller's tale. There is however a slight suggestion that folk memories of Minoan Crete may have played some part in shaping the description of an island stretching out to the east, in which Zeus was peculiarly honoured, in which there was a place called Asterusia,[14] and in which men were once powerful enough to have been deified. These patterns from Crete imposed on an island in the south-east show that the island is wholly fictitious.

Euhemerus gave his theories that 'all the accepted deities were generals, admirals and kings who lived a long time ago'[15] within a political framework. In so doing he wrote in some sense the first Utopia. For Antisthenes and Plato had sought to idealize the system of administration, but they did not idealize those external and adventitious circumstances which are outside the control of man. On the Sacred Isle enough frankincense grows to supply all the religions of the world. The myrrh is harvested twice a year. The cypresses grow to an unusual height. The palm-trees have gigantic trunks and fruit of unusual quality. Vines grow in considerable number and variety. Water is plentiful; one spring gives immediate rise to a navigable river. The sheep have fleeces of extraordinary softness. There are abundant mines of gold, silver, bronze, tin and iron.

The debt here is to Homer's Phaeacia.[16] There are however clear echoes of Plato's Atlantis, which was also the Sacred Isle, and was, like Panchaïa, associated with the sun, which also bore aromatic substances in profusion, and was rich in fruit and in metallic ores, which also had springs of water of unusual quality nurturing trees of unusual height, which also had a temple of considerable size with height proportionate to its other measurements, and which also was ruled by kings, who did not have power over life and death.[17] But Euhemerus fails to face the possibility that, even given ideal external conditions, the character of the men and nature of the commonwealth may yet degenerate, a fact which Plato with his deeper understanding of human nature fully foresees. So that Euhemerus is in this sense the first Utopian, father of all those who have set their ideals outside the bounds and difficulties of ordinary human living, and is responsible for turning political theory from its more obviously practical task of improving the existing politic to that of setting out an ideal, of which men may dream, but because it denies that Nature (including human nature) has her ruthless side, they will not realize.

Being a Utopian Euhemerus invents his place-names.[18] His choice seems governed by three main considerations. The names are linked with Greek names; they use typically Greek suffixes (*-ara, -akia, -usia, -is*). Pan-ara is a glorified form of Meg-ara; Dalis recalls Elis; Hyracia Ambracia. Secondly, his names are connected with the peoples of the island (native Panchaïans, and immigrant 'Oceanites', Indians, Scythians and Cretans). Asterusia is Cretan; Hyracia has Cretan echoes. The last is also reminiscent of Hyrcanis, perhaps associated with Indians and Scythians. The Indian Doanes may be at the back of Doia. Thirdly, there is a flavour of archaism and religion. *Pan-* is an archaic prefix, as in Panormus. *Chaios* means good, and is Doric and archaic. Asterusia is linked to star-worship. Dalis echoes Delos and Doia Dodona. Other associations are lost, but Hyracia must derive from *hyrax*, a shrew, and Dalis may denote brightness.

Some points in the ordering of the society call for a closer examination. The first is the class structure of his society. There were three divisions, the first consisting of priests and magistrates, the second of farmers, the third of soldiers and herdsmen.[19] Various triple divisions had been known in the past, that of Hippodamus of Miletus,[20] and the caste system of India and Egypt,[21] but Euhemerus' division is all his own. There is no indication of economic or social privilege attaching to membership of these castes. To this there is one exception: the priests receive a double share in the apportioning and live in exceptional luxury, but as this does not apply to the magistrates the distinction is not coterminous with the class distinction. The basis of the distinction between the classes is not entirely clear. The third class ministers to the first two: the soldiers' task is specifically said to be the protection of the farmers, and the chief function of the herdsmen is to tend the sacrificial animals. There is no mention of slavery, and we may assume that it was non-existent. All the inhabitants of Panara alike are known as 'Suppliants of Zeus of the Three Tribes'; there is no distinction between citizen and non-citizen.

Secondly, though Euhemerus' state is Utopian he does not fall into the error of many Utopians and isolate it from the rest of the world. Neither Diogenes nor Euhemerus was a cosmopolitan in the political sense. The community of Panchaïa has to have soldiers to protect its agriculture from brigands. It trades directly with Arabia, and indirectly with Phoenicia, Coele-Syria, Egypt and thus the rest of the civilized world. The Sacred Inscription is written in Egyptian hieroglyphics. Celtic torques are worn. Persian fashions may be seen in the ear-rings and the priests' caps. Thoas, king of the Tauric Chersonesus, seems to have visited Panchaïa. The gods came there from Crete, and Zeus in his wanderings visited many other countries, including Syria, Cilicia, and Babylon. Somewhere Euhemerus wrote about the pyramids of Egypt and the history of the Jews.[22] But though Panchaïa is a single state among others, it is cosmopolitan in the sense that no peoples are excluded. In addition to the natives there are the Cretans representing the east, Scythians the North, and Oceanites the unknown people surrounding all. The three known peoples form a single tribe, the Doians.[23] This is an impressive testimony to Alexander's work, for Euhemerus here takes it up and goes beyond it.

Thirdly – and the point is relevant to the development of Stoic cosmopolitanism – Euhemerus, rationalist as he was, adopted some of the external paraphernalia of Babylonian astrology. Thus it was from Babylon that Zeus came to Panchaïa; the name of the sacred stream was 'Water of the Sun'; according to Pliny the City of the Sun stood near to Panchaïa;[24] one of the principal cities was called Asterusia; the name of the great mountain was Heaven's throne (though this is rationalized). Ideas such as those of just apportioning, equality of the sexes, communistic sharing, are often found associated with the Sun, which shines alike on just and unjust and enters palaces and cesspools without being defiled. Further in his treatment of the gods Euhemerus shows an interest in the sun, moon and stars. Harmony, which Cleanthes' divine sun established, was a flute girl who contracted an alliance with Cadmus.[25] Sol was the son of Oceanus.[26] Heaven, or Uranus, was an astronomer who climbed to the top of the mountain just mentioned, and from there surveyed the heaven and the stars. Elsewhere it is Venus who first determines the stars and demonstrates them to Mercury.[27] The two sentences are apparently contradictory, but whether in their contexts they would be resolved, or Hyginus is misquoting, or *The Sacred Inscription* consisted of contradictory myths, Euhemerus' astronomical interests and his linking of them with the establishment of Panchaïa are clear.

Fourthly, Euhemerus does not neglect economics. There appears to be a plenitude of all things necessary to life. The principal food is fruit, especially nuts, but also grapes, dates, and on the Sacred Isle the fruit of the Christ's thorn. The normal crops are produced by the farmers and provide a staple diet. O meat-eating there is no indication either way, but there are plenty of animals both wild and domestic. Cannibalism was strictly forbidden.[28] For drink there is the fruit of the Christ's thorn again, and the great profusion of grape-vines, but also the water of the sacred stream which is very sweet. The influence of

Diogenes and Crates, both water-drinkers, is evident here. The clothing is made of wool, and being for an ideal community it is especially soft, though Euhemerus does not go so far as Vergil and picture the sheep with their fleeces ready-dyed. The priests may wear linen which is regarded as a great luxury. (In Lucian's satire its place is taken by glass.[29]) Men and women wear similar shoes,[30] (the specification implies that their clothing is different) of variegated colours; the priests similar sandals. Gold ornaments are common to everyone, though the priests refrain from ear-rings, but though they reject this Persian fashion they adopt the Persian cap. For the rest there is a wealth of gold, silver copper, tin and iron, the gold and silver being used for dedicating offerings and ornamentation. Stone is used for public building, and white marble for the temple. The Sacred Isle produces incense in profusion.

Private property is practically abolished, the only private possessions being a house and garden. This is Ptolemaic. Everything else is distributed from the national exchequer. As in the Soviet Union, within limits the reward is proportionate to service and responsibility. The resources are estimated in goods, that is the things which are actually necessary to living, and according to their quantity in a given year (or possibly half-year, since the myrrh at least gives two harvests), a basic share is allocated. This is doubled for the priests, and increased for those of the farmers, and possibly the herdsmen, who have produced outstandingly good results. The king of the Sacred Isle similarly received his tithe of all the fruits, the immemorial system in Asia. Euhemerus is either being very woolly here, or is concerned merely to lay down principles which will in practice be imperfectly worked out. The principles are important – that everyone shall have a fair share relative to the actual resources, that those with special responsibility shall receive more, that there shall be adequate incentives for good work. Aristotle in discussing community of land and of crops raised the difficulty of how to achieve an equitable division whether strictly egalitarian or not, without aggrieving the best workers.[31] This is Euhemerus' solution. But in practice it would not be possible to put all the food in the country together and issue a yearly ration in the crude manner in which he conceives it; the incentives he offers, prizes for the best ten farmers only, would be largely ineffective, and in any event the inevitably different conditions on each farm would make judgement of the best farmer impossible. But there are the glimmerings of the Stakhanovite idea. In all this there is no place for currency, and one would suppose that Euhemerus, like Zeno and unlike Diogenes, did away with it. He says however that the soldiers do receive allowances but these we must suppose to mean allowances in kind.

Panchaïa has a small trade with the outside world. Export of its mineral resources is strictly forbidden. The Sacred Isle exports frankincense and myrrh, but there is no indication of the consequent imports, and probably Euhemerus did not consider them. From both these points it seems that he regarded Panchaïa as self-supporting, and so evaded one of the more difficult political problems, that of preserving the internal integrity of a nation which is dependent on the outside world. This is the reason why the priests may not roam abroad. Panchaïa is static; it is perfect, and any change from without would be a change for the worse. Similar taboos are found historically among the Mossynoeci and the Sabaeans.[32]

Finally, a word about government. The Sacred Isle itself is a monarchy. But the part of Panchaïa around the city of Panara is ruled by a different system. There the inhabitants of the city form the ultimately responsible body. They make their own laws and elect three ministers to serve them annually. They may apparently be from any of the three classes. But the effective power is in the hands of the priests, who have no official political status. Here again the parallel with the USSR is illuminating, where the Communist Party, not being an official organ within the constitution, is none the less the effective voice in government, Stalin having for a long time been secretary of the Party and holding no constitutional position at all. The Ministers 'voluntarily refer the most important business' to this intellectual élite. The ministers themselves have plenary powers, but the capital punishment has been abolished except for behaviour on the part of the priests which may be deemed traitorous, namely the attempt to leave the precincts of their authority within twenty-five miles of the great temple. Euhemerus is thus an early adherent to the 'mixed' constitution popularized by Aristotle and the later Stoics. His important original contribution lies in the suggestion that the expert should have no constitutional position, but should, by being consulted voluntarily, exercise none the less a decisive influence upon the affairs of state.

Euhemerus' political ideas had slight influence. They were propounded only incidentally to his rationalistic fervour. They are careless but suggestive, original but unrealistic. But though the ideas themselves made but little impact, his Utopianism passed through Iambulus to More and Campanella and many later writers. We may sum up his work as a typical and important specimen of what Chassang has called 'le roman philosophique'.[33]

Cassander had an eccentric brother named Alexarchus. He is a footnote on the pages of history, but a not uninteresting one. The literary evidence about him is scanty. The most important passage comes from Athenaeus, and is derived from Heracleides Lembus. It tells us that Alexarchus was Cassander's brother and founded Uranopolis, or the City of Heaven, and introduced a peculiar vocabulary with archaic diction and compound epithets.[34] Athenaeus records a letter he wrote to the neighbouring city of Cassandreia. It is written in very odd Greek, and Athenaeus, or Heracleides, comments 'I don't believe that even the Delphic Oracle could make any sense of this letter.'[35] Tarn tried to build a large thesis on a small foundation: the letter seems to begin: 'Alexarchus to the chiefs of the Brethren, rejoicing.'[36] But the word 'brethren', itself an emendation, is naturally applied to the citizens of his brother's foundation, and is nothing to do with the brotherhood of man.[37] Similarly the language is garbled Greek, not a blending of international languages. Other slighter references tell us that Alexarchus was a language expert in virtue of his knowledge, and transformed himself into the sun, that he wrote a letter in which Dionysus was identified with the Egyptian Arsaphes, and that Uranopolis was on the isthmus linking Athos with the mainland, near where Xerxes tried to dig his canal; it had a circuit of thirty stades, or about four miles.[38] It may well be a refoundation of Sane, but only excavation will solve the problem of the history of that region. The name Uranopolis belongs also to a city of Pamphylia.[39] This may well have been another of Cassander's foundations, perhaps for his other brother Pleistarchus, or perhaps even colonized from Alexarchus' city. Fortunately we have in addition the evidence of some very remarkable coins.[40] These bear instead of the expected *Uranopolitai* 'Citizens of Uranopolis' the name *Uranidai* 'Children of Heaven'. The dominant figure is that of Aphrodite Urania. She is one form of the ubiquitous Mother Goddess of the Near East, and her title is derived from the Semitic *Meleket Aschamain*, 'the queen of heaven' whom Jeremiah scorned.[41] According to the Greek religious historians, the worship of Aphrodite Urania was established at Cythera by the Phoenicians, and it may have followed the purple trade.[42] We do not know how it reached the northern parts, but Herodotus thought of it as already established in Scythia.[43] Gardner thought that she came into Thrace as a consort of Ares, the local sun-god.[44] It is likely that the goddess was there well before Alexarchus.[45] Aphrodite Urania, as her name suggests, acquired, if she did not always possess, an astral significance: in some traditions she is identified with the moon, and associated with the sun.[46] Furthermore, although it was seemingly Aphrodite Urania who was worshipped at Corinth,[47] in general Aphrodite Urania, not least in the philosophical traditions deriving from Socrates, is a divinity contrasting with Aphrodite Pandemos or Aphrodite Apostrophia, and involving some kind of higher moral response.[48]

Typical coins show the goddess holding a sceptre and seated on a globe. She wears a long chiton and peplos fastened on the right shoulder. Sometimes there is a headdress topped by a star. In the field stands a star-topped cone. There is sometimes a lighted torch. The obverse of the coin is regularly taken up with astral symbolism: sun, moon and five stars; a radiate globe, presumably representing the sun; an eight-rayed star with a crescent presumably the sun and moon. This symbolism has many links. In the first place it is associated with the traditions of Macedon. A star is to be seen on the coins of almost all Macedonian monarchs from Philip to Perseus, and Cassander was assiduous in claiming this symbolism for himself; Gardner thought it the symbol of Ares, sun-god and war-god.[49] Still, Uranopolis was the only Macedonian city to claim this type for her own. Secondly there are images associated with Aphrodite Urania, notably the cone, which appears in the field and is reflected in the headdress. Some interpreters have seen in this an allusion to Mt Athos. But one form under which the goddess was worshipped was that of a conical or pyramidal betyl, and Roscher thought this the most primitive form of the cult.[50] Conical stones, apparently serving as idols, were found at Golgi in Cyprus, and in the Phoenician temples of Malta, and on Sinai in the shrine of the 'Mistress of Torquoise'; similarly at Byblus a cone was the emblem of Astarte.[51] Maximus of Tyre says that the image of Aphrodite at Paphos is like a white pyramid. Other evidence suggests rather a cone, curved, and tapering from the bottom upwards.[52] In a fourth-century inscription at Epidaurus five triangles, stylized cones or pyramids, appear as the symbol of Aphrodite Urania.[53] The star symbol is also associated with Aphrodite Urania, among the Sauromates, for instance, and on the coins of Julia Domna. Thirdly there is symbolism related to the sun, and in view of the literary evidence perhaps representing Alexarchus himself.

We have then a city of an unusual name, the City of Heaven, citizens uniquely called Children of Heaven, a ruler identified with the sun, a patron-goddess who provides a link with the Near East and who is in some circles associated with ethical ideas, a deal of astral symbolism, and a new language. This emerges from the same circle as a rationalist who produces a theoretical Utopia with similar astral symbolism, a similar attempt to depict a community which reaches out beyond the traditional Greek boundaries, a clear power structure, and interesting economic provisions. It is at least possible that Alexarchus was trying out some of Euhemerus' formulae, and one wonders what was the economic structure of Uranopolis; the language seems to have been his own idea. Certainly there was at this time a ferment of idealistic, Utopian thinking. Uranopolis is our only example of a practical attempt to produce a foundation of a new kind to incorporate the values of a new age, and we could wish that we knew more of it.

CHAPTER XIII

THE EARLY STOICS

ZENO, THE FOUNDER OF THE STOICS, brought into Greek philosophy the element of orientalism. He was the son of Manasses, born in Citium, a Greek city of Cyprus, occupied by Phoenician settlers.[1] He was swarthy and ascetic to look upon, but despite his foreign appearance he was able to establish himself in Athens as a man of power and insight. He first looked to obtain wisdom from the writings of the past, such as Xenophon's reminiscences of Socrates. Then he began to feel a personal need for living men realizing in his time the ideals he found among the dead, and attached himself to Crates the Cynic, who became the greatest single influence upon his life, even after he had passed from him to Stilpo, Xenocrates and Polemo; he had too much native modesty fully to accept the Cynic shamelessness.[2]

It was at this period that he composed an ideal commonwealth, called in rivalry to Plato *The Republic*. The genuineness of the work is attested by Chrysippus,[3] though it may have suffered interpolation.[4] He wrote it, we are told, while still under Cynic influence, 'hanging on to the dog's tail',[5] and later apologists excuse its excesses on grounds of his youth.[6] H. C. Baldry has made a model study of all that is known for sure of the work.[7] Baldry decided not to integrate the passages explicitly ascribed to *The Republic* with general accounts of Zeno's political thought. In one sense this is obviously safe; at the same time, except for the apologia noted above, later sources do not speak of a development or contrast in his political thought. It is not illegitimate to reinforce what is specific to *The Republic* by other allusions.

Zeno's political thought may be traced to a variety of sources. First he perhaps owed to the Orient his religious ethic. The ethical approach accorded with his Greek predecessors. 'Cities should be adorned not with offerings but with the virtues of the inhabitants,' he said.[8] The difference was that it was religious not humanistic. Further the religion was not the conventional Greek religion, and in *The Republic* depended not at all on the temples familiar to the Greeks.[9] Zeno favoured instead the universal gods, the sun, moon and stars. These derived ultimately from Babylonian astrology,[10] though this aspect was less prominent in Zeno than in Cleanthes. To Zeno they were manifestations of the divine fire, examples of an ordered commonwealth, powers of the whole universe;[11] and we must not forget the traditional association of the sun with justice. They possessed thought and intelligence, and the whole universe was disposed and governed like a well-ordered community. The universe in fact is one common city of gods and men.[12] It is hard to think that these are later thoughts, irrelevant to *The Republic*, especially as Plutarch explicitly speaks of the Republic as embracing all men, a single world-order, a flock nurtured by one common law or pasture (there is a Greek pun on *nomos*).[13] At the same time it is just to say that there is no mention of these deities in the passages identified as from *The Republic*, only of Love (*Eros*), as provider of unity, freedom and safety.[14] The religious ethic remains clear.

Next came Cynic influence, obvious in a work 'written under the Dog's tail'. Not only so; behind the Cynics lay Antisthenes, who 'laid the foundations of the commonwealths' of Diogenes and Zeno alike.[15] In Zeno's work 'the teachings of Antisthenes and Diogenes were brought together'.[16] He took from them community of wives and children, a critical attitude to slavery, indifference to worldly values, a high place for wisdom, a critical attitude to Plato, and a reinforcement to his moralism.

Thirdly, we cannot neglect the influence of Alexander. We may discount Tarn's picture of Alexander as a cosmopolitan idealist; we may accept that there was genuine cosmopolitanism in Greece before the time of Alexander; still, Alexander did fling back the frontiers. This meant on the one hand that the historic rôle of the city-state in its old form was played out; it meant that those who had once felt that they were in control of their own destiny now felt themselves in the grip of world forces too large for them to handle. So a moral answer had to be found for the individual in his helplessness. At the same time the world rulers might use a mentor, or an ideal might be held before them. Positively, it forced new thinkers to think on a world scale.

Fourthly, Plato stands in the background of all Utopian, indeed of all political thinking. Negatively, we are told that Zeno used to write in opposition to Plato's *Republic*;[17] it was not the city of Zeus. Other criticisms to some extent arose from historical changes, the fact that the city-state in its old form was not enough, or the greater emphasis on individual as against civic virtue. It is significant that the temples, law courts and gymnasia abolished by Zeno all appear in Plato's *The Laws*.[18] Positively, the Stoics found much to learn in Plato, the idea of a philosopher-king, the notion that each individual, whatever his function, was an integral part of the community (Zeno made a punning variant; the individual was not a *meros* but a *melos*, not a part but a limb), and the exaltation of Eros.[19]

Fifthly, Heraclitus is in the background of the Stoic thought, especially from the time of Cleanthes. The influence on Zeno, especially in the early period, is less striking, but Zeno's treatment of law does seem derived from Heraclitus' 'All human laws are nourished from one divine law'.[20]

Plutarch asserts the dependence of Zeno's state on Lycurgus' Sparta.[21] The principal points of contact were the continued basis of the city as the local unit of government within the world communities, within these cities the domination of the mass of ordinary people by a small oligarchy of sages, and the single-mindedness of the community.

When we look at the nature of the proposals we find a religious and moralizing approach. Zeno's characteristic later view was that the Universe, Diospolis or Megalopolis or Cosmopolis, is a community of gods and men, the sun, moon and stars, the months and years, and the air itself being divine. These views are not explicit in the references to *The Republic*, nor are they excluded. The immediate guiding forces on the minds of men are Reason, the divine element dwelling in the mind, or rather being itself the mind,[22] and Love, the bringer of friendship, freedom, and above all, concord, and serving the salvation of the city.[23] So reason and the passions co-operate for the common good. The result of this world view is that Zeno is no longer concerned solely with a single city-state. Individuals were no longer to be divided from one another, each with his own petty idea of justice, but they would be united in a single community, its life and order single and simple, pasturing on universal law like a herd.[24] The typical quality of the new community is to be *homonoia*, concord, something between fellowship and single-mindedness[25]. Now Zeno was not without feeling for the sense of belonging to a particular city; he was proud of belonging to Citium.[26] So he does speak of 'the city',[27] and the parallel with Lycurgus' Sparta would be ludicrous if that were not true. Equally, he lays down what shall be done in 'the cities'.[28] One significant passage says that money would not be needed for going abroad.[29] The implication is that we have a number of different cities, worldwide, all united in a common rejection of currency. Hence too, in part, the abolition of those state institutions which proved divisive – temples, law-courts, gymnasia, as well as currency;[30] all pertain to state government and all must be removed. Tarn was wrong to refuse to admit the cosmopolitanism of Zeno's Republic and the relevance of the Plutarch quotation.[31] The natural interpretation is a world community comprising an indefinite number of individual cities.

Education was inescapably important to Zeno's scheme. We know that it was discussed at the beginning of *The Republic*, and that he dismissed the ordinary curriculum of the Greeks as worthless;[32] hence also the abolition of the law-courts, the main repository of the fruits of literary education, and of the gymnasia, the scene of continuous physical education. For the rest we have to go outside *The Republic*. But we know that he set store by education,[33] and held that it needed inborn grace of character, a reasonable amount of discipline, and a teacher who would give tirelessly and unsparingly; and that he regarded the object of education as a virtuous character.[34] Stein in fact suggested that Zeno's works on education, *On the Greek System of Education, On Listening to Poetry* and *Homeric Problems*, were complementary to *The Republic*.[35] It is significant that the very title of the first shows Zeno as a non-Greek standing outside the system. Farrington has suggested that Diodorus' account of the Chaldaeans is taken from Zeno's treatise.[36] The criticism of the Greeks and the application of the term 'ungrudging' to the teacher support this view. The passage in sum emphasizes the need from childhood for education directed systematically towards intellectual certainty and a total view of life by dedicated instructors. But it is the single-mindedness of the Chaldaean system which appeals to Zeno, not the end product of astrology, however sympathetic the later Stoics might be to this. We know in fact from the other works that Zeno was sympathetic to music,[37] poetry and logic. In fact with the establishment of his school in 301 BC, perhaps to meet the changed conditions of service of the ephebes[38] he replaced the old division of letters, 'music', physical training by logic, physics, ethics.

Zeno's attitude to government, slavery and the class system has been much misunderstood. Zeller and most subsequent commentators have treated his Republic as a 'polity of the wise'. The matter remains controversial, but the evidence seems to point in the other direction. There is a contradiction in the passages assigned to *The Republic*: in one all men are citizens; in another only the wise have the qualities needed for a harmonious whole.[39] Now Zeno repeatedly said that the good alone were kings, and the wicked (that is, on the principle *omnia peccata paria*, the rest of mankind) alone slaves. He was not merely speaking in metaphors; he was implying that in an ideal community this would be so. The Stoics did not attack the institution of monarchy; they complained that the wrong people became kings; this was the burden of 'the philosophical opposition to the principate' in the first century AD. The worthy, the *spoudaioi*, alone were happy, prosperous, blessed, fortunate, pious, godly, noble; they alone had a grasp of sovereignty, military leadership, politics, domestic economy, business. It is nonsense to say that the Stoics had no business with kingship. They were always talking about it, and Zeno was for ever hanging round kings, Antigonus or Ptolemy Philadelphus. It is wrong to say that Stoic political philosophy was egalitarian.[40] It is reasonable to discern a sympathy for monarchy in its early history.[41] About slavery the Stoics were uneasy; it was not in accordance with nature; but they never assailed it as an institution. In a passage which is perhaps not Zeno's, but which he might not have disowned, he recognizes three types of slavery.[42] The first, the absence of the power of independent action, is evil, but it is an evil which comes from within. The second is subordination and is not evil. The third involves the ownership of the slave's body as well as his subordination; its correlative is overlordship; and it too is evil. Thus despotism is condemned, but not sovereignty. We may conclude that Zeno's ideal community is ruled by sages, a multi-sovereignty; the others are there but subordinate.

A number of the surviving passages concern sex, but this emphasis may be due to later critics rather than to Zeno.[43] Community of wives was a feature of the Republic, associated with a free choice of partners on both sides, but apparently confined to the wise. The result would be that all children would receive an equal degree of paternal affection, and jealousy due to adultery would be abolished. There are no signs of the safeguards and strictures with which Plato hedged round his own scheme. Zeno regarded the accepted attitude to sex as conventional and sought to create a natural attitude by removing all artificial inhibitions. The evidence is not quite clear, but he perhaps permitted a combination of controlled marriage with promiscuity outside. Men and women would wear the same dress and no part of the body was to remain covered (Zeller's suggestion that this applied merely to gymnastics was an un-happy one: Zeno abolished the gymnasia); this is again life 'according to nature'. Homosexuality is positively encouraged; Zeno is here close to Plato. About the economic ordinances we know little. Zeno in practice did not espouse Cynic poverty, though he was always frugal; in his advanced theory everything concerning money was a matter of indifference except its legitimate and honourable use.[44] Money was in fact irrelevant to true living, and could be dispensed with; it was needed neither for exchange at home nor travel and trade abroad.[45] There is no indication of any alternative. Presumably the sages practised communism among themselves and an equitable distribution among their subordinates, and, the commonwealth being world wide, this took place on a world-wide scale. There is however one further indication of Zeno's economic outlook. He shared the upper-class Greek prejudice against artisans, and one part of his attitude to the building of temples was that the work of artisans was unworthy of the gods; intellectual effort alone was worthy of God's presence.[46] Clearly then material work will have been confined to a minimum, and concentrated in the subordinate classes.

'All human laws are nourished from the same divine law.'[47] Natural law to Zeno was divine, and the divine law was the basis of all earthly justice. But there were no law-courts in the Republic, so presumably no human law to administer; the wisdom of the sages lived and ordered the commonwealth by direct contact with the law of heaven.

Here then is the weakness of Zeno's scheme. It was an ideal; he gave no indication of transition from the present to the ideal, and had no thought (un-like Plato) that once the philosophic commonwealth were established there could be degeneration from it. Zeno's Utopia was a Utopia, a vision to guide and reform contemporary politics.

Between Zeno and Chrysippus came Cleanthes, like Zeno a foreigner, unlike him a proletarian. Cleanthes was industrious, slow to learn, tenacious of what he acquired, and not afraid of innovation. His political thought started from Diogenes and Zeno, and we know that in his work *On the Cloak* he spoke approvingly of Diogenes' *Republic*.[48] This work is not mentioned by Diogenes Laertius, who lists other works relevant to politics, *The Statesman, On the Laws, On Administering Justice*, and *On Kingship*; Plutarch too attests his interest in political questions.[49] We have also a citation in Stobaeus: 'If a city is a domestic contrivance in which men may take refuge and exact and receive their just dues, then surely a city is something civilized? But a city is such a domestic contrivance, therefore it is something civilized!'[50] We have no con-text for the remark, but plainly it gives some sort of sanction to political life. Beyond this his writings show a concern for education, with a strongly moralis-tic bias.

One of Cleanthes' main innovations is his exaltation of the sun and the heavenly bodies generally, under the power of Zeus who is identified with the universe.[51] The sun is the ruler of the world, director of the universe, disposer of all, torchbearer for the mysteries of life; it is slightly ironical that Cleanthes assailed Aristarchus for his heliocentric theory.[52] This predominance of the sun is linked with Cleanthes' predilection for Heraclitus, and with the introduction of Babylonian astrology. For political thought in general, and Utopian thought in particular it is of the utmost importance. The sun plays for Cleanthes the rôle which is assigned to Love in Zeno's *Republic*. The political associations of the sun are with monarchy and justice. The Sassanid rulers, like the Pharaohs of Egypt, proclaimed themselves 'brothers of the sun and moon'; the Seleucid kingdom was dedicated to Helios-Apollo, and the sovereigns were honoured as his representatives and wore the radiate crown as symbol of their sovereignty and simulacrum of the god. The sun was the arbiter of the Fortune of kings, who ruled by his grace, the Hvaremo or aureole which the Greeks rendered by Tyche. Later Philo constantly compares the sovereignty of the sun with that of the Great King, and Julian of Laodicea calls the sun 'the king and ruler of the whole world'.[53] The resemblance between these and Stoic ideas is patent, and Dio of Prusa has no hesitation in using a myth of the Magi as an allegory of Stoic cosmology.[54] To one who like Cleanthes came from Assos Persian thought would be familiar. Similarly in Persia *The Acts of Pusai* called the sun 'judge of the whole earth who sees righteousness and pronounces judgement'; the Jew Malachi, who knew the Persians, speaks of 'the sun of justice'.[55] It was the sun who dispensed justice, guaranteed equity, held the balance straight; men waited for the sun-king to descend from heaven and establish justice. To the Greeks the sun in his impartiality was the guarantor of freedom. At Troezen an altar to the Sun of Freedom commemorated the deliverance from Xerxes;[56] to Artemidorus it was he who set free the slaves.[57] Cleanthes was ambiguous in his political attitudes. He had no room for democracy,[58] any more than Heraclitus had; this is represented in his insistence on monarchy. But he had a practical sympathy for honest toil, poverty and the lot of the slave; and this is represented in the office of the sun as dispenser of justice. In general we can say that the foundations of Cleanthes' political theory were profoundly religious, they were astrological to a degree to which Zeno's were not, and their practical marks were monarchy and justice. Cleanthes did not himself construct a Utopia, but his work has its place in the development of Utopian thought.

It was Chrysippus in the view of later generations who established the Stoic school firmly for the future; 'if there had been no Chrysippus there would have been no Porch.' It was not so much that he diverged from Zeno and Cleanthes, though later critics tend to make much of his divergences.[59] It was that his colossal output of more than 705 books developed, systematized and popularized the thought of his predecessors.[60]

He wrote a Utopia, inevitably called *The Republic*, but we do not know very much about it. There were other political works too, *On the City and Law, On Justice* and others. It is uncertain how much we may extrapolate. We know for example that he was consistent in a number of works in opposing the taboo on incest,[61] but we obviously cannot be in general certain that a philosopher so long-lived would not vary his views or that an author so voluminous would not, like Cicero, find different points appealing to him in different contexts.

We can make some safe observations. Like Cleanthes, he was religious and moralistic in his approach. Plutarch says that he wrote nothing about law and politics without writing in the forefront Zeus, Destiny and Providence, the Unity and Finitude of the world, and the single power which holds it together.[62] There is no beginning for righteousness except in God. Call him what you will, Zeus, Common Nature, Fate or Necessity, the same is Lawfulness (*eunomia*), Justice (*dike*), Concord (*homonoia*), Peace (*eirene*). The Universe is a city, the stars are citizens, and were citizens before man existed. They are magistrates, the sun is a counsellor, the evening star a government official.[63] Chrysippus' whole political approach is governed by his vision of the universe as the community of gods and men. Yet this of itself creates a tension in his thought. For in the perfection of the universe vice is left to men. [64] Chrysippus was a pessimist about human nature. He did not take part in politics because if he did evil he would be unacceptable to the gods, if well, unacceptable to his fellow citizens.[65] So for him, in explicit conflict with Plato and Aristotle, virtue, righteousness, justice (*dikaiosune*) is individual, not social; animals live socially but have no *dikaiosune*.[66] In *Demonstrations* a discussion of law led not to political theory but to the damage an unjust man does to himself.[67] Yet this very pessimism about the contemporary scene also drove Chrysippus in the direction of Utopianism. And his religion directed him to cosmopolitanism.

The ideal rule is kingship, as Zeus is lord and governor of all.[68] Chrysippus had a healthy contempt for the monarchs of his day, dedicating none of his works to them, and refusing to go to Ptolemy,[69] but this represents no rejection of monarchy as an ideal, but an attack on round pegs in holes which only the four-square man could fit. As Zeus and Reason are one and the same, so the kingship in the cities of men should rest upon the sage. So, although Chrysippus in his pessimism tended to praise political quietism, he also said that the sage would accept a kingdom.[70] The wise man alone is free, and because kingship is irresponsible rule, he alone can maintain it; knowledge of good and evil is an indispensable attribute of the ruler, and he alone has it.[71] Not many are wise, and it is possible that in Chrysippus' Utopia the sages were distributed round the cities as kings, themselves forming a kind of United Nations of the wise, sharing in the divine commonwealth. Equally, a plurality of sages in any one political unit would point to oligarchy rather than monarchy; and the fact that, as we shall see in a moment, Chrysippus believed in the educability of all those possessed of reason, carries with it some kind of democratic implications. Later Stoics fostered the theory of the mixed constitution. Chrysippus did not, but we can trace a line of descent from his thought.

The unworthy have no share in government. In Cosmopolis they are cityless and homeless;[72] the words in which Diogenes gloried have become a term of shame. But equally all those and only those who have a share of reason and intelligence also partake of law and citizen rights in some sense;[73] there is an explicit contrast with Sparta, where the Helots, having no power to become citizens, become instead enemies of the state, and Chrysippus is effectively the first of the Utopians to turn his back upon Sparta. Chrysippus' ideal common-wealth was not a community of sages, but a community of ordinary human beings governed by a sage or sages, a community under law, in which the ordinary members exercised no political responsibility but with the potential of becoming sages.

It is here that education counts. The fundamental difficulty faced by Chry-sippus in dealing with education is raised by Alexander of Aphrodisias.[74] There is no intermediary state between virtue and vice, reason and unreason; yet children go through a process of acquiring reason. Chrysippus specifically says that virtue does not come by nature; it is by a process of learning that men become noble; virtue in short is teachable.[75] Nor will this teaching come from the traditional form of education, though Chrysippus held, as against Zeno, that this was not entirely profitless. He perhaps followed Zeno in abolish-ing gymnasia, favouring more practical forms of exercise and training.[76] He believed in logic as helping the power of discrimination,[77] and thought that poetry, properly taught, could be used as a part of moral education.[78] For-tunately Quintilian has preserved for us some of his other educational principles. 'Some people have thought children younger than seven incapable of assimilat-ing letters. Better are those who, like Chrysippus, wish no period to lack supervision. He gave the children for three years to the care of nurses, but even then thought they could form the infant mind by the best methods.'[79] Beyond this we know that he did not object to corporal punishment, recom-mended music in coping with infants, and found a place in the curriculum for lessons in gesticulation.[80] All this is not explicitly associated with *The Republic*, but in view of the long association of education and Utopia it is unlikely that he left it out, or that the principles inculcated were very different.

Chrysippus said that the nurses should be sages if possible.[81] He was the first of the Stoics to say explicitly that men and women are alike in virtue, and both should philosophize.[82] In this respect he is returning from Zeno to Plato, perhaps with Hipparchia in his mind. His community is a community of men and women as partners in the state. Like Zeno he allowed in *The Republic* community of wives with a free choice of partners. He also permitted, and, according to one source, enjoined incest in *The Republic*.[83] This was part of a reversion to Diogenes and the Cynic flouting of convention; Chrysippus actually wrote six books *Against Convention*, and followed Diogenes in approv-ing cannibalism (though this probably did not appear in *The Republic*).[84] We can thus trace a readiness to shock his readers out of convention, and at the same time a positive desire to find what is according to nature; in *The Republic* he attempts to outline the social place of the sexes according to nature.

Similarly Chrysippus made a great advance on current thinking about sla-very in insisting that the difference between the slave and the free employee is one of degree, not of kind; the slave is a workman hired *ad infinitum*.[85] The radical distinction is between men and the lower animals.[86] It is reasonable to attribute to Chrysippus the attack on the idea that slaves have no share in reason or law, and the maxim that slaves ought to philosophize.[87] Unfortunately we do not know whether this led him to abolish slavery in his Utopia. Probably not, or we should hear of it. But slaves equally with any of the citizens were potential sages and potential rulers.

Economically we know that in *The Republic* Chrysippus gave no place to luxury. He upbraided those who reared peacocks and nightingales; these things would have no part in his city. His citizens would never act from pleasure; they would be contented with the simplest needs and with satisfying them in the simplest way.[88] He is sarcastic about excessive splendour, saying 'We are near to painting dung-heaps', and criticizing farmers for 'beautifying' their work with creepers and myrtles. Plutarch comments with some justice that it is absurd to praise God for his creation and remove from the citizens those parts of creation which delight the eye and ear, to praise nature for the tail of the peacock in all its glory and exclude it from the city, to maintain that bugs are created profitably and bees unprofitably. As Kenneth Hare put it centuries later:

> The Puritan through life's sweet garden goes
> To pluck the thorn, and cast away the rose,
> And hopes to please by this peculiar whim
> The God who fashioned it and gave it him.

For Chrysippus this was a matter of the indifference of beauty; he would have answered, like the Puritan, that these things, becoming ends in themselves, stand between us and God. In the world as it is there are legitimate differences of private circumstances, since these are irrelevant.[89] From the ideal commonwealth the effect of these things will be excluded. We can legitimately attribute to Chrysippus the idea of a polity as one of men living a noble life together and sharing all things. It is not an ideal of narrow egalitarianism, but one of men of different gifts each contributing what he has to give to the common stock.

Chrysippus also elucidated the Stoic concept of law, though it seems that he did not elaborate a legislative scheme in *The Republic*.[90] There is one eternal law, fated necessity, the eternal truth of things to come. This law is Zeus. Law is the king of all human and divine affairs. It should have the authority to ordain what is good and evil, it should be the canon of right and wrong, instructing those creatures which are by nature political what they should and should not do.[91] Justice, law and right reason all exist by nature, since reason is given by nature, and therefore right reason, and therefore law, which is right reason in the realm of commanding and forbidding. It is the law which by its forbidding voice calls men away from wrongdoing.[92] The nature of man is such that a kind of code of law is operative between the individual and the human race; justice consists in maintaining this, injustice in departing from it.[93] The task of the statesman is to apply this law to the community of which he is a part. The Stoics defined a city as an assemblage of men ordered by law. The state lacking law could not exist.[94] But no existing constitution has grasped and applied the eternal law, and Diogenianus attacks Chrysippus for his criticism of these.[95] Yet Chrysippus was right, and in his vision of the perfect commonwealth, the sage would perfectly apply the eternal law. There and there only would the laws of God and man become one.

At this point we may briefly summarize the Stoic contribution to Hellenistic political thought. One thing is certain, even if it were not firmly attested by Philodemus, the basis of it all is Zeno.[96] He formulated a proper Utopia; in this Cleanthes did not follow, though Chrysippus did. The foundations of their thought are moralistic and pietistic with an increasing place for astrology, and an increasing appeal to the authority of Heraclitus. The structure of the ideal society is built upon the absolute cleavage between the worthy who alone are fit to govern and the unworthy who are fit only to serve. Consequently the earliest strain of thought is oligarchical and with the influence of astrology monarchical; the associations of early Stoicism with the ideal of kingship are too clear to be denied. Maturity softens such hard and absolute judgements, and experience brings a spirit of compromise. Events outside revealed the dissolution of Alexander's empire; within the school a developing educational theory based on logic, physics and ethics narrowed the cleavage between the two classes. If we set aside the mere attack on conventionalism, deriving, as so much else, from the Cynics, we see that the really significant source of Stoic thought was Alexander, his achievement and his failure. In his absolute government the Stoic sage had seen the diadem he alone was fitted to wear; but subsequent years brought disillusionment with such absolute powers, and the school gradually set before themselves the ideal of a mixed constitution, implicit in Chrysippus, explicit in Poseidonius, in which, as in a theatre, each had his place. 'God, the eternal dramatist, has cast you for some part in his drama, and hands you the role. It may turn out that you are cast for a triumphant king; it may be for a slave who dies of torture. What does that matter to the good actor? He can play either part, his only business is to accept the role given him, and to perform it well.'[97] King, baron, commoner, each has a part to play in life and his contribution to the state. But hence comes the first tension in Stoic thought, since the wise man alone is fit to rule, but is also called to play the part in which he finds himself. And secondly Alexander gave a glimpse of the historical possibility of a brotherhood of all mankind, but Greek thought was still bounded by the city-state, and harked back to Sparta and to Plato. Thus Euhemerus can realize his cosmopolis only upon a limited island which has relations with other communities. In Stoic thought this tension too became acute. They had a glorious and grandiose vision of the city of God, of which the other cities were but as dwelling places.[98] But what became of the loyalty to the city of Cecrops? Ideally the wider loyalty was realized in the narrower. The good citizen was to submit to the law of his state; you served your country best by fulfilling your proper function, and the world by serving your country.[99] Emperor and slave alike could commend that to their disciples. And it was easy to construct a Utopia in which the harmony between the laws of God and man was unblemished. But the tension could not be so easily relaxed, and the growing interest in law results from the failure to achieve a full integration in this matter. A third tension results from the failure of a primitive communism to satisfy the economic aspirations of man. Hence from the earliest stage where the ideal is pure moneyless communism by the connecting thread of the indifference of wealth we pass to a stage where men's wealth may legitimately vary as God wills. Again the tension rests between the ideal and the duty of accepting the actual. But in recognizing these tensions we are only doing credit to a group of thinkers who by putting forward ideas far in advance of their time involved themselves in such contradiction. The rule of the wisest, and the responsibility of all men; a world-wide cosmopolitanism, and a unit in which men may be brothers in practice; the theoretical uselessness of money, and an indifference to its actual existence; these reconciliations were never fully effected by the Stoics; they have not been effected since.

CHAPTER XIV

THE HELLENISTIC ROMANCERS

PLATO BY HIS ACCOUNT OF ATLANTIS had set a popular pattern in the dramatic presentation of political thought. Euhemerus in the changed situation after the death of Alexander had capitalized upon this. Contact with distant peoples had led to a renewal of curiosity. Hecataeus, Leon and Megasthenes all helped to spread new knowledge, which whetted others' appetites.[1] There was some tendency to idealize remote peoples, as Onesicritus did with the Indians and Hecataeus with the Cimmerians.[2] Quite reputable historians and geographers might incorporate fictitious Utopias in otherwise sober works; those with a political view to put over, especially one which, though they might not admit it, was escapist, added verisimilitude by giving it a remote but plausible location in time and space.

We must begin with a brief mention of a passage from Theopompus recorded by Aelian.[3] According to this passage, Europe, Asia and Africa were really islands, and the only continent was outside our familiar world. This was of limitless size. All its animals were on a large scale; its human beings were twice our size and lived twice as long. There were many cities and differing ways of life, and the laws were diametrically opposed to ours. There were two great cities, Machimos (Military) and Eusebes (Pious). The inhabitants of the latter lived in peace, and natural wealth; they gathered their food without need to plough or sow. They were free from disease, happy, and free from injustice; the gods did not scorn to move among them. The others were militaristic, aggressive, imperialist. Their population numbered 2,000,000. They were subject to disease, but more frequently died in war, although they were impervious to iron. Their wealth lay in gold and silver. They tried to reach our islands, and reached the outpost of the Hyperboreans. There was also a people called Meropes. They had a number of large cities, including one called Anostos (The City of No Return) which was shrouded in a mixture of mist and a fiery turbidity. There were two rivers, Pleasure and Grief, and by them trees the size of a large plane-tree. Those who tasted the fruit of the trees by the River of Grief were reduced to tears for the rest of their lives. The other trees had the opposite effect. They made a man young again, restored his lost faculties and reversed the direction of his life so that he ended in babyhood.

We have hardly enough to make much of this.[4] There are certain reminiscences of Plato, both of *The Republic* and of his Atlantis, perhaps also of *Phaedo*,[5] and there are traditional legends, as of the Hyperboreans, recollections of the ubiquitous Homer, traveller's tales, and familiar accounts of nature-peoples. There have been attempts at actual geographical identification, but they become blurred. Remote parts of Africa have been suggested, and fiery turbidity might be Mt Cameroon in eruption.[6] So has England: mist and turbidity, neither daylight nor darkness, fits well some ancient impressions of England, but the ruddy effect is more difficult to explain. Rohde may be right in seeing a source in Hecataeus' account of the Cimmerians. Hirzel saw Cynic influence also. There was certainly a strong tendency in Theopompus towards moralizing, a favourable attitude to Antisthenes and a strongly critical attitude to Plato, which is by no means incompatible with the borrowing of motifs. But moralizing and criticism of Plato may belong to Isocrates as well as to Antisthenes or Diogenes. No doubt when Theopompus was writing it was impossible to escape entirely the impact of the Cynics. But it would be a mistake to suppose that Theopompus' excursion into Utopianism was a piece of Cynic propaganda. No Cynic would have written Theopompus' forty-eight laboured volumes. It seems rather to derive from a love of a good story combined with a general desire to point a moral and adorn a tale.

A romancer who merits brief notice is Dionysius Scytobrachion or Leatherarm.[7] We know little about him.[8] He may have been born in Mytilene. He seems to have worked and written in Alexandria. He was by profession a grammarian, with an interest in implausible etymologies. He was familiar with Euhemerus, and followed Euhemerus in his views of the origin of the gods,[9] and it was no doubt Panchaïa which gave him the idea of including in his hotch-potch two Utopias. We cannot, however, trace any social purpose underlying these; Scytobrachion seems to have been concerned merely to entertain. Similarly, we cannot associate him with any philosophical school or standpoint, other than that of Euhemerus.

The first of these is Hespera.[10] It lies in the mythical marsh Tritonis to the west, near Ethiopia (which means no more than the land of the Negroes) and the Atlas range. It is a large island. The inhabitants live from the milk and meat of goats and sheep and from fruit, but do not know corn: they thus fall into the category of primitive nature peoples. Rather oddly for such people, (but like the West African Yorubas), they live in cities. One of these, Mene, the Moon-Town, is sacred, rich in precious stones, and with vents of volcanic fire. This is inhabited by Ethiopian 'Fish-eaters'. The rest of the island has been subjugated by militaristic Amazons, who built their capital on a headland and called it Cherronesus. From here they entered upon a career of conquest of the peoples of Africa (Libya) within range, and upon further adventures including a campaign against the great civilization of Atlantis. There is an account of this campaign; the Amazon forces, 30,000 infantry with the unusually high proportion of 3,000 cavalry, with shields of snakeskin, swords and lances, and the use of bow and arrow after a sudden wheeling movement; the ruthless treatment of the captured city of Cerne, and subsequent campaign against the Gorgons.

There are a number of points in this curious description which call for comment.[11] First is the geographical location. Scytobrachion follows Euhemerus in placing his Utopia on the fringes of the known world, but where Euhemerus chooses the east, he chooses the west. It is possible, as Schwartz has suggested, that he was interested in contemporary concern with the circumnavigation of Africa; more probably, he was simply choosing a location diametrically opposed to that used by Euhemerus. Secondly, we note that he uses the people of traditional mythology to occupy his Utopia, adding the Ichthyophagi to the Amazons, and linking in allusions to Perseus and Heracles, and Horus and Isis, as well as to the legendary origins of Mytilene and Samothrace. Thirdly, we observe that here as elsewhere Scytobrachion is alert to the history of the recent past and contemporary present. The Amazon queen Myrina is a female Alexander, and her dominance is suggested by such personalities as Olympias and Arsinoe. The Amazons found cities and name them after their chief officers, like the Alexandrias and Antiochs and Ptolemais and Seleuceias of the Hellenistic age, and they refer to the land they occupy as 'spear-won' in orthodox Ptolemaic vocabulary. But of course the most interesting aspect of this Utopia is the dominance of women, and the fascination of the idea for Scytobrachion recurs in his account of Dionysus.

The other Utopia is Nysa.[12] This is linked with the first through common association with the river Triton. It lies on an island in the river, and is protected from intruders by precipitous cliffs. This is one of those Utopian lands where nature is bountiful. The soil is rich and well watered. There are fruittrees in abundance, and the vine grows wild. The air is healthful. There are springs of delicious water, rocks of varied colours, song-birds, fragrant shrubs, flowers that never wither and leaves that never fall. It was in a cave in this marvellous place that Dionysus was reared.

Here there is less that calls for comment, but we may notice the typically Utopian attribution of long life and health to the inhabitants, though Scytobrachion follows Euhemerus in not exaggerating these beyond the bounds of possibility. The perfection of nature goes back, as we have seen, to Homer. The description of the site with its protecting precipices, narrow entrance, coloured rocks and marvellous cave, perhaps owes something to Petra, which must have come into prominence about this time: it is typical of Scytobrachion to build his fantasies upon actuality.

More interesting than these is Iambulus, whose Utopia is fairly fully cited by Diodorus.[13] Iambulus was a merchant who was captured by brigands in Arabia, and kidnapped from the brigands by some Negroes to be used for the purification of their land. He and one companion were placed in a boat with six months' provisions, and set to sail southwards till they reached a happy island with kindly inhabitants amongst whom they would live in blessedness. If the envoys reached the island safely the Negroes would enjoy peace and prosperity for six hundred years. If they turned back in cowardice they would bring disaster on the whole nation, and be punished accordingly.

They sailed through stormy seas, and after four months reached the island which was round with a circumference of 600 miles. The inhabitants welcomed them. The inhabitants were physically all alike, over six feet tall, with pliant bones and an impregnable grasp, hairless except for the head, of exceptional beauty, and with a divided vocal system which enabled them to carry on two conversations simultaneously.[14] They lived at the equator, with equal days and nights and no midday shadow. They enjoyed a mild climate with fruit all the year round. They lived in extended families of about 400 people. Their lives were lives of leisure, for the crops grew without tendance, some being unfamiliar; one gave a white fruit which would swell in water, and was used for a kind of bread. There were hot and cold springs in profusion.

The people were keenly interested in education, especially astronomy. They used an alphabet of twenty-eight letters, with seven signs each having four positions. They wrote in vertical columns. There was little disease, and they lived to 150; anyone diseased or crippled, or reaching the upper limit of age, was expected to engage in voluntary euthanasia, by lying on a bed of plants which brought on drowsiness. They did not marry but held wives and children in common.

The island contained remarkable animals. One with four eyes and four mouths, and large numbers of feet enabling it to move rapidly in any direction, had blood of magical healing properties. Each commune kept a large bird which would take babies on its back for a flight to test their spiritual disposition. Political authority in each commune rested with the oldest member.

The island was one of seven, all of like size and equidistant from one another and following similar practices. The sea around the island was sweet to the taste, and with high tides. Many familiar stars were not visible. The people lived simply. They worshipped the sky, sun and heavenly bodies. They made their clothes by extracting a downy substance from a kind of reed. The work was shared round all except the senior citizens. On festivals they sang hymns to the gods, and especially to the sun, after whom the people and the islands were named.

Iambulus and his companion stayed for seven years, but were then banished, seemingly because they had not attained to the perfection of the islanders and might become a corrupting influence. After four months they were shipwrecked on the shores of India. The companion was drowned. Iambulus reached Palibothra where he found a king well disposed to the Greeks and interested in education, who gave him a safe-conduct.

Iambulus was evidently a real person and was perhaps a merchant who had travelled widely himself and was in touch with others who had travelled more widely. The equatorial region is known to be habitable. There is knowledge that in parts of the world the Bears are not visible. The tides are higher than in the Mediterranean. There is knowledge of lakes of fresh water large enough to be seas. There seems to be a vague knowledge of the mass-cultivation of cotton, rice and opium-poppy. There is no understanding of the monsoon – that did not come till later – but the journeys out and back are of equal duration. There is perhaps a vague knowledge of Ceylon (Onesicritus estimated it as

5000 stadia, i.e. about 600 miles in size) and the Borneo islands, but it is certainly only vague, as Rohde has shown.[15] Among much fantasy there is a core of fact. We can identify his date reasonably closely. The *terminus a quo* is Megasthenes' account of India in about 290; the *terminus ad quem* is the limit of Diodorus' information in the mid-first century BC. H. J. Rose suggested that Iambulus' attribution of a temperate climate to the equator was derived from Poseidonius.[16] This is quite impossible; by then the plants of which Iambulus speaks vaguely were well known. In any case this view of the equatorial climate is found in Eratosthenes, and no doubt goes back to Dalion or the expedition of Alexander.[17] It is also hard not to think that Aristonicus owed something to Iambulus' Island of the Sun and Children of the Sun.[18] There seems, as we shall see, to be Stoic influence on Iambulus, but it belongs to the early Utopian Stoics, not to the later thinkers. The Indian king at Palibothra must be one of the three great Mauryas, Tschangragupta (315–291), Vindusara (291–263) or Asoka (262–226), though this does not preclude the work being later; but it is unlikely to be appreciably later than 200 BC. The limited knowledge of eastern plants also suggests a third-century date. But it seems that Iambulus is not familiar with the work of Eratosthenes (fl. *c.* 235 BC). Eratosthenes knew that the Sun was not always overhead at the equator; further, Eratosthenes gave the length of Taprobane as 8000 stades or about 1000 miles. It is thus a reasonable presumption that Iambulus was writing between 250 and 225 BC. He belongs to the constructive period of Hellenistic thought, and it is significant that with him the sequence of Utopias comes to an end.

Iambulus' Utopia is a patchwork from various sources. In form, but in little else, it derives directly from Euhemerus. Iambulus first visits Arabia, and then after various adventures reaches an island set in the ocean far to the south. Euhemerus associated Panchaïa with the sun; he had his 'City of the Sun' and 'Water of the Sun'. Iambulus makes the relation more explicit, and is frankly astrological in his approach. Astronomy was the keen interest of some of the so-called gods who resided in early days in Panchaïa; it was the most important object of education in the Islands of the Sun. The springs on both islands are of unusual sweetness; fruit-trees and vines grow in profusion; in Euhemerus the myrrh gives its crop twice a year, in Iambulus the fruit is ripe all the year round; in both there are reminiscences of Phaeacia, and Iambulus quotes from that part of *The Odyssey*. Neither admitted slavery. Both are interested in the question of writing; Panchaïa uses something like Egyptian hieroglyphics, the Children of the Sun write vertically in columns like the Chinese, but unlike them have definite letter forms. But the most important fact is that both communities are set outside the historical scene, and enjoy external conditions of life which are openly Utopian.

Iambulus' debt to the Stoics is a more contentious question. Bidez, Rohde and Susemihl all claimed him as Stoic. Tarn rejected this in his later work, but too sweepingly, and partly on erroneous grounds; he did not do more than show that there were non-Stoic elements.[19] It is *a priori* likely that a Utopian writer of this period would be familiar with the Cynic and Stoic Utopias.

Certainly we receive the impression from Lucian that later generations regarded Utopian writing as something of a Stoic speciality.[20] Despite some recent interpreters also it is hard not to accept some link between the Stoic Blossius, Iambulus' Utopia and Aristonicus' Sun-State.[21] Iambulus' Utopia is certainly a very successful picture of the life according to nature. The astrological approach is Stoic. The Children of the Sun worship the all-embracing aether, the sun and other heavenly bodies: Zeno spoke of the Aether as the highest of the gods, source of all things, and Cleanthes emphasized the centrality of the sun and the political implications of this.[22] The singing of hymns also sounds very Stoic.[23] The place of Concord in the community is a commonplace of Hellenistic thought, but it is specifically found in Zeno. There is some presumptive evidence of the absence of temples, law-courts and gymnasia, as in Zeno's Republic. Community of wives too, though found in Plato and among various nature peoples, is most obviously derived from the Cynic-Stoic Utopias. The simplicity of life is also characteristically Cynic-Stoic. Stoic permission of suicide is certainly nothing to do with voluntary death at 150, but it is not so irrelevant to the voluntary death of the crippled and diseased.[24] On the other hand the disposal of the dead in the sea is not part of Cynic or Stoic indifference to the fate of the corpse.[25] On the contrary the disposal is meticulous. 'The sea washes away all men's evils.'[26] 'The water of the sea is naturally purificatory.'[27] The kingship is also, as we have seen, despite Tarn, Stoic. The authority in each commune rests with the oldest member who exercises it like a king. This is closely parallel to Zeno's government by an oligarchy of sages each of whom possessed kingly powers. So too is the equality of the citizens, considered as a fellowship of the 'worthy', and the expulsion of Iambulus and his companion, presumably as 'unworthy' would fit this concept, though of the Utopias we know it fits better that of Diogenes who advocated the expulsion of the insensate and folly-stricken.[28]

Apart from Euhemerus and the Stoics, Iambulus is aware of Aristotle's *Politics* and finds in it useful illustrations; it is presumably from here that the rotation of tasks is taken.[29] Sometimes however he seems to be deliberately contradicting Aristotle. He has none of Aristotle's interest in property,[30] and whereas Aristotle says 'No state is composed of equals',[31] Iambulus' citizens are equal even physically.

To these philosophical sources we can add a certain number of legends, fantasies and travellers' tales: we have already noted that many primitive tribes were believed to practise community of wives, and crops growing of their own accord are a commonplace of envisioned paradises.[32] Only one fantasy can be traced to a certain source: at Ceos there was said to have been a law prescribing death at the age of 60, so that the food supply should suffice.[33]

The first fact about the Islands of the Sun is their Utopian nature. It is true that the adventure story shows an advance in geographical knowledge since Euhemerus. But it is certainly a mistake to try to take accurate geographical bearings. Authentic elements mingle with fantasy. The Children of the Sun display their equality by a physical equality. Their bodies are unusually large, their bones unusually pliant, their tongues and ears peculiarly formed, their grasp impregnable, their life of great length. The animals upon the island are, as the author rightly says, incredible. There is the creature with four eyes and mouths whose blood has magical healing properties, and the bird which flies with the babies on its back (Can this be linked with the mythology of the stork?). The water from the hot springs never cools unless it is mixed with cold. The sea is sweet to taste. The fruit-trees bear all the year round, and many of the crops grow without tendance. The people themselves live in perfect happiness and unblemished bliss. Disease is absent. They are the sort of community the Stoics might have expected a community of sages, all joyfully accepting the law of Destiny, to become. They are completely severed from the outside world, amazed to receive intruders, and when they do they put them on a period of probation, at the end of which they are rejected, not apparently for any monstrous act against the commonwealth, but because they had not attained to the perfection of that people.

Secondly the astrological tendencies of the early Stoics are here completed and fully developed. The land is called 'The Islands of the Sun', the people 'The Children of the Sun'. All the islands are round like the sun, and an equal distance apart, and there are seven of them, the number of the principal heavenly bodies. In like manner Iambulus' period of probation is seven years. The period of bliss, lasting 600 years, accorded to the Ethiopians by Iambulus' safe arrival, is the same in length as the lesser of Berossus' great years and was adopted by the Jews for their great year.[34] The islands are situated upon the equator, and the sun at mid-day stands directly overhead. The temperature is equable and day and night are the same length. Similarly the moon's influence may be seen in the strong ebb and flow of the tides around the island, a phenomenon which is linked with the interment of the dead, and the growth and diminishing of the reeds which supply their sustenance. They worship the All-Embracer (Aether or perhaps Heaven), and the heavenly bodies, especially the Sun, to whose honour they speak praises and sing hymns. Astronomy is the principal subject of their education. The astrological outlook is reflected in the equalitarian organization of the community. The people are nearly identical in form, stature and beauty; they live to an equal age at which they take their own lives. This similarity in general appearance is commonly attributed to primitive peoples, by Hippocrates to the Scythians, by Philostratus to the Ethiopians, by Tacitus and Juvenal to the Germans, by Juvenal to the inhabitants of Meroe.[35] They prize Concord above all things, appear to have no private property, and hold their wives and children in common. They take it in turn to perform the duties and offices of the community, and when they die are all alike entrusted to the indifferent power of the sea, rather as the A.B. and the Admiral become one in a 'sailor's grave'. All the islands are alike in constitution and custom.

The third point of predominant importance is the emphasis laid upon education. In the short and perhaps garbled summary given by Diodorus at each stage the significance of education is stressed, no fewer altogether than three times in independent contexts. At the beginning the only facts we are told about Iambulus are that he was a trader and interested in education.[36] At the end all we know about the Indian king is that he was friendly to the Greeks and interested in education.[37] The interest of the islanders in education is one of the traits especially recorded.[38] It is at least possible that the full work contained some kind of contrast between three systems of education, Greek, Asiatic and ideal. At that we can only guess. Of the islanders' system we have only a very abbreviated account, but we can see its general trend. Two facts predominate. It is directed to teaching about the fundamentals of religion and life, and to the formation of sterling character. It is expressly stated that astronomy is the most important subject of education,[39] for the rest the fantastic story of the children on the backs of the birds implies that tests of character were a fundamental feature of their thought in this realm. As to other subjects, their inborn physical prowess may have absolved them from the need of physical training, especially in view of the absence of disease and the extermination of the crippled or infirm. Of utilitarian subjects writing is the only one which was certainly admitted; astronomy would seem to imply mathematics, but that must be uncertain. But in general such subjects would be subsidiary to the main purpose of education, though the islanders are interested in education of all kinds.

Fourthly, the kind of life Iambulus envisages for his islanders reveals what he considers to be the ideal life a man should live. It is free from toilsome occupations. Most of the crops grow of their own accord. Farming is for the most part simple gardening. There is no great complexity about the preparation of food or clothing. Of housing we have no indication.

But Iambulus recognizes that some work will have to be done, and that, like the responsibility of public office (or possibly religious duties), is undertaken by the whole community in rotation. Such tasks are the catching of fish, and the practice of the crafts. Their life is extremely simple. Their food is varied, and like the Catholics, and indeed so many of us, only for other reasons, they appear to have a meatless day. But the preparation of the food is simple. The complexities of civilization are almost entirely absent. The community is one, and they appear neither to have nor to want privacy, but to live in clans of 400 or so members. All this natural good fortune and simplicity of life gives them a considerable amount of leisure, and it is here that Iambulus' vision proves either totally inadequate or immensely profound. For the occupation of this leisure they while away their time in the meadows. That is all. This may mean that Iambulus has entirely failed to face the fundamental problem which confronts him, namely, given ideal external conditions and a freedom from obsession with the daily round and common task, what is the real purpose of man's existence here on earth? But it may be that he has faced this and given his answer; that in the simplicity of children who would never be bored if left free in the fields, is found the true meaning of life; that the thing of importance is to be one of a fellowship, and that fellowship if real manifests itself in conversation and in the simple act of being together; that the purpose of man's life, as Epictetus said, much later, is to know and to sing the praises of God.[40]

CHAPTER XV

THE REVOLUTION AT SPARTA

THE THIRD CENTURY was a period of economic decline for Greece – on the whole, for there were brief periods of recovery.[1] The centres of prosperity which were now Alexandria, Antioch, Rhodes, and Pergamum, benefited from being closer to the new trade-routes, and benefited also from the concentration of power and economic resources. Local industry and agriculture expanded in Egypt, Syria and Asia Minor, to the detriment of agriculture and industry in Greece. Egypt developed the vine and the olive. By 250 the period of natural expansion of the new kingdoms was coming to an end, but the centralized control made protection almost inevitable, and imports from Greece were heavily taxed.

In general the century saw falling wages and rising prices. On Delos workers in the tile industry at the end of the fourth century were receiving 15 obols for 6 pairs; in 250 BC the rate was 4 obols for 6 pairs. In 281 BC two tool-sharpeners named Dexios and Heraclides were being paid 1 obol per job. Two years later Heraclides was sacked; five years later Dexios was doing all the work for ½ obol per job. Varnishers' rates halved between 282 and 250 BC. Stonemasons working on inscriptions saw their rates plummet from 1½ drachmae (9 obols) per 100 letters to 6 obols per 350 letters, less than a fifth of the old rate. Prices of food and drink fluctuated enormously with variable harvests, but the general tendency was upwards. The flood of money through Alexander's conquests caused a violent rise in prices in wheat and oil. During the first half of the third century they tended to fall, though they never reached the fourth-century level. This was the period when money was flowing from Greece into the new kingdoms through emigration and investment. This process came to a halt in about 250; after that prices began to rise again.

It has been calculated that 100–200 drachmae a year was a subsistence wage for a single man, 200–300 for a man and wife, and about 400 with the addition of two children. On Delos, where rents soared through the century, Dexios the tool-sharpener managed only 54½ drachmae a year, a carpenter named Theodemus 106, a mason named Nicon 187. And Delos was an area of relative prosperity. In Greece proper it must have been worse. The lack of purchasing power inhibited the development of cottage industries. Land was mortgaged. A law was passed at Sparta by an ephor or ex-ephor named Epitadeus legalizing the alienation of land, perhaps so as to encourage emigration;[2] from the loss of Messenia in 370 there must have been increasing pressure on relatively small land resources. In general over all the mainland of Greece the rich landowners were becoming fewer and richer. Many of those who had once been powerful were in their debt. There was a small middle class, mostly of aliens with trading interests in the new capitals. The peasants and artisans were living near the bone. Unemployment was widespread. It was a situation in which change had to come, from above or below.

The revolution of Agis and Cleomenes at Sparta is difficult to evaluate. The ancient evidence is tendentious.[3] Polybius, whose practice did not always come up to his principles, is biassed in favour of Aratus, and thus against Cleomenes. Our main source, Plutarch, took his basic narrative from the Athenian Phylarchus, who may have had some Cynic sympathies, and was a strong apologist for the revolution. We are thus confronted with two sources leaning in different directions. There were others, and Plutarch no doubt had access to some of them, including Sphaerus himself, the Stoic philosopher who was somehow involved.

Agis IV came to power in 244. He was not yet twenty. He had been brought up in luxury. Now he espoused the asceticism of the traditional rough cloak and rough bread. His aim was a redistribution of land and the cancellation of debts,[4] and the restoration of equality and common meals. He planned to have 4,500 lots round Sparta for the Spartiates and 15,000 farther out for the *perioeci*.[5] These are in precise proportion, appropriate to the reduced population, to the 9,000 for Spartiates and 30,000 for *perioeci* of the traditional Lycurgan scheme.[6] But Sparta had fallen on bad times. There were only 700 Spartiate families left, according to Phylarchus (and not more than 100 of these in possession of estates).[7] The number of Spartiates would therefore have to be built up by recruitment from the *perioeci* and aliens. Of Agis' sincerity there is no doubt. He distributed his own land freely and encouraged those close to him to do the same. Agis won the enthusiastic support of the poor; the privileged called on the other king, the conservative Leonidas, to oppose him. A debate split the country, but means were found to discredit and depose Leonidas; Agis was instrumental in saving his life. But he was naive. His uncle Agesilaus and other senior members of the Establishment were sunk in debt. They reversed his programme. In place of the redistribution of land, followed by the cancellation of debts to enable the mortgaged land to be a genuine benefit to the new tenants, they began by cancelling debts – which they owed – and then refused to redistribute the land. Agis lost support, and then, disastrously, had to leave his reforms for the pressures of the military situation. While he was away his power was undermined; on his return he was trapped and put to death.

What influenced Agis? He was undoubtedly humanitarian in character. We need not be so steeped in behaviourist theory as not to accept that a sensitive person, however unpromising his upbringing, might not come to sympathize with the oppressed, and find his own solutions. But not in a vacuum. Clearly, according to our evidence Agis was inspired by the example of Lycurgus; his final defence was that he had acted in imitation of Lycurgus.[8] He was thus primarily a Spartan traditionalist, who was hoping to restore the ancient justice and so the ancient glory to his country in reaction against the decay and corruption of centuries. In addition, he was living in a revolutionary age, and the revolutionaries favoured abolition of debts, redistribution of land and property, and liberation of slaves. Agis does not seem to have touched the last, but in the other two he is in accord with the general revolutionary demands which must have been infectious from one state to another. Aratus, leader of the Achaean League and the federalist movement, was a supporter of the *status quo*. Macedon was opposed to revolution. The revolutionaries must have welcomed the adhesion of Agis. But something else too was in the air. We have seen it in the philosophical Utopias, which sometimes broke through class barriers and sometimes through national barriers. Agis was a Spartan nationalist, but he did propose to enfranchise aliens. This looks like an idea from a philosophic source, and it is likely to have been transmitted by the Stoic Sphaerus, who was at court as tutor to Leonidas' son Cleomenes.

Those who, like T.W. Africa, seek to play down the influence of Sphaerus, and suggest that the philosophical impulse behind the revolution, such as it was, was Cynic rather than Stoic, seem insufficiently aware of the differences within the Porch itself.[9] Zeno, after all, wrote his *Republic* 'under the tail of the Dog'.[10] There was always a radical wing of the Stoics who are almost indistinguishable from the Cynics; witness, among others, Musonius or Epictetus. Concord (*homonoia*), community (*koinonia*) and equality (*isotes*) were always Stoic catchphrases. Plainly, the revolution was complex; precisely for that reason it is a mistake to deny Sphaerus his part in it. Specifically, he is stated to have taken a constructive interest in the reform of the general way of life.[11] But we have noticed the proposal to enlarge the citizen body by *perioeci* and aliens. Leonidas protested that this was un-Spartan, as indeed it was. If Agis and Cleomenes were merely Spartan nationalists and traditionalists, this would have been a very odd move. But it accords well with Stoic universalism.

It is significant to note the later relationship of Cleomenes to Heracles. The kings of Sparta were traditionally descended from Heracles,[12] Polybius amusingly remarks that one usurper became a descendant of Heracles by distributing money amongst the ephors.[13] So Plutarch tells us that when envoys were confronted with Cleomenes 'who was really a king and not just called king' 'they could not resist him and said that he alone was of the stock of Heracles.'[14] Cleomenes put the image of Heracles on his coins.[15] Heracles was the type of the Stoic sage who is also the only true king; Polybius, even, can accept the image: his final comment on Cleomenes is that he was 'a born leader and king by nature'.[16]

We do not know much about this Sphaerus.[17] Diogenes Laertius tells us that he studied under Zeno and Cleanthes, and went as visiting philosopher to the court of Ptolemy III of Egypt.[18] He wrote treatises on Monarchy, on Spartan Institutions, on Socrates and on Lycurgus.[19] We have two well-known anecdotes of him at the Court of Ptolemy IV. One tells how he was deceived into taking a wax fruit, and explained that he had assented not to the proposition 'This is a real fruit' but to the proposition 'This is probably a real fruit'. The other is his brilliantly ambiguous remark that being what he was, Ptolemy was a king indeed (or as well).[20] It is odd that Tarn treats this as showing that Sphaerus had a general contempt for kings;[21] if he had he would hardly have been so enthusiastic a supporter of Cleomenes.[22] For this last is really the one certain fact we know about him, and if we have to choose between fact and anecdote the anecdote will have to go. But in fact the anecdote can stand; its ambiguity contains no generalization. It is merely tendentious of T.W. Africa to say that Sphaerus was brought into his narrative by Plutarch to balance Blossius in the story of the Gracchi; one might equally say that Blossius' rôle in the story of the Gracchi shows that a Stoic such as Sphaerus was capable of sustaining a similar rôle. Sphaerus' position at Sparta is certain. It is important, however, to establish a chronology. Sphaerus must have been born in the 280s to study under Zeno (d. 263). We do not know when he came to Sparta, but Cleomenes must have been born about 260, so Sphaerus will have been tutoring him in the 240s. Some time before Cleanthes died in 232 he sent him to Egypt to the court of Ptolemy III. This makes it highly probable that he withdrew from Sparta after the death of Agis, and this again makes it more likely that he was involved with Agis. Cleomenes then recalled him at some point, and his presence in Egypt under Ptolemy IV makes it likely that he was close enough to Cleomenes to go there with him.

The conservative Leonidas had been exiled and brought back. He thought to heal the breach in the state, and secure the power and prestige of his family, by marrying his young son Cleomenes to Agis' widowed queen Agiatis. The girl appears to us in retrospect one of the more remarkable women of antiquity. She was beautiful to look on, unassuming in character, and with a will of steel and an enthusiasm for justice and for the greatness of Sparta. She communicated that enthusiasm to her husband. She made him see that greatness walked hand in hand with justice.

Cleomenes bided his time. For eight years after his accession in 237 he learned his trade of ruling. Then he provoked a war with the Achaean League. The citizen army was taken on campaign. The king returned with a mercenary force, ousted the ephors, claiming that they had been instituted to support the kings and were otiose if they were not doing so,[23] and exiled eighty citizens on whose sympathy he could not rely. The total loss of life was 14.

Now he cancelled debts and redistributed the land. It is characteristic of the man and his belief in his revolution that he reserved 80 lots for the exiles. 4,000 lots were made available for Spartiates; the numbers were made up, as Agis had proposed, from *perioeci* and aliens. It was perhaps now that Alexander of Aetolia dramatized the situation in an epigram:[24]

Time-honoured Sardis, land of my fathers, had I grown up in you,
    I would have been a eunuch in Cybele's service,
in cloth of gold, beating the ribboned tambourine. As it is, my name

is Alcman, Sparta of the tripods my city.
I have learned to know the Muses of Helicon, and they have made me
greater than a dictator like Dascyles or Gyges.

Like Agis before him, Cleomenes set the example of sincerity, and like Agis, he appealed to Lycurgus. He restored the ancient way of life, and it is significant that he had Sphaerus at his elbow for this.[25] This time the main opponents of reform were out of the way, and Cleomenes was no man's tool. The changes were carried through and greeted with enthusiasm, Cleomenes' own simplicity, self-discipline and accessibility being an example and encouragement. He established a citizen army, sustained by the ancient discipline, and seems to have been remarkably successful in ridding them of camp-followers, army brothels, and, in general, of relaxations which he regarded as enervating.

The success of Cleomenes was infectious: he had turned a dream into a reality. The cry 'Cancellation of debts and redistribution of land' broke through in other cities. Those in power began to make concessions. In Boeotia an otherwise unknown Opheltas was instrumental in the use of state resources to help the needy.[26] At Megalopolis an aristocrat named Cercidas was one of the leaders in opposing the onrush of Cleomenes' nationalism.[27] He was the emissary who drew in Macedon, and he was commander of the Megalopolitan army. One of his fragments attacks Sphaerus' character; the motivation was no doubt political, and is further evidence of the importance of the Stoic at Cleomenes' court.[28] Cercidas was, oddly, also a Cynic, who would, one would have thought, have renounced wealth, nationalism and military service. Instead he is found, whether now, or as some think later,[29] after Cleomenes' defeat, warning the ruling class to be generous and help the poor before they are overwhelmed. He versifies the complaint of the poor.

> Turn
> the greedy cormorant,
> the millionaire Xenon,
> to poverty. Give us
> the riches that flow
> uselessly from him.
> What can prevent –
> should anyone ask –
> (it's easy for God
> to bring to completion
> whatever he wills)
> God from stripping
> of his swinish wealth
> the filthy profiteer,
> the halfpenny-miser,
> who wastes his possessions
> in riotous living,
> or from giving the frugal
> who eat from a common bowl
> the money he squanders?

Is the eye of Justice
withered to blindness?
Does the sun look aside
with his single eye?
Is Right in her glory
shrouded in mist? . . .
Victory is ours
and with her Fair-Sharing
(she is a goddess)
and Vengeance on earth.
The winds of heaven
blow favourably for us.
Honour the goddess,
mortals. *They* prosper,
but a sudden stormwind
drowns them in their pride.
The whirlpool will never
vomit them out.[30]

'The sun look aside.' It is hard not to think that Iambulus was one factor moulding this demand for equity.

It was tragic that the two great Greeks of the time should clash. Aratus of Sicyon had liberated his city from autocracy. He was himself incorruptible. He believed passionately in political freedom; he saw that in the conditions of the day this was best fostered by federalism, and from 245 he was the dominant figure in the Achaean League. In economic redress he had no interest. In Cleomenes a passion for economic justice was overlaid with Spartan nationalism. Aratus was seen as the liberator from Macedon. Cleomenes was seen as the liberator from injustice. Mantinea called him in; he expelled the Achaean garrison and restored their laws and constitution.[31] From this came full-scale war with the Achaeans. Cleomenes won Argos, where even Aratus had failed. He won Corinth from Aratus. He ravaged Sicyon. Aratus saw his lifework slipping away from him. He preferred to sell it back to Macedon than see it taken from him by Sparta. He called in Antigonus Doson. Not even Cleomenes' vitality and military skill could stand up to Macedon. He lost Argos, partly because he had been too busy with the war to institute the expected economic changes; the significant fact is that they were expected. He negotiated with Egypt, and they let him down. He allowed 2,000 Helots to buy their freedom, used the money and the enfranchised men to form a new army, and sacked Megalopolis. For a brief period it almost seemed that he might still hold the field, but at Sellasia in 222, outnumbered by nearly two to one, he lost the day. His revolution was undone. He refused suicide, because Sparta still needed him, and retreated to Egypt. But the Egyptian politicians were not adventuring for lost causes. He made a quixotic attempt to raise the revolutionary flag in the streets of Alexandria, was frustrated in an assault on the prison, and died by his own hand. He was not forgotten. Even in his frustrations he had seemed to the people of Alexandria a dominant figure, 'a lion among sheep'.[32] Now in death they accorded him heroic honours.[33]

It is no doubt easy to romanticize Cleomenes.[34] But it is equally easy to demythologize him. Neither fits the facts. He was no doubt a tough Spartan nationalist, but he was also an idealist. Perhaps the two most interesting facts in his career are that the Argives expected him to bring swift economic justice and that he failed to do so.[35] Human beings are seldom simple: motives are difficult to disentangle. Did Cleomenes foster social revolution at Sparta out of personal ambition, as a means to Spartan imperialism or out of sympathy with the oppressed? Did he stand for revolutionary change elsewhere because he had espoused an ideology of revolution from which he could not escape, as a weapon in defence of resurgent Sparta against the Achaeans, as a weapon in a personal duel with Aratus, or because he wanted to liberate the oppressed? No doubt all the motives were there. But Plutarch's narrative makes it clear that the two chief influences upon him were the gentle determination of Agiatis and the philosophy of Sphaerus,[36] and it would be certainly wrong to disallow to Cleomenes a vision of justice.

The power passed to a usurper who went by the name of Lycurgus: the name may have been part of his usurpation, which he won by bribery.[37] The other king was a minor. Lycurgus embraced Cleomenes' nationalism without his radicalism, and turned the Spartans once more against Macedon and the Achaeans.[38] While he was campaigning a revolutionary member of the royal house named Chilon took up the radical cudgel. He followed Cleomenes in proclaiming a redistribution of the land as his policy, rallied some two hundred supporters, and assassinated the ephors.[39] He was unsuccessful. The situation was strangely ambiguous. Cleomenes' supporters were divided between Chilon's radicalism and Lycurgus' nationalism, his opponents were naturally equally opposed to Chilon. One curious feature of the whole story is that Chilon took refuge in Achaea.

As a postscript, the picture of revolution at Sparta should be completed by a brief account of Nabis.[40] Nabis has had a bad press; there was no Phylarchus to panegyrize him. He appears in our sources as a cruel and ruthless tyrant, murderer and bandit. Plainly here there is no question of a direct philosophic influence guiding reform. Yet this very fact makes the reforms more striking; and he had the examples of Agis and Cleomenes before him. Not merely the examples. He had sons of marriageable age in 198; he himself must have lived through the period of Cleomenes' reforms, and could hardly have been untouched by them. Nabis plainly played politics tough. That he played it with skill is seen in his survival for fourteen years. That he played it with the approval of the citizens is seen in that the Assembly rejected Flamininus' terms when Nabis' policy incurred the hostility of Rome. Nabis was of royal blood, and linked by marriage with power in Argos. He used a bodyguard of mercenaries to seize power, and eliminated his ward Pelops. Once in power he redistributed the land, in whole or part, and liberated and enfranchised Helots. This made him less dependent on mercenaries. There is even some talk of a redistribution of families.[41] This might be a treatment of wives as chattels (which would not well accord with Spartan traditionalism). It might merely reflect the sexual violence often associated with periods of upheaval, but might equally misrepresent an essay in communism of families. Furthermore, he extended his revolution to Argos, when he secured power there, as Cleomenes had failed to do. His revolution was a popular one, and when the people of Argos might have defected from him they did not do so. Historians from the Establishment tell us that he attracted to his cause crooks and criminals, bandits and pirates from all over Greece. This sounds suspiciously like the possessors' account of the dispossessed.

Nabis by a combination of popular reform, force and diplomacy succeeded for a time. Like Cleomenes he combined reformist zeal with Spartan nationalism. He assailed Megalopolis and the Achaeans. He developed a fleet, then lost it as part of a settlement with Rome. He tried to reassert his power with the backing of the Aetolians, but again was pulled up short by the Achaea-Rome alliance. At this point his Aetolian allies treacherously assassinated him. That he was no mere tyrant is seen in the reprisals taken by the Spartans against his assassins. The reason for the murder is not clear; one suspects that Nabis was playing some dangerous double game of diplomacy. But with him died Spartan independence, and the last hope of the revolution.

CHAPTER XVI

BLOSSIUS, TIBERIUS GRACCHUS AND ARISTONICUS

CAIUS BLOSSIUS CAME FROM CUMAE, and whatever is uncertain about him he was certainly a Stoic. He studied under Antipater of Tarsus, and his name is linked with that of Panaetius (who at one time studied at Pergamum) and Diophanes of Mytilene.[1] He thus had associations both with Italy and the east. At Rome he had powerful protectors, being a *hospes* of the family of Scaevola.[2] It was well for him. Blossius' association first with Tiberius Gracchus and then with Aristonicus show his political concern. He was not a red revolutionary or Karl Marx's 'Hellenic prototype'.[3] He believed in social justice, and he believed that it could and should be brought in by a wise monarch; for this rôle he cast his protégés, with himself as the *rector's rector*. It is significant that he ignored the pretensions of the Sicilian slave-king Eunus, and after the Gracchan débâcle went over to Aristonicus. There was an element of social snobbery about the Stoics; despite Epictetus (and at this time he lay far in the future) it was easier for them to believe that a king might be (in their sense) a 'slave' than that a slave might be (in their sense) a 'king'.

Dudley in an article which combines ingenuity and caution has put together all we know or can reasonably deduce about the life of Blossius.[4] His family may have been of Sabellian stock. Marius Blossius was *praetor Campanus* in 216 BC and one of those who proposed to treat with Hannibal.[5] Six years later, after the revolt of Cumae, the Blossii brothers were leaders of a conspiracy to burn down the city.[6] We know of the family as one of the great Campanian families.[7] They were plainly not by tradition pro-Roman, but allied to the dissident democrats, and this may have predisposed the young philosopher in favour of the more radical wing of Stoicism. It is possible that the pro-Roman policy followed by the senate of Cumae may have influenced him to leave for Athens; for it was there almost certainly that he pursued his studies. At what point he came to Rome and how he became associated with the Gracchi we do not know, but it is reasonable to assume that Scaevola or his brother P. Licinius Crassus Mucianus, both of whom appeared in support of Gracchus' legislation, provided the link, and his influence was sufficient to suggest that he was one of those Greek teachers to whom Cornelia entrusted the education of her sons. We can be certain on the evidence that Blossius originated Tiberius' programme of land reform. Plutarch tells us as much,[8] and narrates further how the philosopher scorned evil omens which sapped the politician's confidence.[9] Plutarch's evidence is buttressed by that of Cicero, who had no sympathy for schemes of radical reform, and says of Blossius 'He was the leader not the follower in Tiberius Gracchus' excesses, and revealed himself the instigator rather than the associate of his madness.'[10] Tiberius' proposals, as we shall see, were hardly extremist, excessive or crazy; indeed they – whatever be said of the method of their introduction – were a model of cool reasonableness. In this, and in the basic concern for social and economic justice we can see the hand of the Stoic.

The position in Rome in 133 BC was perilous. By the middle of the previous century this small, tough city-state had become the dominant power in the Italian peninsula. By the end of the century she had defeated Carthage in the struggle for the western Mediterranean, and was ineluctably being drawn into the East. The next half-century saw the Romans, as the Greek Polybius put it, 'bring nearly the whole of the inhabited world under their government and theirs alone, an achievement without parallel in human history'.[11] The expansion was slow and reluctant. Rome was governed by a handful of aristocratic families; across a century 10 of these families monopolized half of the consulships, and 26 three-quarters and more.[12] To expand responsibilities meant extending the number of offices to be held. The aristocracy eventually solved this by extending the period during which a man might hold office, so that he was allowed a further period not as consul or praetor, but in lieu of consul or praetor (*pro consule, pro praetore*). So 146 BC saw the sacking of Carthage and Corinth, and the establishment of new provinces under direct government from Rome. Still it was clear that the machinery of state was creaking at the joints, and the expansion over the Mediterranean itself led to the prosperity of new middle-class business interests (*equites*) probing at the power of the landed aristocracy, who by the Lex Claudia of 218 BC were allowed to have only limited commercial interests.

Changing economic conditions led to hardship among the small farmers in Italy. In this there were four main factors. First, as Rome had expanded through Italy she confiscated about a third of the conquered territories. Some of this common land (*ager publicus*) was leased to a legal limit of 500 *iugera*, that is about 300 acres. But this limitation had been neglected, as had the conditions of lease generally, and what emerged was comparable to the enclosures during the sixteenth and eighteenth centuries in England, and the *de facto* enlargement of already large estates (*latifundia* as they were later called). Years after, Pliny looked back and said that to those who were prepared to acknowledge the truth it was the great estates which were the ruin of Italy.[13] How large they were we do not know, but a century later we know of estates of 400,000 iugera.[14] Secondly, the continual years of war pressed most hardly on the smallholder. If he was conscripted his land might fall into dereliction, whereas the rich could afford a farm manager (*vilicus*). Furthermore, war and conquest brought in fresh floods of slaves which began to oust free labour. Thirdly, the settlement of the Mediterranean in 146 BC meant that grain from overseas which in the first part of the century had been used for military provisions now began to find a market in Rome, and some of the other ports. Transport by sea was relatively cheap. Small farmers around Rome in particular, who had once had a ready market for their corn, found themselves squeezed out by the produce of Sicily and Sardinia. Fourthly, it is a general principle of economics that 'to him that hath shall be given; from him that hath not shall be taken away even that which he hath.' The rich can ride a bad year more easily than the poor, and in a bad year the small farmer easily slips under the thumb of the great landowner. There was a drift to the city, a depopulation of the land, and a swelling in the numbers of the urban paupers. The problem was even alarming the military authorities, since military service was confined to those with property, and these drifters were dropping below the requisite level.

Tiberius Gracchus[15] was son of Tiberius Sempronius Gracchus, consul in 177 and again in 163, and Scipio Africanus' daughter Cornelia. Young Tiberius was born about the time of his father's second consulate. He was not ten when his father died, and was brought up by his remarkable mother, with the help of Greek tutors, who may reasonably be supposed to have included Blossius. At the age of ten Tiberius became an augur. He served as a young officer in the siege of Carthage in 146, and strengthened his political position by marrying the daughter of the *doyen* of the Senate, Appius Claudius Pulcher. He was quaestor in 137 and served in Spain. This was a formative period for him. He was 26 and still impressionable. His journey to Spain took him through some of the depopulated territory, and past the large slave-estates in Etruria. In Spain in a difficult situation he negotiated an agreement with the Spaniards. The Senate scandalously repudiated this agreement and handed his superior officer Hostilius Mancinus over to the Spaniards; Tiberius narrowly escaped a similar fate. He returned to Rome with no cause to love or trust the Senate.[16]

In 133 Tiberius became Tribune of the People, and used his position to introduce a *lex agraria* controlling the amount of *ager publicus* held in one estate. Laelius had tried something similar seven years before, and received the name of 'Wise' for not pressing it.[17] Tiberius produced a skilful and statesmanlike measure. The legal limit, as we have seen, was 500 *iugera*. To sweeten the pill, he proposed the extension of this by 250 *iugera* for each son up to a total maximum of 1000 *iugera*; further that within the legal limit the land should be freehold not leasehold. This was considerable compensation, and the opposition was indication just how large and absolute were some of the enclosures. The rest of the land would be returned to the State, and allocated in inalienable lots of (probably) up to 30 *iugera* with a reasonable rental.[18] The practical value of the move is shown by the fact that between 131 and 125 BC the census figures rose by some 75,000, an increase largely attributable to the work of redistribution originated by Tiberius' bill. Despite the moderation of the proposals, Tiberius was expecting obstruction from vested interests in the Senate, such as Laelius had experienced. He therefore moved his measure in the Assembly of

the Commons without referring it first to the Senate. This was perfectly constitutional, but scarcely calculated to win the goodwill of the Establishment,
who put up his fellow-tribune, M. Octavius, to interpose his veto. Tiberius
tried to persuade Octavius to withdraw; he tried to create a bargaining position
by himself obstructing other business; he even consented to the matter going
to the Senate, but it was by then too late. All progress seemed blocked. He took
the dangerous precedent of persuading the Commons to depose Octavius, who
was arguably exceeding his office by opposing the will of the people.[19] The
veto once removed, the bill was passed. Now a commission had to be established to carry out the terms of the bill. Tiberius proposed himself, his brother
Gaius, and his father-in-law Appius Claudius Pulcher.[20] The Senate tried to
hamstring them financially, but some unexpected news from the East came
to their rescue.

Attalus III of Pergamum was a curious eccentric, 'strange, bizarre, enig-
matical', a 'perplexing personality'.[21] T. W. Africa writes pungently of him:
'According to legend, Attalus lacked few of the stock villainies of a stage tyrant.
Misanthropic and slightly mad, he murdered his relatives and mourned them
excessively, dabbled in science and metallurgy, and distilled deadly poisons
from a garden of noxious plants. However, Attalus was also a capable adminis-
trator who managed his realm efficiently. Since the kingdom was a centre of
trade and industry, the crown derived revenue from the production of pitch,
parchment, and textiles, but the chief source of royal income were the great
farms and grazing lands worked by semi-serfs and royal slaves.'[22] Attalus died
childless. He had long had close relations with Rome and Rome had supported
Pergamum against rival powers. He 'left the Romans his heirs'.[23] The will was
a strange one, but it is not to be explained in terms of imaginary motives of
far-sighted statesmanship,[24] or petty rancour towards either his likely successor,[25] or his subjects.[26] Its authenticity was challenged in antiquity, but it has
been confirmed by inscriptional evidence.[27] It seems that what he left to the
Romans was in fact his private possessions[28] – his royal estates and personal
treasures – and that he intended the city to enjoy an independent democratic
constitution together with control of the territory round about.[29] The Greek
cities, and of course the temple precincts, were explicitly excluded from the
bequest, a nicety which the inheritors ignored.

The will was brought to Rome by Eudemus for ratification. He arrived in
the early summer of 133 BC at a tense moment. Tiberius Gracchus had passed
his agrarian law. Tiberius' father had had connections with Pergamum, and
Eudemus naturally contacted him. The will was additional fuel to Tiberius'
fire. In the first place the money involved would enable the smallholders, bene-
fiting under the agrarian law, to have capital for the provision of livestock and
necessary equipment, and Tiberius was quick to introduce a bill to this effect.
In the second place, here was another whip to thrash the Senate; the words
'Let the Roman people be my heir' were explosive. So Tiberius' popularity
with the people soared, and his standing with the senate sank. They said that
Eudemus had given him a diadem and purple robe, and that he, Tiberius,

would assume the mantle of Attalus at Rome. This was mud-slinging, but
some stuck, and the aristocrats resolved to dispose of their enemy at the next
elections. Tiberius was standing for office again; re-election was not unconstitutional, but it was without precedent for two centuries. He was suspected of
aiming at *regnum*. There was some kind of disturbance: we can hardly fail to
suspect that it was provoked by the aristocracy. The Senate called on Scaevola,
the consul, to intervene: he refused to commit or sanction any illegality. P.
Scipio Nasica had no such scruples; he led a lynching mob, and when the mob
was over Tiberius and three hundred of his followers lay dead.

Tiberius was murdered, and his faction scattered. The Senate, as T. W. Africa
put it, 'scrupulously purged the radical wing of the popular party but daintily
ignored the better-born Gracchans, Scaevola, Crassus, and Gaius Gracchus'.[30]
Blossius was hauled before a tribunal; the consuls, P. Laenas and P. Rupilius,
were present; also C. Laelius and Scipio Nasica. There was a theory, which
the Gracchans themselves had formulated, that the legality of a tribune's
exercise of his power depended on the public interest.[31] The tribunal – or perhaps Laelius privately[32] – offered this to Blossius as an escape clause, and asked
him whether he would have obeyed if Tiberius had ordered him to set fire to
the Capitol. It was a barbed question, as one of Blossius' ancestors had been
executed for arson. It says much for Blossius' courage, and for his personal devotion to Tiberius as a 'philosopher-king' (we must remember that Laelius on
the tribunal bore the title *sapiens* for dropping his scheme of land reform in the
face of opposition), that he answered 'Yes'. He was protected by powerful
interests, and the Romans respected courage when they saw it, and he was
possibly pardoned and certainly allowed to go free.[33] He went to Pergamum.

Eumenes II had left a bastard son named Aristonicus. His mother came from
Ephesus, and his grandmother played the harp.[34] We know little about him,
but the fact that Blossius ranged himself beside him suggests that he had already come under Stoic influence of a radical kind. That he was a man of
uncommon quality is obvious. The unsympathetic historian Magie, who
without any justification describes him as 'wholly unfitted to be king of Pergamum', admits his 'boldness and ability',[35] and Florus describes him as a
young man of royal blood and fierce disposition.[36] Aristonicus was no doubt
motivated by personal resentment at being passed over; after all he was half-
royal. There is no question of his revolution being instigated by Blossius; it
was under way before Tiberius' death.[37] Aristonicus played on the emotions of
the time. He was not the first or last pretender of the period, but he was perhaps the ablest and certainly the most interesting. Hostility to and suspicion of
Rome was an easy and sincere emotion. The eradication of Carthage and Corinth was not long past, and men had only to use their eyes to see how Rome
emptied the coffers of her provinces and filled the slave-market. Alongside
this, whether from idealism or expediency, or a mixture of both, Aristonicus
appealed to the spirit of social justice which was always latent in the Hellenistic
Age. The upper classes in Pergamum resisted him, and preferred to ally themselves with Rome. He won some support among the slaves and lower classes,

more among the serfs of the interior. He also found valuable allies among the Thracians.

The smouldering discontents blazed high. Leucae fell;[38] Phocaea acknowledged the claims of Aristonicus.[39] He had ships and a foothold on the coast. Samos, Myndus, Colophon and (perhaps) Notium succumbed.[40] His fleets were storming down the coast of Caria; his allies were harrying the Chersonese. He had his fifth column in Pergamum itself; deserters to him were increasing. Rome was dilatory; the client-kings, Mithridates V of Pontus, Ariarathes V of Cappadocia, Nicomedes II of Bithynia, and Pylaemenes of Paphlagonia, fearing revolution and aware of Rome's power, closed ranks against the usurper, and watched and waited. Pergamum began to panic. The power of the social appeal of Aristonicus is seen in a remarkable counterblast issued in the city at this date; even through its fragmentary and uncertain text we can discern its object:

'. . . Because King Attalus Motherlover and Benefactor, when he was removed from mankind, left our fatherland free and specified it and the public domain (and the Romans must ratify the bequest) and it is necessary for the public safety for the subjugated population to share citizenship in general harmony, the People made this decree. With good fortune, the People ordain to grant citizenship to the following: the resident aliens carried in the rolls; the soldiers settled in the city and its territory; and the Macedonians, Mysians, and Masdyans (?); . . . and resident troops throughout the city and its territory and their women and children, also those registered in the garrison of the old city. Into the rolls of resident aliens are entered the children of freedmen and the royal and public slaves, young and old, with their wives, except those royal slaves purchased in the reigns of Brotherlover[41] and Motherlover. But those inhabitants, who since the death of the king have gone out of the city to the country, are declared outlaws and their property is to be confiscated by the city . . .'[42] It is not unduly cynical to think that this extraordinary generosity must have been called out by an extraordinary crisis.

Rome had sent out Scipio Nasica to organize the new province, but Nasica died in Asia.[43] The consuls for 131 were P. Licinius Crassus (who had once supported Gracchus) and L. Valerius Flaccus. Crassus, rich, noble, eloquent, skilled in law, and *pontifex maximus*[44] received the command, was defeated while invading Leucae, and captured by the Thracians, whom he improvidently insulted with fatal consequences. The threat from Rome was deferred, but Ephesus had not succumbed to Aristonicus' persuasion or power and resented his naval exploits. Roused to action they defeated his fleet at Cyme,[45] and destroyed his command of the coast.

There follows the most remarkable episode in this train of remarkable episodes. At this point Aristonicus was compelled to rethink his position, and at this point Blossius arrived. The next we hear is recounted by Strabo. 'Going up into the interior, he' (Aristonicus) 'quickly collected a vast number of propertyless men and also slaves bewitched by liberty whom he called suncitizens.'[46] They stormed Apollonis and Thyateira. Pergamum was again in

danger. The revolutionary troops reached Cyzicus and Sestus.[47] Plainly the
movement acquired a fresh impetus. This was not yet the vitality of despair. It
is associated with the arrival of Blossius and the proclamation of the Sun-state.
But Rome was too strong. Crassus was succeeded by M. Perperna, consul for
130, fresh from his victory over Eunus in Sicily. He cornered Aristonicus at
Stratoniceia on the Caicus, and starved him into surrender. Aristonicus was
sent to Rome, where he was murdered in prison at the Senate's orders.[48] Blossius did not trust the clemency of Rome a second time and took the Stoic way
of suicide.[49] Perperna sent Attalus' treasure to Rome, and later moralists com-
plain about the ensuing corruption.[50] His successor, M. Aquilius, overpowered
the remnant of the Sun-citizens by poisoning their water supply;[51] the inhabitants of Pergamum showed their gratitude by worshipping him as a Benefactor
God.[52]

The Sun, 'whom the wise men call the king of the gods and the father of all
things'[53] is, as we have seen, a natural guardian of justice, and in Asia Minor and
Thrace, solar cults were widespread. T. W. Africa has rightly pointed to the
expediential element in Aristonicus' proclamation of a City of the Sun; it
would make a natural and familiar appeal alike to the peasants whom he was
arousing and to his Thracian mercenaries.[54] But he is less wise in refusing to
accept the inspiration of Iambulus. More than one City of the Sun – Helio-
polis – was known to the ancient world, but they were not communities dedicated to social justice. The sun had long been worshipped in Asia Minor, but
he had not sparked off a social revolution. This City of the Sun was different.
The difference is the sort of difference which we see in Iambulus. No doubt
Africa is right in saying that 'a literary parable would hardly provide a work-
able program for a struggling revolution much less suffice to inflame an illiterate peasantry'. But a literary parable may provide the inspiration for the
leader of a revolution, and ideals have more force, whether on the sons of
kings or an illiterate peasantry, than historians always allow. Furthermore, the
transformation of the revolution is associated with the arrival of Blossius.
Blossius was a Stoic, and we have seen evidence that Iambulus stands within
the Stoic tradition. We do not know enough about Aristonicus to know how
far his reasons for embracing a City of the Sun were pragmatic. We can be
certain that Blossius presented him with something which was rooted in
philosophical idealism. 'To pull the oppressed out of their apathetic lethargy'
wrote Bidez 'required a great mystical impulse, in which the Stoic missionaries
took the initiative.'[55]

But though we need not accept Africa's rather cynical repudiation of idealism
as a motive in politics, it would be a pity not to quote his brilliant summary.
'Presumably Aristonicus aimed at public welfare and the betterment of the
Pergamene poor but within the contemporary framework of monarchy, a
benevolent despotism (at least in prospect) with the king no longer the shearer
but the shepherd of his flock. Apart from the immediate violence of the class
war, the bourgeoisie of Pergamum feared confiscation of their wealth, not universal suffrage, for Aristonicus threatened, not social democracy, but redistri-

bution of the profits of society, a by no means unique occurrence in Greek history. Perhaps with success the pretender might have proved more king than benefactor, since he saw himself as a prince unjustly deprived of a rightful throne by a wicked relative, a not unusual situation in Near Eastern fact and legend. While he challenged an oppressive social order and the imperial might of Rome, Aristonicus embodied both the Hellenistic ideal monarch counselled by a sage and the vastly older tradition of the hidden hero, a king's son of doubtful birth, raised in obscurity and striving to wrest his father's throne from usurpers. Probably Aristonicus hoped to realize the aim of 'perpetual peace for his subjects and swift redress in his courts' but he also knew that the son would come into his kingdom only as the Sun in his zenith.'[56]

CHAPTER XVII

THE MESSIANIC KINGDOM[1]

WE MUST NOW TURN ASIDE to look at a quite small community in Palestine, who spread through the eastern Mediterranean during the Hellenistic Age, and carried within themselves the seeds of three of the great world religions. That people was the Jews.

With their history we are not much concerned. At some time in the second half of the second millennium BC they migrated from Egypt and settled in Palestine. Back beyond that are folk memories, and it is reasonable to accept a much earlier migration from Mesopotamia. The eventual settlement in Palestine placed the Jewish tribes first in the middle of a group of rival tribes, warring with one another, and then as an uneasy buffer state between empires. From the east came the Assyrians, Babylonians and Persians; to the south Egypt stretched her sleepy limbs and from time to time reasserted her power. Later Alexander burst in and his Successors; later still Rome. The Jewish people enjoyed periods of independence or quasi-independence; they suffered periods of exile and dispersion. Their unity, their very being as a people, depended on their religion. In the course of their migration from Egypt they had adopted and been adopted by Yahweh, a god worshipped by the Kenites. This covenant relationship meant that Yahweh, unlike most tribal gods, was independent of his people; so it held within it the possibility of universalism. Further, from the first the covenant involved moral demands, the Ten Commandments, the Torah or Law. Here too was the foundation on which were built the prophetic demands for social justice and personal responsibility.

Among the myths passed down from one generation to another was the myth of Paradise or the Golden Age. The most famous and familiar version of this is in the early chapters of *Genesis*.[2] There the first man and the first woman live in a beautiful garden; there is reason however to think that the restriction to a single couple arises from an adaptation of the story to the creation myth.[3] The garden is God's garden; he walks there in the cool of the evening. It is well watered; there are many trees; they are beautiful to contemplate, and bear fruit in abundance. Not that it requires no attention, but maintaining it is co-operating with natural goodness, not struggling against adversity.[4] The river which waters the garden branches into four great rivers, and gold and precious stones lie in their course; the garden therefore lies in the mountains. There man once lived at peace and in harmony with the animals. Man and woman lived together innocent, naked and unashamed; they were, in the strict sense of the word, uninhibited.

This primal Utopia is naturally echoed in later prophetic and poetic writing. There is a curious relic of it in the forty-eighth psalm. This is about the Jerusalem Temple. It is about God's city (God's dwelling-place?) on his holy mountain (where the garden lay?). The hill (of Zion) is described as beautiful and elevated, the cynosure of the world. It might be an exalted account of Jerusalem. But the mountain is described as in the far north, and we realize that it is an old account of Paradise applied to Jerusalem.[5] So too Ezekiel sketches a picture of Eden, the garden of God set on the mountain of God, rich in gold and precious stones (the products of the lower reaches of the river in *Genesis* are brought back into the garden), where man lived in innocence and righteousness, wise and beautiful, in harmony with the spiritual powers.[6]

It is natural that such a Paradise myth should, like Janus, face both ways. It is a dream of the past, tinged with regret; it is a dream of the future, tinged with hope. This is the force of a number of passages in *The Book of Isaiah*. In one, just as mankind has passed from Yahweh's garden into a wilderness, the prophet shows Yahweh turning the desert places back into Eden.[7] Three of the most famous visions of the future seem to hark back to a myth of the Golden Age. In the first the nations come in peace to Yahweh's mountain, and turn their weapons of war to instruments of farming.[8] Yahweh's mountain is, as we have seen, ambiguous between the primal Paradise and the actual mountain on which stood the historic Jerusalem. In apocalyptic literature the use of weapons is taught by Azael, 'the tenth ruler';[9] in other words the vision of a world without them is a restoration of a Golden Age. So too another well-loved passage tells how under the guidance of a righteous ruler, 'they shall not hurt or destroy in all my holy mountain'. The animals live in harmony with one another and with mankind, as in Eden. The idea of the knowledge of Yahweh flooding through the land seems also to be a restoration of the Paradise which was lost by eating the forbidden fruit of the knowledge of good and evil.[10] Yet again the vision of the coming of Yahweh incorporates material from the original Golden Age, as the wilderness becomes a garden, and God walks there, the conflict between men and animals is over, suffering and weariness fall away, and peace and contentment are over all.[11]

At some point – the idea was well established by the time of Amos in the eighth century BC[12] – there emerged a popular expectation denoted by the words 'The Day of Yahweh'.[13] Amos has a very different vision of the Day of Yahweh from those he is addressing: he sees it as a judgement upon the wicked, and not least the wicked among the Israelites: but by reading between the lines, and – almost – by turning his picture upside down, we can see the ideas which he is combating. The Day of Yahweh, alike for the people and for the prophets, meant the direct intervention of Yahweh in human history and the assertion of his power. On that day Yahweh would pass through the midst of his people,[14] as he once walked in the garden. To the popular mind the Day of Yahweh meant the triumph of his people, and that triumph was seen as the restoration of the Golden Age. The labour of husbandry would be past, the land would be well watered, there would be no danger from wild animals, the peoples would live at peace with one another, sickness and death would disappear, all would be light and joy. In answering this Amos attacks those who have lived on Yahweh's mountain as if the Golden Age of prosperity had come for them, while ignoring the fact that it had not come for all, and by their violence and injustice denying the values which Yahweh's presence would assert.[15] The river which will flow again with the coming of Yahweh will be the river of justice.[16] The prophets do not deny the ultimate restoration of the Golden Age, but it will come only through a process of purgation, and this period of tribulation becomes a notable feature of late apocalyptic.

Whether in the popular picture or in the profound ethical challenge offered by the prophets, the Day of Yahweh leads to the establishment of the Kingdom of God, a phrase not in fact used in the Old Testament, but a concept clearly enough there. Gradually the idea emerged that the Kingdom would be inaugurated and administered by Yahweh's anointed vicegerent, the Messiah (another term not prominent in the Old Testament, but important later: it means 'anointed', Christ in Greek, and is derived from the anointing of the kings). The concept of the righteous kingdom thus depends on the ideal king. He is well depicted by Isaiah in a number of passages.[17] He is of the house of David, in line of descent from the idealized king. He is described as 'in purpose wonderful, in battle God-like, Father for all time, Prince of peace' – the last phrase is so familiar that we miss the colossal paradox of it. His reign is marked by justice, righteousness and peace. For this he has to see deeper than most. It is not that wickedness no longer exists, but that it is discerned and controlled, so that the under-privileged have an equal chance. More remarkable is the effect on his subjects: their eyes and ears are alert to the truth, impetuous judgement gives way to good sense, the faltering tongues to clear speech, and they discriminate between fools and wise, crooks and good citizens. Jeremiah foresees a king of David's line, maintaining law and justice, peace and security.[18]

From the time of Jeremiah onward the vision of the coming kingdom becomes a part of apocalyptic and eschatological literature. We can trace three great changes of emphasis. First, there is a new emphasis on the individual. The phrase 'the kingdom of God' is itself ambiguous, for it may denote the community which is obedient to God as king, or it may denote the kingship or sovereignty of God. In Jeremiah the new covenant, the new law, is within men, written on their hearts.[19] Jesus seemingly echoes this when he says 'The kingdom of God is within you', though the words are ambiguous.[20] In this way the submission of individuals to the kingship of God is the prerequisite of the establishment of the divine community. Secondly, whereas the earliest vision of the kingdom was the triumph of Israel, and this is found in a thinker of the stature of Ezekiel, and continued in men of more constrained humanity than his, the later picture sees the kingdom as world-wide and all-embracing. Thirdly, the kingdom becomes eschatological; that is to say that its realization lies not in the world we know but in a transformed universe. These developments have their evident historical source in the period of Jewish impotence, even though they are anticipated earlier. The Fall of Jerusalem and the Exile led inevitably to smaller dependence on the political community and greater emphasis on the individual. The Dispersion led to a greater involvement with other peoples and a less exclusive attitude. Political weakness led to a projection of political hopes on to eternity.

The apocalyptic hopes of the Jews during the Hellenistic Age are remarkably conveyed in 1 *Enoch* 37–71. Here the king who shall come is given four titles: Messiah or Anointed, Righteous, Elect, and Son of Man. That these are key terms is well seen in that the early Christians applied all of them to Jesus.[21] According to this vision the Messiah existed before the creation of the world. He comes as judge (though in some sections Yahweh is the judge). He will be a staff to the righteous, a light to the Gentiles and a hope to those in distress. Before him tyrants will disappear without trace. So will come peace, and the Messiah's days of glory. Wisdom will cover the land as the waters cover the sea. Unrighteousness will vanish before the righteous judge. Nature itself will be transformed, and the light of the original creation, the light of the primeval garden, will shine on the holy. Men are restored to fellowship with spiritual beings. The dead rise. The life of men is transvaluated. 'There shall be no iron for war, and no material for a coat of mail; metal shall be of no value, tin shall be of no service or esteem and lead shall not be desired. All these things shall perish and be destroyed from the face of the earth, when the Elect One shall appear before the face of the God of Spirits.'[22] It is the restoration of the Golden Age, the kingdom of rest and peace.

In *The Psalms of Solomon* also there is a striking account of the Messianic deliverance. In one sense it belongs to a concrete historical situation. The Maccabean priest-rulers have become corrupt and fallen before Rome, but the Roman conqueror will himself fall, and the Messiah will bring an age of blessing upon Israel under the kingship of Yahweh. He is of the house of David. He will break the Gentile oppressors with a rod of iron, and hold them in subjection, till they come freely to see the glory of Yahweh. He will be the just ruler of an exclusive Israel, in which the land is fairly distributed, and justice is established. His power will depend on God, not on arms or gold. His judgements will be wise, equitable and just. He will be pure of sin; in others sin will not cease to exist, but it will receive appropriate treatment.

> Happy are they that shall be born in those days,
> to see the good fortune from Yahweh
>   which he will bring to pass for the generation to come,
> under the rod of discipline of Yahweh's Anointed
>   in the fear of his God,
> in the spirit of wisdom, righteousness and might,
> to direct men in works of righteousness
>   by the fear of God,
> to establish them all before Yahweh,
> a good generation in the fear of God in the days of mercy.[23]

Evidence of the continuing vision may be extracted from Philo, writing in the first century AD.[24] Philo's thinking, for all his Alexandrianism, is deeply rooted in the Old Testament. He shares in the vision and hope of the Messianic kingdom. We can establish a number of facts about this vision. First, the kingdom is the gift of God. Second, it is primarily a blessing upon Israel. Third, it will extend throughout the world. Fourth, the moral superiority of the new generation of Israel will be such that the other peoples will submit from awe. Fifth, there will be an era of peace. Finally, the new age will be marked by the restoration of nature to the conditions of Eden, the free growth of the fruits of the earth, the disappearance of disease, and the re-establishment of peaceable community between men and animals.

Although there was this tendency to take an eschatological view of what had been a historical hope, concrete historical expectations appeared and re-appeared. Even Cyrus is called the Messiah,[25] Cyrus who in conquering Babylon, and making possible the return from exile, seemed to be opening up a new kingdom founded on penitence for the past, a kingdom, it was hoped, of righteousness. When that hope failed of its immediate fulfilment, one of the later leaders of the returning exiles, Zerubbabel, who built the Second Temple and tried to restore the city walls, was identified with the Messiah,[26] and thought to be God's instrument in establishing a kingdom whose prosperity should compensate for previous adversity, where young and old might live in peace and security, and where the whole world might find its religious centre.[27] We do not know how Zerubbabel fell, but these expectations also were doomed. Similarly the Maccabean stand against idolatry, and their temporary achievement of a measure of independence, led to an outburst of Messianic prophecies, Here, for example, is an idealized picture of the land when Simon was high priest:

They farmed their land in peace,
the earth produced her crops,
the trees in the field their fruit.

The old men sat in the streets
and conversed about their blessings.
The young men were finely dressed
but not in battle-armour. . . .[28]

Simon gave the land back its peace;
there were great rejoicings through the land.
For every man sat under his own vine and fig-tree
and they had none to fear.

In those days every enemy vanished,
every hostile king was defeated.

Simon protected the poor among the people,
he observed the law closely,
he rid the country of lawless and wicked men.[29]

Similarly his successor John Hyrcanus is exalted, as holding the three functions of the Messiah, prophet, priest and king, as a righteous judge, as the instrument of enlightenment for the Gentiles, as the bringer of peace, justice and prosperity.[30] So again with the coming of Rome there was a whole succession of pretenders to the Messianic position of liberator, as Gamaliel reminded the Sanhedrin on a celebrated occasion.[31] R. Akiba even saw the ill-fated Bar-Kochba as the Messiah, and coins were struck proclaiming the redemption of Israel.[32]

The Dead Sea Scrolls reinforce our picture of this atmosphere without adding very much to it.[33] Remarkable is the clearcut contrast between the Way of Light and the Way of Darkness, the Spirit of Light and the Spirit of Darkness, and Children of Light and the Children of Darkness. A historical dimension is given in the person – or persons, for arguably the title has been accorded to more than one individual – of the Teacher of Righteousness, who is set against the Wicked Priest. Various attempts at identification have been made: the most that can be said for certain is that the events referred to must belong to the later Maccabean period. The Teacher of Righteousness is not himself a Messianic figure. In the *Damascus Document* he seems to be the prophet who proclaims the Messiah's coming. There will in fact be two Messiahs, one from the house of Aaron, one from the house of Israel, one priestly and one lay. This, though unusual, is not unique, being found also in *The Testament of Levi* and in rabbinic speculation. The expected pattern is one of forty years of trouble after the death of the Teacher, ending with the destruction of the powers of darkness, the reign of the two Messiahs, and peace on earth. This is the Time of Favour. There is a fragment of a *Manual of Discipline for the Future Congregation of Israel*. This lays great stress on education in the Covenant. At twenty a young man will be examined as to his fitness to full membership of the community; he is to have no sexual relations before that age. At twenty-five he becomes eligible for office. At thirty he may join the bench of judges and hold military command. Plainly this is not an eschatological sketch: it pertains to an intermediate period when the congregation of Israel is united, but the battle is not yet won, and there is not yet peace on earth. There is provision for common meals, but these are not Messianic banquets. Of the ultimate vision there is little detailed indication.

Jesus of Nazareth, condemned by the Jews for the blasphemy of claiming to be the Messiah, and executed by the Romans with the death appropriate to the leader of a liberation movement, belongs to the same pattern.[34] Jesus was seemingly the first in the prophetic line to identify the Messiah with the Suffering Servant of *Isaiah*.[35] The story of the Temptation shows Jesus rejecting some of the traditional and popular views of the Messiah. Yet some of the traits are strong. Luke, himself politically eirenic, put the birth of Jesus in the context of two revolutionary songs,[36] speaking of economic justice, the breaking of the power of rulers, deliverance from enemies, security and righteousness. So too Jesus in his first sermon in the synagogue at Nazareth spoke of economic and social justice.[37] Jesus in fact proclaimed the approach of the kingdom of God,[38] and sometimes spoke as if it had already arrived.[39] There seem to have been seven elements in Jesus' understanding of the kingdom. The first is that the Messianic hope has to do with this world: witness, among much else, the prayer 'Thy kingdom come; thy will be done on earth as it is in heaven'.[40] The second is that the way of violent uprising as a means of political liberation was both alien to Jesus' understanding of God and unrealistic in practice.[41] The third is that the coming of the kingdom, while it is in one sense an act of God in response to a crisis, is in another sense a comprehensive process of natural growth, and Jesus insists on this in parable after parable.[42] The fourth is that Jesus established a new community in the hope that they would be the nucleus of the kingdom (in one sense of that word), a community of men and women who hold a common purse, who are given a new way of life (Jesus took the disciples apart before speaking the words we call the Sermon on the Mount[43]), who are taught that the first would be last and the last first (that is to say that the familiar social values were reversed), and who emerged with a new system of their own for fostering economic justice.[44] The fifth is that Jesus saw his mission as beginning with the Jews,[45] but also that he saw it as expanding to take in the Gentiles as well.[46] The sixth is that there is an inescapable eschatological element in the teaching of Jesus about the kingdom. It was to Schweitzer's credit to restore this to its proper place; unfortunately in so doing he treated Jesus' approach as exclusively eschatological. For, finally, there is, equally inescapably, the conviction that the kingdom, at least in the sense of kingship, of God is present; it is, Jesus claimed, realized in his own obedience to God. It is this that C. H. Dodd has taught us to call 'realized eschatology'.[47] To put it differently, at the last the hoped-for community, which would serve through suffering, shrank to one man, Jesus himself. But the insights were social and communal insights. To sum up the whole matter, the ideal kingdom of God for Jesus involved alike the obedience of the individual, social action, and, for its ultimate fulfilment, the cataclysmic revelation of God. And it is significant, in the light of the ideals of the Hellenistic Age, that Jesus' standard of the impartiality of Christian love is the sun who shines impartially upon just and unjust alike.[48]

We can now essay some brief generalizations about the ideal commonwealth of the Jews. First, in a way that is true of none of the others we have been studying, the kingdom comes for the Jews by the absolute act of God. It is true that in some of the Greek Utopias the Sun plays a characterizing rôle in the new community, but his power is much more passively exercised; he is in the background, not the foreground. Secondly, the ideal commonwealth is a monarchy, and an absolute monarchy, with Yahweh as king; it matters little whether he is seen as ruling directly or through the Messiah as his representative. The Jews had no interest in democracy as a principle, or in constitution-mongering of any kind. Thirdly, there is a profound interest in economic justice, in equality before the law and the consequent use of the law to promote morality, and in peace (which in Hebrew is not just the absence of war, but a positive state of economic, political and social well-being which contains no seeds of discontent or strife). Fourthly, there is a concentration on the ideal state of Israel, and a strong tendency to see other nations as unjust oppressors of the people of God; at the same time some of the more radical prophets look to the moral power of the new Israel to radiate out into a worldwide community of peace and justice. Finally, although Messianism is at all times politically relevant, not least as the inspiration of liberation movements, there is a certain nostalgia for a mythical golden age and a consequent projection forward of the dreams of political independence and economic and social justice eschatologically on to a mythical future.

CHAPTER XVIII

VISIONS OF THE LATE REPUBLIC

THE SUPPRESSION OF TIBERIUS GRACCHUS could not suppress the demand for change. His land commission did its work, or some of its work, despite obstruction from wealthy Italians backed by Scipio Aemilianus. M. Fulvius Flaccus began a move to both economic privilege and Roman justice in proposing a choice between economic privilege and Roman citizenship. The senate resisted this; Fregellae revolted and was crushed; but the senate perhaps now granted citizenship to the local magistrates in cities with Latin rights. The extension of citizenship which was in the end to make the world (*orbem*) a single city (*urbem*) was on its way.

Tiberius' brother Gaius, a skilled politician and orator, instituted further reforms. He remains an enigmatic figure in an enigmatic period; we can make no sure analysis even of his immediate programme, let alone his ultimate aim. He reinforced his brother's agrarian reforms, and developed them by overseas settlement; he subsidized the urban poor, and he checked the dominance of the senate. But he did this by fostering the power of the business men, and at the expense of more remote subject-peoples in Asia. His support of the Italians made him unpopular; he resisted with violence opposition to his schemes and met a violent end, like his brother. The Gracchi were seared deep into the heart of Rome. Blossius' influence may have affected Gaius during a formative period. In his legislation of 123–2 BC is no trace of Utopian vision, only of a firm grasp of immediately pressing problems with some indifference to some more distant implications of his policies. The lesson learned from the period of the Gracchi was in the end a lesson that had been better unlearned. It was the power of violence. The next century belongs to the men of violence; the violence escalated, as it always does. The pendulum swung, and first one faction and then another saw their leaders wiped out. Marius, Saturninus, Sulla, Pompey, Caesar – they were all men of blood, and the result of their violence was the destruction of the republic.

The demand of the Italians for citizen rights was beginning to sharpen. It was sheer folly of the senate in 95 to be legalistic about some Italians who had been enjoying these rights. M. Livius Drusus in 91 tried to extend the citizenship. The senatorial aristocrats were naturally conservative and against him. So were the commons, who feared to be ousted from their own more circumscribed privileges. Drusus was murdered, and the Italians rose in revolt. The Social

War was destructive of life and agriculture. The senate's hand was effectually forced; in conceding citizenship to those allies who did not rise they gave away their case, though they did their best to make the concession politically valueless by ensuring that the new citizens could always be controlled. But the concession was made; it was extended to all Italy, and before the end of the century the Roman citizenship was being extended to individuals and communities much further afield.

Another ground for discontent was slavery; it was a festering sore on the body of antiquity. There had been sporadic risings against the brutality of masters in the earlier part of the second century. About the time of Tiberius Gracchus the situation exploded into life at several points in the Mediterranean world, in Pergamum as we have seen, in the slave market of Delos, in Attica (where the mine slaves had a particularly hard lot),[1] in Italy at Minturnae and Sinuessa,[2] and in Sicily. It looks at first blush like a conspiracy, the work of a revolutionary international, and there have been those to put forward such a view. But this view is ill-supported by evidence, and such a world-wide conspiracy of slaves would be almost unthinkable. It seems rather that in human history there is such a thing as the ripeness or fullness of time, the *kairos*, when similar events take place in different places without immediate connection. So it must have been at this moment. And if it is true that the movement at Pergamum was actuated in part by a kind of Utopian idealism, it is at least possible that this was equally true of some of the other uprisings.

We know little enough about them. The most challenging, and the one about which we are best informed, was the one in Sicily.[3] Towards the end of 135 BC a Syrian slave named Eunus masterminded an uprising in Enna. What we know of Eunus suggests that he was more of a prophet than statesman or general; he was a charismatic leader, endowed with a magnetic personality, something of a visionary, and either a man of religion or at least a man who knew how to exploit the religiosity of others. They sacked Enna, sparing only those who had been humane masters or had the skill to make weapons for their new overlords. Eunus now established himself as king with the title Antiochus, and his followers took the name of 'Syrians'; a coin survives struck with the name of Antiochus.[4] Probably there is no more to this than a memory of his Syrian past, and a system which was a counterblast to Rome. There is no sign, beyond the freeing of the slaves, of a new order of society. Eunus withdrew to the ultimate sovereignty. A council controlled the activities of administration and military preparation, in which the lead was taken by one Achaeus. Meantime there was a successful *coup* in Agrigentum, led by a Cilician named Cleon. But Eunus had a *mystique*, and Cleon joined him instead of rivalling him. The allies secured Tauromenium and Catana. They behaved with exemplary moderation and statesmanship, and were obviously seeking to build up support for an independent régime in Sicily. What would have happened had they been successful we cannot tell. The Romans descended upon this. L. Hypsaeus was defeated, C. Fulvius Flaccus was held at arm's length, L. Calpurnius Piso penetrated to the walls of Enna, where sling bolts bearing his name have been found but won no decisive victory, and it was only with P. Rupilius, after four separate years' campaigns, that the slaves were defeated. This suggests able leadership, a remarkable solidarity with no fifth column, and something positive to fight for. One curious and unexplained fact is that Eunus, who was captured, was not executed, but died a natural death as a prisoner. We have a distinct sense that there was more to the First Servile War than meets the eye.

Thirty years later there was a fresh uprising in Sicily.[5] Again it was not completely isolated; there were movements in the mines of Attica, in Italy at Nuceria and Capua, and an odd enterprise led by an *eques* named T. Vettius who tried to escape from the consequences of a bankruptcy induced by extravagance in love by raising an independent army of slaves. The Sicilian business was sparked off by a decree freeing slaves who were citizens of allied states. This caused such excitement among the slaves in Sicily that the process of liberation had to be suspended, and this in turn provoked an uprising. There were curious parallels with the earlier revolt.[6] The leader, a man named Salvius, proclaimed himself king with the title of Tryphon. The most interesting feature of our record is that his capital of Triocala is described in language which owes a debt to Utopian writing. The 'three beauties' are an abundance of springwater of exceptional sweetness, a locality rich in vines and olives and with marvellous potentialities for farmers, and outstanding security with its impregnable cliffs.[7] Salvius was supported by an independent movement led by a Cilician named Athenion. But Salvius was not Eunus, and there was some rivalry between the leaders, though the measure of their support may be gauged from the fact that it once again took four years before the rising was quelled.

Almost exactly another thirty years passed before the third and greatest of these risings. This started in Capua, and the genius behind it was a Thracian gladiator named Spartacus, who lent his name to the Spartacist revolutionaries of 1919.[8] In 73 BC Spartacus led an escape of gladiators and established his headquarters in the crater of Vesuvius, which was of course inactive. Here he attracted other runaways, and defeated the Romans sent after him and his forces grew to some 70,000. He made little appeal to the urban slaves but had a great appeal to those who were suffering in the countryside. His own plan was to march across Italy and through the Alps; from there Gauls, Germans and Thracians had a reasonable chance of dispersing to their homelands. This made more sense than a similar proposal would have done with Eunus, who would have had a hazardous sea voyage to Syria. Spartacus knew his limitations. His followers and associates did not, and a Gaul named Crixus led a party dedicated to looting and self-aggrandisement. Spartacus forced an entry to the north, but the forces demanding that they stay in Italy were too strong. He toyed with the possibility of securing Rome, but decided instead to seek a base in Sicily. It proved abortive. There were quarrels in the liberation movement and they succumbed to a coalition of Crassus and Pompey, and the Via Appia was soon lined with six thousand crosses. Spartacus has acquired his own legendary dimensions. Even in antiquity they told stories of how his mantic wife foretold his greatness, because a snake coiled round him as he slept.[9] His actual historical importance is negligible. His importance here is also negative; it consists precisely in the fact that he was not, despite Arthur Koestler,[10] a Utopian, but a practical man with limited objectives.

Four men of this period must be specially mentioned here. The first is P. Sertorius.[11] He was a Sabine, who had been one of Marius' officers, but had stood against his excesses as he stood against Sulla; through the period of civil war he pursued the reputation for moderation and integrity.[12] When Sulla came to power he withdrew to Spain, and, harried there by Sulla's troops, he sailed with a company of 3,000 first for Carthage and then for Mauretania. Pushed from pillar to post he sailed out through the straits of Gibraltar into the Atlantic. Here he fell in with some sailors who told him of islands a thousand miles or so off the coast of Africa called the Islands of the Blessed. They said that the islands enjoyed a moderate rainfall, gentle breezes, healthful air, and little change of season. The soil was fertile and excellent for crops; more, it bore by natural growth produce adequate in quantity and quality to feed a people without need for laborious work. They might in short be thought of as the plain of Elysium and the home of the blessed in Homer's poetry. Whether these islands were just a sailor's yarn, or represent a vague knowledge of Madeira or the Canaries or even the Azores, it is hard to say; probably fact is interwoven with myth. Sertorius was fascinated by these stories and yearned to colonize these islands and to lead a life free from political oppression and endless wars. Some of his followers were more interested in riches than in peace, and he had to give up his scheme.[13] He settled for a while in Tingis-Tangier, before responding to an urgent call to return to Spain. There for eight years he held out, not, as he would claim, against Rome, for he was a loyal Roman, but against those who had wrongfully usurped the power in Rome. During this period we may note his claim to divine favour illustrated by his famous white fawn; his reputation for moderation and equity; the establishment of a school at Osca for the children of Celtiberian chiefs; the loyalty he commanded.

Sertorius is for us one of the great rebels, and in the end only a footnote on the pages of history. Mommsen described him as 'a man who under more fortunate circumstances would perhaps have become the regenerator of his country.'[14] Fated to a life of war, he never encountered those circumstances. But we can trace a strong vein of practical idealism when opportunity afforded. And the dream of Utopia is a bizarre pendant to a tragic career. For it is a Utopia in the Phaeacian tradition, where Nature is kindly and food grows without tendance. There is political idealism too, freedom from dictatorship, and the desire to establish a democracy, *demos*, perhaps with himself as a kind of Pericles, a monarchical symbol of justice, and a democratic symbol of equity. And there is some indication of an almost mystical belief in a religious destiny for himself.

The second of these figures is L. Sergius Catilina.[15] He must here be mentioned, because there has been some attempt to portray him as an idealistic revolutionary. We do well to treat with caution the extreme rhetoric of his great opponent. But in his younger days Catiline had been one of Sulla's right-hand men, bloodthirsty in proscription. He was a spendthrift aristocrat and a man of violence, and for all his undoubted personal attractions was hardly sincere in his later pose of radicalism. In his pursuit of power he turned to the discontented, and claimed that his own economic straits made him a reliable champion of those who were in similar straits. His programme was in fact debt-cancellation and the redistribution of land. This was genuinely attractive to the peasant-farmers of Italy, but they were not a significant factor in consular elections. It had no appeal to the urban proletariat. It had a considerable appeal to the impoverished section of the aristocracy; as an election-asset it was reactionary not progressive.[16] When Catiline failed at the polls and tried a military coup, he found little support in Rome or the areas in the vicinity, except for Etruria, where he had personal influence. His associates, realizing that it was further afield that the discontent increased, tried to rouse a delegation of dissatisfied Gauls, who made a shrewd calculation and sold their knowledge to the government. The conspiracy was suppressed without difficulty. The catchwords of Catiline's policy remind us of Agis; but Agesilaus supported those same catchwords. Catiline was no idealist, but it is significant that he thought a policy which included the familiar appeal to social justice worth making.

Cicero is more important.[17] Unlike Catiline, he did not belong to the senatorial order. He was a 'new man', of equestrian birth, who stood for the cooperation of the aristocrats and the middle class, 'the concord of the orders': *concordia* is the Greek *homonoia*, but here strictly circumscribed. For the commons he had nothing but contempt, 'the dregs of Romulus', 'the miserable half-starved mob, with their mass-meetings, sucking the blood of the treasury.'[18] He was strongly opposed to democracy; the people were incapable of taking rational decisions; they were unstable and easily swayed by demagogues.[19] They should therefore be given only sufficient power to keep them from dissatisfaction. Cicero's political ideal was *cum dignitate otium*.[20] The phrase is not easily to be translated. *Otium* is a condition of political tranquillity, containing strong implications of conservatism and the maintenance of the *status quo*; *dignitas* points to a class-structure under the guidance of an aristocracy, to which however a Cicero could always be admitted on merit. He expands this in his defence of Sestius, and summarizes the foundations by which such an enlightened aristocracy may maintain its power unquestioned. These are religious observances, auspices, the powers of the magistrates, the authority of the senate, the laws, tradition, the law-courts and official interpretation of the law, credit, the provinces, the allies, the good reputation of imperial government, military power, and the treasury. To maintain all these requires high qualities of character, high ability, and high perseverance.

There is no Utopianism here; there is a strong practical Roman bent. Cicero did however put himself in the direct line of Utopians by electing to follow Plato in writing two works entitled *The Republic* and *The Laws*.[21] *The Republic* was written between 55 and 51 BC, during a period when Cicero's political wings were clipped, but before he left politics for writing during the period of Caesar's sole rule.[22] It is hard to know whether we are to treat *The Republic* as a serious attempt to influence practical politics, or as an escape into the world of the ideal. Unlike Plato, Cicero chooses a dramatic date outside his own lifetime, in 129 BC, significantly between the Gracchi, that is within the sphere alike of Utopia and practical politics; his *dramatis personae* include Scipio Aemilianus, who plays the rôle of Socrates, and C. Laelius.

The work is unfortunately fragmentary, but we are still in the preface when our manuscript begins, and Cicero defends the profession of patriotic statesmanship and practical politics in a strongly personal way. He then passes to the dialogue proper. A reference to Panaetius is perhaps introduced to indicate one of Cicero's chief sources.[23] After a leisured introduction, which is partly designed for dramatic flavour, and partly to anticipate and balance Scipio's dream at the end, Laelius invites Scipio to give his view on the state (*de republica*).[24] Scipio then defines the state as *res populi*, the state or concern of a people, a people being defined as a congregation of a large number of persons brought together by a common mind about law and an agreement to share in that which is mutually advantageous. The stress on law is important, and characteristic of the Roman and the lawyer; elsewhere he calls the state *iuris societas*, a community bound together by law.[26] He takes for granted the traditional Greek classification of constitutions into monarchy, aristocracy and democracy, holding the last as the worst of the three. All are important; the first two do not allow sufficient responsibility to the ordinary citizens, the third in pursuit of equality eliminates proper distinctions. All may degenerate, into tyranny, plutocracy and mob-rule. Scipio expresses a marginal preference for kingship: it reflects the rule of Jupiter in the universe, and makes possible a benevolent paternalism. But the ideal constitution is a blend of all three; Rome has it and will serve as a basis for discussion on the ideal state.[27] (A century and a half later Tacitus wryly commented that the mixed constitution was easier to praise than to secure.)[28] The second book then contains a summary of the history of Rome, from which it seems to go on to an account of the ideal statesman. This is unfortunately largely lost; we can hardly say more than that he is supposed to be a model to his fellow citizens.[29]

Only at the end of the second book is the question of justice raised.[30] Nothing shows more clearly the essential difference between Cicero and Plato than this delay. Plato is alienated from the Athens of his day, and starts from an absolute search for justice; Cicero is absorbed by his own Rome and is seeking to draw political lessons from that fact. And this is in general true of the Romans: their contribution to Utopian thinking is Rome.

The third book opens with some reflections by Cicero on the nature of man, his weakness at birth, the countervailing gift of the divine spirit,[31] the power of reason, and its highest expression in practical statesmanship. Cicero, like Plato, then allows a case for injustice to be put. It is in fact based on the Sceptic Carneades.[32] It is answered by Laelius and Scipio without difficulty in terms of

Stoic universal law;[33] in the course of his answer Cicero establishes and lays down for posterity the doctrine of the just war, which the Christians, when they attained power, somewhat strangely arrogated to themselves.[34]

The next two books are unfortunately in a very fragmentary form; the fragments are tantalizing in the extreme. The fourth book dealt among other things with the class structure of society and the education of the young. The class structure of the ideal society appears to be that of Rome. but Cicero sees Plato's Guardians in the senators and 'knights', and the third class in the *plebs*. He is critical of the structures and practices of the Greek states, and seems to reject both Spartan and Platonic communism, eliminating Plato from his ideal city as Plato eliminated Homer.[35] Education seems to be directed to moral training and simple living. The most remarkable fragment of the book runs 'I don't like seeing the same people rulers of the world and its tax-collectors.'[36] This is Plato's divorce of economic from political power, but how Cicero applied it to his ideal Rome we do not know: perhaps the senators became the Guardians proper and the knights were left with a wider economic rôle.

The fifth book again began with Cicero speaking in his own voice. It is an encomium of the ancient Roman virtues. The meagre remains of the rest are important because it was here that he developed the idea of a director of the state, *rector* or *moderator*, a man of all the qualities, wise, courageous, hard-working and devoted to the common good. One of his greatest skills is to be the power to anticipate disruptive emergencies.[38] He is to have the vision of a Marcellus and the policy of a Maximus. He is to cultivate a laconical eloquence. He must be versed in law, and understand Greek.[37] He is to be brought up on glory. Exactly what Cicero meant by this *rector* has been a matter for considerable debate. Reitzenstein thought that he was making a general plea for someone like an Augustus to intervene in the crisis at Rome; Meyer suggested that he was writing in specific support of Pompey; Heinze argued against any monarchical concept and thought that he was giving general definition to a class of people.[39] We have no evidence to give a determinate solution. But I would suggest first that Cicero is trying to find a place for the 'kingly' man from Plato's *Statesman*; secondly, that he is drawing on a tradition also represented by a fragment of Diotogenes, a Pythagorean writer on kingship,[40] who also draws parallels with the pilot's pursuit of a safe voyage, the doctor's of a healthy patient, and the general's of victory, but that this does not mean that he is idealizing monarchy but rather seeking to fit into the anti-monarchical Roman system the virtues associated with monarchy. Cicero has in mind the rôle he assigned to Brutus in the establishment of the Roman republic ('. . . outstanding in ability and courage, he was only a private citizen but took on himself the whole weight of government, and was the first in our country to show that no-one is only a private citizen when it comes to protecting the liberty of the citizen-body'[41]) and also the historical part played by Cato the censor;[42] fourthly, that it is hard not to think that somewhere at the back of his mind Cicero is casting himself hopefully for the rôle; this last leaves the ambiguity between the active statesman and the philosophical *éminence grise*. He thus is not in any sense an absolute ruler, with or without a constitutional position. He is much more the elder statesman, who is listened to for what he is.

Finally the last and most famous book contains the account of Scipio's dream and takes the statesman's reward beyond the grave, so that his achievement is seen *sub specie aeternitatis*.

If the truth must be told Cicero's Utopia is but a pale shadow of Plato's and the fragmentary character of *The Republic* makes it difficult to assess in detail. Many readers prefer the greater practicality of *The Laws*. The model is still in some sense Plato, though Cicero is elaborating, not modifying his ideal state, and the inevitable link with Roman law means that he is less reliant on the Greeks. The first book however is introductory and theoretical, and is patently derived from some Greek source or sources, whether Panaetius, Antiochus of Ascalon or some other.[43] Cicero, his brother Quintus and his friend Atticus are the interlocutors, A leisured introduction sets the scene, but Cicero soon makes it clear that his theme is no ideal system of law but the familiar *ius civile*,[44] though it is to fit into a wider pattern. Law is defined as practical wisdom whose material force is to command right action and ban wrong action.[45] This is Stoic enough, but it is a practical Roman who suggests that the right of justice lies in law, even if he does go on immediately to the universal law of Nature. Justice then is rooted in Nature; but Cicero's aim is practical not theoretical: it is directed to strengthening constitutional government, to establishing political stability, and to curing the ills of mankind.[46] Not all that is found in state-law is just; this further confirms that justice must be derived from natural law not civil law: the distinction is again a Stoic one. State laws must therefore be judged by the standard of justice, not the other way round, and justice is to be pursued for its own sake. Cicero has a curious anticipation of the epigram 'Honesty is the best policy, but the man who acts on that principle is not an honest man.'[47]

The second book deals with the religious institutions of the ideal commonwealth. It is, Cicero claims, essential that the citizens be convinced from the outset that the gods are lords of the universe and in control, that they are benefactors, and that they take cognizance of piety and impiety.[48] This follows Plato, but it also follows the practice of the Roman establishment, who, however sceptical they might be themselves, saw the political value of religion.[49] So Cicero in archaic language drafts legislation defining the proper attitude to worship. Wrong actions will be punished by men, wrong attitudes by God. He then expounds his laws. Most interesting is the classification of gods: first the traditional gods; then those whose meritorious qualities have won them a place in heaven, from Hercules to Quirinus (the way is thus open for others to be added, from Julius on, though Cicero would have abhorred the thought); then those personified qualities which lead men to heaven, Intellect, Virtue, Piety, Faith; finally, the ancestors. Cicero goes against Roman practice in not allowing personified powers of evil, and not permitting the introduction of new gods on private initiative. But in general he is concerned to mention the familiar offices and familiar rituals, and Quintus in fact says 'It seems to me that this religious system of yours is not so very different from the laws of Numa and our own practices.'[50]

The third book in turn outlines the political institutions of the ideal commonwealth. Once again Quintus comments on their similarity to Roman institutions,[51] and Marcus claims that the Roman system does in fact conform to the balanced type of constitution approved in *The Republic*. There is great stress laid on the magistrates, who are described as the voice of the law.[52] They determine the constitution of the state.[53] Cicero's variants from Roman practice are for the most part slight, but the proposal that censors exercise power continuously for periods of five years greatly increases their power, and at the same time minority control of the state.[54] Cicero oddly clutters up his ideal state with the residue of the quarrels of patricians and plebeians. It is in one sense his concession to democracy, but, when pressed by Quintus, he explains that the function of the tribunes in his constitution is not to defend the people but to keep them under control.[55] A pious hope expresses the need for calm and sedate behaviour in assemblies of the commons:[56] as well offer such a prescription to a modern football crowd. Only at one point does Cicero allow that early Utopian writers have anything useful to contribute, and even then he may be basing his views on practice rather than theory. He concedes the value of *nomophylakes*, guardians of the laws; the censors will have to execute their responsibilities.[57]

Here the treatise, as we have it, breaks off. We know that Cicero began writing it in 52 and took it up again in 46–5; we know also that it was not published in 44.[58] It is likely that the fourth book dealt with the administration of justice. We have fragments of a fifth, and it seems most probable that six were planned,[59] but we do not know whether they were completed.

Cicero's work is important for its limitations. Not for him the high speculations of a Plato or the romantic imagination of an Iambulus. His feet were rooted in Roman soil, and he cannot see far beyond the institutions of Rome. Yet he saw far enough to touch the future as he failed to control the present. His concept of the *rector*, although he did not intend it that way, did in fact humanize the principate and influence it for good; the *prudentia* he assigned to his ideal statesman is precisely the *providentia* which Tiberius so proudly claimed.[60] Further, although Cicero had no notion of institutions which might serve the world, he did place the institutions of Rome in the context of the universal law of Nature. 'There is in fact a true law – right reason acting in accordance with nature. It reaches out to every man, it is unchanging and everlasting. Positively, it summons men to do their duty; negatively, it deters them from crime. In both it influences the righteous and has no effect on the wicked. It is an offence to oppose this law; it is not permissible to repeal any section of it; it is not possible to annul it. Neither senate nor people can absolve us from this law, and we need no outside exposition to interpret it to us. This law will not vary from Rome to Athens, or from present to future. There will be one single eternal unchangeable law for all peoples at all times, and, as we might say, one common master and ruler of all, God, the author, interpreter and promulgator of this law. Anyone who will not obey this law is trying to escape from himself; he is denying his human nature; and he will suffer the worst of all penalties, even if he succeeds in escaping all the other commonly conceived punishments.'[61] These are Stoic commonplaces, but it was Cicero who transmitted them to Rome, and in so doing helped the mental revolution which transmuted the city into the world and the world into the city. It was this which won him the tribute of his great adversary, Caesar, 'It is better to extend the frontiers of the mind than to push back the boundaries of empire.'[62]

Caesar is indeed the fourth who must have a place here, though only briefly, seeing that he like Catiline, has been claimed as a visionary and an idealist without justification.[63] As consul in 59 – the consulship of Julius and of Caesar – he was much concerned with his bargain with Pompey and Crassus, and with strengthening his own position; more statesmanlike measures dealt with the colonization of Novum Comum, with bribes and elections, and with the publication of senatorial proceedings. But there is no sign of an overriding vision. The civil war was nothing to do with political idealism but was fought for his personal safety; the stress on his country's honour is the merest propaganda, and in any case refers to the actuality of the present rather than the vision of the future.[64] More significant are Caesar's words, recorded by Cicero, that his natural span of life and his honour had had their due.[65] There is no consummatory purpose there. Caesar found himself in sole power through the folly of his opponents. In power his measures were opportunist and unsystematic: the reform of the calendar; sumptuary laws; schemes for public works; revision of debt, carried out with extreme moderation; careful control of the corn supply; the development of colonies; the reform of local government; the restriction of the *collegia*: the abolition of the tax-farming in Asia; schemes for traffic and transport, like the Corinthian canal; the extension of the senate; the introduction of non-Italians. These measures show strong individuality but not systematic reform. He was not afraid to curb the commons by restricting the corn dole, the businessmen over the tax-farming, the aristocrats through the sumptuary laws. His only immediate plan was to revert to the life of a soldier and, like Alexander, march east to conquer Parthia. Comparisons are misleading. Gracchus had a clear-cut programme; Caesar did not. Marius had no political acumen; Caesar did. Sulla was ruthless; Caesar knew when it was politic to be clement. Pompey was indecisive; whatever Caesar was, he was not that. Cicero had a philosophical plan for the permanent ordering of the state; Caesar's legislation was *ad hoc*. As Syme says, 'Caesar was not a revolutionary. If he had begun a revolution, his next act was to stem its advance, to consolidate the existing order.'[66]

Caesar was murdered, and civil war and ruthless executions followed. Then came an uneasy truce as Octavian, the future Augustus, cold and implacable, was master of Italy, and Antony, warm and wilful, was overlord of the east and philandering with Cleopatra. Antony's brother Lucius made a stand against Octavian in Italy, and was defeated. Antony came west, and in October 40 at Brundisium the two potentates arrived at a new agreement, and Antony married Octavian's sister Octavia. Behind this agreement lay the figure of Pollio, consul in 40, Antony's man but a moderate and a reconciler. Vergil, pacifistic and until recently an Epicurean, wrote Pollio a poem to celebrate the reconciliation and to anticipate the birth of a son who would reunite the Roman world. This is surely the occasion of the poem, which Vergil expounds tactfully; it is the father's prowess which will impose peace on the world, but at the last it is the mother whom he is to recognize with a smile.[67] We call it the Messianic Eclogue, and there is some possibility that Vergil was aware of the prophecies of Isaiah and inserted an allusion to them out of compliment to Pollio.[68] For Pollio had Jewish connections; we actually read in Josephus of Pollio, a Pharisee who advised the Jews to accept Herod as their king.[69] The consul Pollio was a personal friend of Herod, and Herod's sons, Alexander and Aristobulus, came to live with him.[70] And when Vergil refers to the song of Cumae, the Sibylline Oracles themselves have in many instances a strongly Jewish slant. So Vergil sketches an ideal world.

> The last generation of the song of Cumae has now arrived;
> the great cycle of the ages is beginning afresh.
> The maiden Justice is now returning, the rule of Saturn is returning,
> now a new race is being sent from the height of heaven.
> A boy is being born, with whom the race of iron will cease,
> and a race of gold be born throughout the earth.
> Be gracious to his birth, immaculate Lucina; your Apollo rules at last.[71]

Casta fave Lucina: tuus iam regnat Apollo. Lucina is the goddess of childbirth and light, Apollo the god of the sun, and of the arts of peace, and of renewal. All traces of crime shall disappear, and the countries of the earth be rid of continual terror and be brought to peace. The earth will produce her crops untended, the herds will no longer be terrified by lions, snakes and poisonous plants will be unknown, the spices of Mesopotamia will grow in Italy, the fields will be golden with corn, the shrubs red with grapes, the trees will flow with honey. There may be a brief period when the sins of sea-going and suspicion, agriculture and war will continue (this is partly a douche of realism, partly a hankering after epic heroism) but the day will come when the earth will give her sustenance freely and the sheep graze with their fleeces ready dyed (T. E. Page has a quotable comment: 'There is only a step from the sublime to the ridiculous and Virgil has here decidedly taken it.'[72])

> 'Come swiftly, such ages!' the Fates sing to their spindles,
> in harmony with the unchanging power of destiny.[73]

So Vergil makes his contribution to Utopia: the memories of a golden age, a new reign of peace and prosperity for all, Justice descending from heaven, Nature conspiring as in the dreams of Euhemerus or Iambulus and the child growing to kingship under the reign of Apollo the sun-god.[74]

But the child was a girl; no son was born to rule a world brought to peace by his father's valour. Octavia, thoroughly good woman that she was, could not satisfy the more colourful Antony; the memory of Cleopatra stirred in his blood. He and Octavian were temperamentally poles apart, the one impulsive, the other calculating, and he became convinced that ultimately co-operation was impossible. By the end of 37 he had got rid of Octavia and married Cleopatra. Cleopatra was a remarkable woman, one of the most remarkable of all women, and she was for centuries remembered in Egypt as a heroic, legendary figure, 'the most illustrious and wise among women', 'great in herself and in her achievements and in courage and in strength.' 'Rome' wrote Tarn of her, 'who had never condescended to fear any nation or people, did in her time fear two human beings; one was Hannibal, and the other was a woman,'[75] and when Vergil sought to express in epic personification the dangers besetting Rome in her imperial career he summed them up in a woman, Dido. Antony does not seem to have been a man of consuming ambitions. Cleopatra and Octavian were, and he was crushed in the conflict. Cleopatra too had her Utopian vision. She would cast down Rome from heaven to earth, then raise her from earth to heaven, inaugurate a golden age for Asia and Europe alike, and end feud, war and bloodshed.

> Tranquil peace shall journey to the land of Asia.
> Europe shall then be blessed, the atmosphere be fruitful,
> lasting, sturdy, free from storm or hail,
> bearing all creatures of the world, winged and earthbound.
> Blessed above all the man or woman who shall see that day. . . .
> For from the starry sky, in its fullness the rule of law
> and righteousness will descend upon man, and with it
> the saving grace of concord, cherished beyond all else by mortals,
> love, trust, friendship with the stranger. Far from man
> poverty will flee, compulsion will flee,
> and lawlessness, carping, envy, anger, folly,
> murder and deadly strife and bitter conflict,
> robbery by night and every evil – in those days.[76]

So Rome and Alexandria played off the Sibyls against one another, one oracular vision confronting another. The ingredients are the same: peace, the supernatural co-operation of nature, justice descending from the sky, the starry sky (a touch of astrology), concord, economic prosperity, political freedom, and an end to sin and crime. Cleopatra renamed the son she bore Antony, Alexander Helios, Alexander the Sun.[77]

Perhaps it was propaganda only. At least it was worth putting out as propaganda. There was idealism in the air. A Utopian vision struck a responsive chord in others to whom it was shown. Cleopatra's dream was to remain a dream. At Actium Antony's fleet let him down. Apollo, the god of Actium, favoured Octavian. Cleopatra planned on. They might start again in Spain, and follow Sertorius; they might like Iambulus sail into the Indian Ocean and found a new independent kingdom there. But Antony was broken and listless. The advance of Octavian on Alexandria roused him to momentary action and he won a momentary advantage. But there was a noise that night, and Octavian put it about that the sound was of Antony's god, Dionysus-Osiris, abandoning the city.[78] Antony committed suicide and died in Cleopatra's arms. Cleopatra and her conqueror faced one another, and we do not know what passed between them. He gave her room to act, and she took her life. With the rule of the sun still in her mind she chose to be stung by the asp, which ministered to the Sun-god and deified those whom it struck.[79]

> She dared to look on her falling kingdom
> with unchanged expression, courageous to handle
>   fierce asps and drink
>   black poison to her heart,
> with greater power once resolved on death,
> too proud to be carried on cruel warships
>   uncrowned in haughty triumph –
>   that woman not to be crushed.[80]

CHAPTER XIX

THE CITY OF THE WORLD[1]

FROM THE DISASTERS OF THE LATE REPUBLIC Rome recovered, through the practical sagacity of Augustus, carried on by his successors, so that already at the beginning of the first century AD Ovid could write:

> Other peoples are granted land with fixed boundaries.
> For the Romans the limits of city and world are the same.[2]

So Jupiter in Vergil:

> I set no bounds of space or time upon the Romans.
> I have granted them empire without limit.[3]

Imperium sine fine dedi. So Tibullus is the first to speak of Rome the eternal city, *urbs aeterna.*[4]

What Augustus achieved was in its simplest form to organize a system of imperial government, which, though imposed, would work efficiently, and, as is sometimes forgotten, he gave to the city of Rome a municipal administration suited to its size; he began too the process by which the public buildings reflect the size and status of the capital. The republican municipal administration was not abolished, but officials were added in charge of the newly formed praetorian guard, the general city administration, the watch and the corn supply; and officials drawn from the Senate to control the river, the water supply, the public buildings, the roads, the treasuries. Imperially, although there was a formal division between the emperor's provinces and the senate's provinces, the great change was the effective co-ordination of imperial policy through the emperor's oversight.

Although the régime was imposed from outside, two major factors kept the subjects sweet.[5] The first was the genuine local responsibility. The Romans encouraged the self-governing municipality. In the east where they found them, they left them, sometimes as *liberae et immunes,* independent and free from taxation. In the west where they did not find them they developed tribal capitals like Lyons or Tarraco, or founded colonies of veterans like Cologne (Colonia Agrippina) or Merida (Emerita). If there was nothing that could possibly be so developed, then and only then would they use some organization based on tribes and cantons, but it was regarded as a temporary expedient suitable for backward peoples while they were being led into the civilized state of town-dwellers. The theory has lately been adduced that the complex formed by Hadrian's Wall and *vallum* was designed not merely to keep the northerners out but to keep the southerners in.[6] It marked off the extent of those to be 'civilized'. There were certainly recognizable municipalities south of the Wall; none north of it. And the citizens of municipalities were proud of their standing in 'free states' and if they served as local senators (*decuriones, curiales*) or magistrates, are careful to record the fact.

The other factor was the extension of citizenship. We have seen how the laws of 90 and 89 BC met an uprising of Rome's Italian allies by conceding citizenship to all of Italy south of the Po. This established the idea of double citizenship. It was not unknown to Greek communities of the Hellenistic age, whether as part of a federal constitution, a reciprocal arrangement between cities, or an extension of favour to individuals from another community. The immediate strength of the relationship was psychological. It was seldom possible for those from other parts of Italy to go to Rome to exercise their theoretical right to vote, and only relatively few of the wealthy would seek a political career at the capital. But psychologically it was important. Roman citizenship gave status. More, it meant that the subject-cities did not feel themselves as subjects; they were part of the family, so to say. The Hellenistic monarchs had never achieved this. It was a technique which Rome steadily developed across the years. Julius Caesar was charged with using it too freely.[7] Augustus was more cautious; he said that he preferred to see the Treasury lose rather than the citizenship cheapened.[8] But he founded colonies, accepted legionaries into the citizen-body, granted rights to individuals, and to some communities (as in Sicily), allowed Latin rights to other cities (thus giving citizenship to their magistrates), and limited but continued to permit the freeing of slaves, whose grandsons might then become full citizens. Claudius too favoured a generous extension of the citizenship, especially in Gaul.[9] Gradually, Gauls, Spaniards, Africans, Syrians were brought in, though Egyptians on the whole were left outside, and the note of caution is still strongly sounded in the correspondence between Trajan and Pliny.[10] Not till the early third century was the citizenship of Rome made virtually universal among the free inhabitants of the Empire.

In the result it is clear that Romans ruled by consent. In the first century AD the total population of the empire was perhaps 70,000,000. The armed forces numbered not more than a quarter of a million. Senior military and administrative posts, governors, procurators and legionary commanders were not more than a hundred, and probably less than eighty. Even at the end of the second century when the forces had increased to 330,000 and the senior administrative posts to about 250, it seems very small for such a vast domain.[11] One small example from within the empire illustrates this persuasively. From the borders of Egypt to the Atlantic, North Africa was policed by a single legion, nominally 6000 men but actually more like 5000, with auxiliaries making up a total of not more than 10,000. Yet in a small part of this same area, a handful of guerrillas in recent years held at bay the armies of France. Rome conquered unwilling peoples by military power, but she assimilated willing peoples by persuasive and diplomatic policy.

Dreams of Utopia continued into Augustus' reign. It was some time about now that Diodorus Siculus published the world history which he called *The Library*.[12] He had been garnering his material over some thirty years before Actium. Rome was the centre of his activity, though he travelled as far as Egypt. He is, as his title suggests, a scissors-and-paste historian,[13] but not without independent judgement, which affected his selection and presentation. In particular he shows the influence of Stoic universalism, the brotherhood of man under the providence of God. We have from him sympathetic accounts of the sufferings of the underprivileged, miners and other slaves.[14] Further, it is to him that we owe the preservation of the Utopias of Euhemerus and Iambulus.[15] The important fact is that a man of this generation is interested in ideal societies, and knows that his readers will equally respond to them.

Augustus, skilled manipulator of public opinion that he was, knew well how to play on this mood of idealism. In 17 BC he celebrated the Ludi Saeculares. For this we happen to have the account of the ritual by a historian of the fifth century AD, Zosimus, together with the oracle enjoining the celebration: an inscription of major importance, consisting of a letter of Augustus giving instructions as to the celebration, two senatorial decrees and a series of records of the quindecimvirs; and Horace's hymn.[16] The *saeculum* was the lifetime of the oldest person, 100 or 110 years, and the festival was based on the thought that the evil of the previous generation must be purged away and give place to a new period of innocence. There are traces of such a festival in 463, 363 and 263. In 249 however the need was felt to inaugurate a new *saeculum*. The first Punic War was pressing on the Romans and there were traces of panic. The ritual, which was Greek, was decreed by a Sibylline oracle. Near the Tiber was a subterranean altar called Tarentum, presumably as representing an access to the lower world. There for three nights black victims were offered to Dis and Proserpina: the idea was no doubt one of death and rebirth. The next celebration was in the key year of 146; why Augustus chose 17 BC we do not know.

Throughout the ceremonies the sacred number 3 is prominent. On May 26–8 the means of purification were distributed by the priests to all free people. On May 31 Augustus and Agrippa offered a sacrifice at Tarentum to the Greek Moirai, on June 1 to Eilithyia, goddess of childbirth, the Lucina of Vergil's poem, heralding a new age, and on June 2 to Mother Earth. The form of prayer is dry and concise; it is a prayer for the general prosperity of the state. The ritual is cathartic and looks to a new age. By day offerings were made to the old Capitoline deities (oddly without Minerva) and to the new deities, though not to Mars or to the divine Julius, who would have been considered inappropriate. On the third day Horace's hymn was sung by twenty-seven boys and twenty-seven girls. It must have been meticulously programmed by Augustus, which explains why it contrives to be both clever and unmemorable. It links the ideas of religion, morality and fertility, all appropriate to the birth of a new age of piety and justice. There is no direct mention of Augustus, only a veiled reference. All the deities involved in the ritual find mention, and with them are linked personifications of the virtues, but the emphasis is on Apollo, Augustus' presiding deity, the god of Actium, the god of light and culture, the god whose temple was Augustus' greatest foundation, as it stood with the great gold figure of the Sun as a charioteer high on its roof. Warde Fowler's suggestion that the hymn was sung twice, once before this temple and once on the Capitol, is very plausible. We must see the Ludi Saeculares as an attempt by Augustus to capitalize on the mood of expectancy, the mood of the Messianic Eclogue, as an affirmation that the Golden Age has now returned.

Together with the Ludi Saeculares should be considered the greatest sculptural monument of the Augustan Age, the Ara Pacis Augustae. The very title is significant in its ambiguity, for Pax speaks both of peace and of the favour of the gods, and the adjectival Augustae links that peace and favour with the emperor without unambiguously naming him as the divine giver. The frieze depicts a religious procession. The emperor himself has stopped to offer a libation. Behind him are the Vestals, the priests and the pontifex maximus: they are followed by the imperial family, the senators, and the people, men, women and children. It is hard not to think that the emperor scripted this personally: it speaks so clearly of so much that he professed and proclaimed. No one knew better the political value of religion; he was careful to foster it; and here is an eloquent tribute to priestly office and liturgical ritual. Politically he appears as *princeps, primus inter pares*. He is no oriental divine monarch receiving homage; Julius had been killed for no more. What we see is in the strict sense a political hierarchy, the emperor, his family, the senate, the people. The senators occupy a disproportionate space. Augustus wished to encourage the illusion, and, within limits, the actuality of continuing senatorial responsibility. After them come the people in their families, standing for the racial purity and increased family life which Augustus sought to foster.

The symbolism is further developed in four panels. On one Aeneas is arriving in Latium and sacrificing to the Penates, a cult which Augustus restored. A second depicts Romulus and Remus suckled by the wolf. In these two we have the emphasis on tradition, the simplicity of the past, and the qualities of piety and courage. A third shows the goddess Rome seated in peace with her armour laid aside; this is subtle propaganda; it tells, as Vergil's poem, of a world brought to peace by military power. Finally there is Mother Earth in all her fertility, she who received sacrifice on the third day of the Ludi Saeculares, standing for the blessings of peace.

Here too Augustus is playing on the vein of idealism, Messianism and the recovery of a lost Golden Age. He is too wise to be extravagant. The ideal is what the ordinary man will see as normalcy writ large. There is a ruling class and privileged subjects; the present is seen as the fulfilment of the past; the themes are religion, peace, an ordered politic, family life, prosperity. Augustus is not so much trying to realize an ideal commonwealth as to idealize the reality he has achieved. But the patterns are related.[17]

We can see another moment of dreaming at the beginning of Nero's reign.[18] Rome had suffered the morose and tactless efficiency of Tiberius, the ruthless megalomania of Caligula, and the uncouth appearance of Claudius, whose genuine capacity for paternalistic government was somewhat obscured by the behaviour of his wives and ministers. Now came this young, seemingly amiable boy, with his artistic sensibilities, under the guidance of the most sententious moral philosopher of the time. Surely a new age was dawning.

> The days of Saturn, the maiden Justice have returned;
> our age has found safety in return to the ways of old.
> The harvester stores his whole crop, hopeful, carefree;
> the wine-god is mature and slow; the herds browse unattended;
> the harvest is not with the sword; towns do not block their walls
> in preparation for ominous war; no woman, dangerous
> in motherhood, brings an enemy to birth. Unarmed our young men
> dig the fields, and the lad trained to the plough's slow movement
> gapes at the sword which hangs in his father's house ...
> Now the earth bears fresh crops in plenty untilled.
> Now the ships are secure, the waves lay anger and penance aside.
> Tigers gnaw the bit. Lions put on the harsh yoke.
> Be gracious, immaculate Lucina; your Apollo rules at last![19]

So a poet of the age echoes Vergil in seeing the advent of Nero as the opening of a Golden Age. Justice returns, peace is universal, the earth gives produce untended, the god of the sun is over all. So too in the nauseating flattery with which Lucan prefaces his *Civil War*, after suggesting that all the carnage was worth while if only to produce a Nero, he looks forward to the emperor's ascent to heaven, to hold Jupiter's sceptre, or to circle the earth in the sun-god's chariot (the allusion is significant: it is found also in the anonymous *Skit on the Death of Claudius*).[20]

> At that moment let mankind look to themselves and lay down
>   their arms!
> Let all the nations love one another! Let him send Peace
>   all through the world
> to shut fast the iron gates of Janus' militarism.

There is the universalism of the Hellenistic Utopias; the Romans place a peculiar and understandable emphasis on peace. So a coin with the head of Nero on one side, and on the reverse a coiled snake with corn and poppyhead, emblems of fertility, shows Nero as the Agathos Daimon, the good genius of the new age.

The reality lies as a sinister ground-bass to the symphony of Seneca's treatise *On Clemency*. Seneca describes his homily as a mirror to reveal the emperor to himself. He is to say to himself: 'Have I out of all mankind been privileged to be chosen as the gods' vicegerent on earth? I have the power of life and death over the nations. In my hand are the destinies and careers of individuals. Through my lips Fortune announces her particular gifts to each. My words afford occasion for joy to states and nations. Without my grace and favour no part of the world can prosper. I have but to nod my head, and thousands of swords, which my peace holds in check, will be drawn. ... But I keep the sword out of sight, I keep it sheathed. ... I wear clemency as my breastplate.'[21] The very commendation of clemency is a reminder of how absolute was the power that wielded it. There is an ambiguity here. Clemency represents the Greek *philanthropia*. In its literal sense this means 'love of mankind', but as the hoped-for attribute of the divine Hellenistic monarch it acquired an inescapable tone of condescension; it meant divinity looking on humanity, not men sharing with one another.[22] Seneca is aware of this absolute power, which can be used for good or evil; he hopes that it will be used for good, but knows that it may not be. An ideal which rests on the integrity of a single individual endowed with absolute power is a fragile one. Suetonius might praise Nero's early attempts to emulate Augustus, his generosity, clemency and affability.[23] But it was not long before temperament and affectation passed into cruelty and debauchery, and Seneca found himself publicly defending the crimes which arose from the failure to follow his advice.[24] Yet the Greeks idolized Nero to the end, and for years dreamed of Nero Redivivus, who would come again and with his second advent inaugurate the age of gold.[25]

There was another strand in Stoicism besides Seneca's conformism.[26] It is exemplified by Thrasea Paetus and Helvidius Priscus, and provided what has been called the philosophic opposition to the principate.[27] It was not in fact opposition to the principate as such. Under the guidance of Poseidonius the Stoics had come to favour the mixed constitution, which brought together the best elements of monarchy, aristocracy and democracy. But throughout, as we have seen, the Stoics saw in kingship government in accordance with nature. It was not only Seneca who said 'The best condition of the state is under a just king'; Musonius Rufus expresses the same sentiment.[28] But monarchy was valid only if the king was just. How then could this be assured? There was some suspicion of Stoic sympathy for republicanism, not surprising in view of the parts played by the Stoic Cato and the Stoicizing Academic Brutus; Thrasea Paetus wrote the biography of Cato and admired both.[29] But the general indication is rather that the radical first-century Stoics stood against actions of which they disapproved, and it was perhaps in these terms – for we do not know the details – that Julius Canus and his associates opposed Caligula, and were executed for their pains. Under Nero Thrasea started his political career in a fairly normal way, but with a reputation for moralism and attention to minor matters. But when the murder of Agrippina was announced and justified to the senate he walked out, 'being unable to say what he wanted and unwilling to say what he might'.[30] Many of his subsequent actions were negative, and although the final charges under which he was executed include the general accusation that he was the centre of revolutionaries looking back to institutions of the past, one of a sect which threw up men like Tubero, Favonius and Brutus, who made a display of liberty to overthrow the empire, the more specific accusations were of his refusal to take the oath, his absence from the public pronouncement of vows, his refusal to sacrifice for the emperor's Safety or his Divine Voice, his absence from the senate for three years, and the fact that all over the empire people were scanning the bulletins avidly following his abstentions.[31]

After Nero's death and the Flavian succession the Stoic opposition continued with Helvidius Priscus in the lead.[32] Partly this consisted in attacks on the *delatores*, the 'informers' who had been responsible for so many Stoic deaths in Nero's reign. Helvidius denounced Marcellus in the senate, and the informer withdrew with the ominous words 'I leave you to your senate, Priscus, play the king in the presence of Caesar'. It was partly residual republicanism; Helvidius wrote in praise of Cato, and, according to Dio, 'cultivated the mob and and was for ever praising democracy and denouncing the monarchy. He banded men together as though it was the function of philosophy to overthrow the established order, insult those in power and bring about a revolution.' No doubt Helvidius stood in the radical tradition of Sphaerus and Blossius; his refusal to address the emperor as anything but 'Vespasian' is curiously Quakerly. But it was partly, it is reasonable to suppose, a policy that monarchy requires the best king, and therefore hereditary succession is to be avoided. We know of a scene in the senate when, after a speech by Helvidius, Vespasian left the senate in tears with the words 'Either my son shall succeed me or no one at all'. It is notable that the Cynics, who were close to the Stoics at this time, opposed the marriage of Titus and Berenice. Vespasian was tolerant; Mucianus was not and Helvidius was eventually executed, and 'the philosophers' banished.

Under Domitian there was further trouble, as well there might be. Opposition was becoming habitual with these radical philosophers, who were to some extent waving the banner of Roman tradition. There were panegyrics of Thrasea and Helvidius; there were also attacks on the morals of the court. It is significant that once the principle of *successio optimi* is accepted at the end of the century, Stoic opposition falls away. The ideal government for the Stoic depends on the ideal ruler.

The period that followed was idealized, albeit with a touch of asperity, by Edward Gibbon. 'If a man were called to fix the period in the history of the world during which the condition of the human race was most happy and prosperous, he would without hesitation name that which elapsed from the death of Domitian to the accession of Commodus. The vast extent of the Roman empire was governed by absolute power, under the guidance of virtue and wisdom. The armies were restrained by the firm but gentle hand of four successive emperors, whose characters and authority commanded involuntary respect. The forms of civil administration were carefully preserved by Nerva, Trajan, Hadrian, and the Antonines, who delighted in the image of liberty, and were pleased with considering themselves as the accountable ministers of the laws. Such princes deserved the honour of restoring the republic had the Romans of their days been capable of enjoying a rational freedom.'[33] It is the appalling fact that, with the possible exception of some periods in the history of China, never since – or, for matter of that, before – has so large an area of

the globe known so long a period of untroubled peace. Travel was swift and
safe. Law developed and became more humane; notable changes were the clear
distinction between intention and act, and the better treatment of slaves. This
was the fulfilment of what the elder Pliny called 'the immeasurable majesty
of the peace of Rome'.[34] But Gibbon had a shrewd eye for weakness. 'A just,
but melancholy reflection embittered, however, the noblest of human enjoy-
ments. They must often have recollected the instability of a happiness which
depended on the character of a single man. . . . The ideal restraints of the senate
and the laws might serve to display the virtues, but could never correct the
vices, of the emperor.' The word 'ideal' there is meticulously chosen. Still, the
achievement was real enough. Rome was the city of the world.

Aelius Aristides, rhetorician and hypochondriac, in his speech to Rome
delivered in AD 143 gives an idealized but not insincere picture of the significance
of Roman imperial rule. 'A common democracy of the world has been established under one, the best ruler and marshal; and all come together into a
common agora, each receiving his due.' He sees the significance of the extension of citizenship: 'Many in each city are fellow citizens of yours, no less than
of their own kin, although some of them have never seen this city.' He sees
the power of the Roman peace: 'As on a holiday the whole civilized world
lays down its ancient burden, iron, and has turned to adornment and all glad
thoughts with power to realize them.' What Rome has brought is freedom
from fear. And he explicitly says that the humane order and harmonious authority of Rome has turned Utopia into reality.[35]

In the second century Lucian in *A True Story* provides evidence that Utopianism was still in the air in the eastern Mediterranean. Not that he himself
was in any sense offering a Utopia, nor that we have any evidence that anyone
else was doing so. But there is a strong element of parody in *A True Story*, and
it is idle to parody unfamiliar works. We can legitimately deduce that a fairly
high proportion of Lucian's readership were familiar either at first or second
hand with Euhemerus and Iambulus.

Euhemerus first. Lucian saw that the main object of Euhemerus' work was
religious not political.[36] So he finds a pillar of bronze inscribed by Heracles
and Dionysus, and other evidences of their real presence, footprints, and a river
of wine: that he is thinking of Euhemerus is shown by the fact that the river is
navigable. A further reminiscence of the Sacred Inscription may be seen in the
inscription of the treaty between the Sunnites and Moonites on a pillar of
electrum set up in mid-air.[37] Stengel considers that the Isle of the Blest owes
something to Panchaïa.[38] In fact there is little direct debt; it is rather to Iambulus that Lucian has gone. The isle is associated with the Arabian spice-lands;
it is holy ground. Myrrh, which grows on the Sacred Isle in profusion, flows
through the Isle of the Blest. The whole picture in each case is blithely idyllic,
and the specific mention of the songbirds is a prominent feature in Euhemerus.
Temples and burnt-offerings, an obvious enough feature, possibly again reflect
Euhemerus' religious purposes. But earlier, inside the whale, there is a passage
clearly calling Panchaïa to mind.[39] There is an extensive forest, containing

many grape-vines which produce wine of great sweetness, and nuts which the sailors eat. There is a spring of beautiful cold water, and bathing there is possible. Birds fly around. Vegetables are grown. And in the middle is a temple to Poseidon. This is clear parody of Euhemerus, sharpened by being set inside the whale. But what is interesting and most important is that Euhemerus' idyllic setting has been transcribed, and something of his ideas on religion has left its mark. But of his political and economic ordinances there is not a trace. Here as elsewhere the influence of Euhemerus' political ideas was negligible.

The reference to Iambulus is explicit; he wrote of many weird discoveries in the ocean, his lies being clear to any reader, but attractive in the reading.[40] But then (the hit is at Plato) falsehood is always a characteristic of those who profess philosophy.[41] And so Lucian begins his story saying that he is truthful at least in admitting that he is a liar. The opening of his adventure is based on Iambulus; they set sail, run into a storm and arrive at an island. After adventures there they visit some islands in the air. There they are met by the Vulture Cavalrymen riding on large three-headed vultures, an improvement on Iambulus' fantasy of the children.[42] These are amazed at their arrival, after so much air to cross. Everything there is of unusual size, which Lucian naturally exaggerates, making the fleas as large as twelve elephants.[43] While there they war with the inhabitants of the sun. This is partly derived from some late Stoics who declared the sun to be inhabited,[44] partly from Iambulus' Children of the Sun. They also visit the moon, whose people have peculiar physical constitutions.[45] Where the Children of the Sun have ears with large openings and a kind of valve, the children of the moon have plane-leaves for ears. Later in the story they sail to a group of five islands, with sweet breezes such as those which blow from the Arabian spice-lands.[46] Here they land on the Isle of the Blest, and are permitted to stay for seven months. A single ruler gives jurisdiction, though he has associates whom he consults. There do not appear to be laws or legal procedure, and this perhaps reflects the type of administration Iambulus proposed. The ruler can enjoin medical treatment (an astonishingly advanced provision even in a skit);[47] banishment seems to be the only penalty. The ground is holy, and the number seven is associated with it. There are seven gates to the city, seven rivers of milk, and the travellers are allowed a seven months' stay. There are also 365 springs of water and as many of honey. The island has the external advantages Iambulus envisaged, and more. There are lush meadows. The fruit-trees bear thirteen times a year, every month and twice in one. Instead of wheat the loaves grow ready-baked. The climate is temperate and constant, there being only one season, and the zephyr being the only wind. For clothes they use delicate purple spider's webs, an improvement on the purpled down of Iambulus. The inhabitants also have their wives in common to the disappearance of jealousy.[48]

In the end despite protestations the visitors are ejected, and after further adventures suffer a final shipwreck.[49] Lucian is a satirist, and chooses his material for his own purposes. His account of Rhadamanthus sitting in judgement like Solomon may throw some light on procedure in the Islands of the Sun. But the important point is that he has shrewdly hit the real weakness of Iambulus' picture, the element of fantasy therein. Political theory which ignores the hard facts of material existence is in the last resort sterile, and wishful thinking is no substitute for the working out of a sound economic structure.

From the end of the second century crisis seized the empire. It was a complex crisis. It was partly economic, and partly military. Disease and depopulation played a part. The total effect was towards both a weakening and strengthening of central authority; weakening in that regions on the periphery like Palmyra or Britain might, at least for a time, assert their independence; strengthening in that individual municipalities could not solve the economic problems or counter the military threats, so that there was a shift from municipal to imperial government. Further, municipal responsibility in a changed economic situation became so pecuniarily exacting that it was a burden to be avoided, not a privilege to be claimed. We have the minutes of a meeting at Hermopolis in AD 192. Some of the details are obscure, but one Achilleus is under pressure to take the office of cosmete. He has calculated that the office of exegete combined with an annual payment of two talents annually – no small sum – would be a better bargain.[50] At much the same time we find a doctor claiming immunity from public service because of his profession.[51] There is an amusing, though rather later example, where one Ptolemy, already High Priest, is nominated Public Banker. He pleads his poverty; the President suggests that a little pressure might be no bad thing; and everyone shouts 'Honest, loyal Ptolemy!' 'Ptolemy won't let his tribe down!'[52]

The beginning of the crisis found a Stoic philosopher on the throne of Rome in the person of Marcus Aurelius.[53] Selected from his youngest days for the highest position, and lauded alike by his contemporaries and posterity, he is in truth a pathetic figure, and it is hard not to feel that he has been overpraised. The wistful agnosticism of his diaries has struck answering chords in the minds of readers across the ages, but there is little to inspire in them. Myers reflected on his position as 'the saint and exemplar of Agnosticism'.[54] Plainly a certain poignancy attaches to Marcus' mention of his political hopes and ideals. It is curious that he never mentions Zeno in any connection. Plato, not Zeno, gave him his political ideal, and he was forever maintaining that political prosperity depended on philosophers achieving authority or those in authority becoming philosophers; the Christian Justin quotes the apophthegm back at the emperor.[55] The cold realism comes in a sentence in the notebooks. 'Do not expect Plato's Republic. Be content if things go forward the smallest fraction.'[56] Marcus would not have so written to himself if he had not had a hankering after Utopia; he more than once rebukes himself for asking for the impossible; in particular you have to work with people as they are.[57] He was interested in the more radical Stoics, Thrasea and Helvidius, whom he groups with Cato, Dion and Brutus. He claimed to have acquired a conception of a state in which there was equality under the law, which was administered according to the principles of equality and equal rights of speech, and in which the monarchy honoured above all the freedom of the subject.[58] The trouble is that it is a muddled conception: monarch and subject are not equal, and Marcus is torn between the practical problems he has inherited and his dreams of perfection. So with his universalism. In theory he is a universalist. The poet calls Athens 'Dear city of Cecrops'; is he, Marcus, not to call the universe 'Dear city of Zeus'?[59] But when it comes to the point his city is Rome in the things which make him Antoninus.[60] This, until the signal for retreat sounds, is his post; it is as a Roman that he is involved with politics.[61] Nothing seems to matter very much. Alexander and his groom perish alike.[62] Asia and Europe are but corners of the universe; the whole sea but a drop of water; Athos but a clod of earth; the whole present but a point of time.[63] No use to play Caesar. Life is short. The only harvest of life on earth is upright character and actions of social value.[64] So the emperor sees himself like a rocky promontory with the waves breaking over him.[65] So the man who wished for peace saw his empire racked by war. The man to whom health was indifferent saw a disastrous plague sweep over his people. The preacher of tolerance did not discourage persecution of the Christians in Lyons and Vienne, in Smyrna, and in Rome itself. The man to whom wealth was indifferent left the state disastrously bankrupt. And, as a crowning irony, the man who taught that the philosopher was a citizen of the universe and above the ties of family, reversed nearly a century's policy of adoptive succession in favour of his worthless son Commodus.

Out of the chaos caused by Commodus and his assassination the Severan dynasty emerged. Caracalla was a man of passionate personal ambition and utter ruthlessness. Yet he is associated with one of the great constructive measures of Roman history. In AD 212 the *Constitutio Antoniniana* conferred the citizenship of Rome on virtually all the free inhabitants of the empire.[66] Perhaps it made little practical difference, except to increase the number of those liable to the duty on inheritances, to tidy up some administrative anomalies, and to open careers in government service to more people. It was not seen by contemporaries as a great revolutionary move, and those in authority took no special pains to commemorate it in the coinage. But there are reasons for associating it with a universal vision of commonwealth. Caracalla idolized Alexander, imitated Alexander's attitudes, took the title of 'the Great', hoped to emulate Alexander's eastern conquests, and fancied himself a reincarnation of the Macedonian who changed the world.[67] Alexander may or may not have been a visionary, but by this time the vision of world unity had been imposed upon him. In the preamble to the decree Caracalla declares that the reason for the extension of citizenship was to show gratitude to the gods in rendering proper service to their majesty by bringing to their worship all his people. One other factor is of some importance. It is under the Severan dynasty that sun-worship in its near-eastern form comes to play a significant part in the state religion; this is clear enough from the coins.[68] Later generations saw Caracalla's act of statesmanship as the decisive moment in transforming the empire into the Stoic ideal of a universal community. At the beginning of the next century on the arch of Galerius at Thessalonica the emperors are attended by the figures of Eirene and Oikoumene, Peace and the Inhabited World. Peace and universalism were the gifts of Rome. Diocletian sees it his responsibility to provide for the whole world.[69] A panegyrist can see the glory of Rome in the universality of the senate.[70]

In the middle of the third century we encounter a curious episode. Plotinus, the great mystical philosopher, was a man who seemed ashamed of being in the body.[71] His life scarcely matters. He was born in Egypt in 205, came to Alexandria to study philosophy at the age of twenty-seven, found an effective teacher in a Platonist named Ammonius, with whom he studied for eleven years, joined Gordian's army somewhat implausibly as means of going east and finding out about Persian and Indian thought, escaped from the débâcle in Mesopotamia to Antioch, and so to Rome at the age of forty, taught for ten years there before putting his thoughts on paper. He was living in what Renan called 'that hell of a half-century' when disaster upon disaster beset the Roman empire. Nothing of this appears in *The Enneads,* unless his very other-worldliness is a reaction to the relativities of human life on earth. For Plotinus' philosophy is about the One, the transcendent First Principle, which is beyond being, and about the need to 'bring back the god in you to the divine in the Whole.'[72] Plotinus may stand in the line of succession from Plato, but he does not share Plato's interest in the contribution which philosophy might make to a healthy politic. He speaks of the political or civil virtues, Ambrose's 'cardinal' virtues, in a discussion which starts from, but sometimes leaves, Plato's *Republic;* they discipline us, teach us system and moderation, help to dispel false opinions, they are a kind of preliminary to the purificatory power of virtue on a higher level.[73] But Plotinus does not really mean by the political virtues anything which affects the structure of the state. They are simply the qualities expressed in social life, in relations with other human beings. Further, where Plato's Academy was a training ground for statesmen and the political advisers, the effect of study with Plotinus was to turn men away from state affairs. A doctor named Zethus had political ambitions; Plotinus was always trying to dissuade him. Senators came to Plotinus; Rogatianus actually sold his property and renounced his rank.[74]

It is the stranger that Plotinus should have been a friend of the emperor Gallienus, though that fascinating man had a streak of genius which in happier times might have been devoted to the sole task of developing the arts of peace. He aspired to be a second Augustus; in his patronage of Greek culture he recalls Hadrian; he directed an artistic revival of the baroque classicism of the Antonine period. Porphyry wrote: 'The Emperor Gallienus and his wife Salonina had the highest regard for Plotinus. He in turn made full use of their friendship. There was a town in Campania which was said to have been a community of philosophers, but which had fallen into decay. Plotinus proposed that they should restore this city, and once they had established it allot to it the surrounding countryside. The settlers were to live under Plato's laws, and the name of the city was to be Platonopolis. Plotinus guaranteed to move there in person with his associates. The philosopher's wish would have easily come true had it not been prevented by the jealousy, hostility or meanness of some courtiers.'[75] It is a curious story. The initiative came from Plotinus' circle; Zoticus versified *The Story of Atlantis*.[76] Whether the community proposed to go all the way with *The Republic* or to essay the less revolutionary but in some ways more repressive constitution of *The Laws* is not clear. Nor is it clear exactly which the town was and what philosophers had lived there, though one would naturally think of Pythagoreans. Nor can we see exactly what Plotinus was driving at. Was it to be a kind of retreat, a city of refuge? Was it to be an example, a demonstration of what could be done even in the third century? Was it directed to the political and economic rehabilitation of one small depressed area? Was it to be an enclave for attaining the One through the first stage of the civic virtues? Was it in fact a despair of practical politics or an assertion of practical politics? The community was not to consist solely of philosopher-kings; that is clear. It is hard to see Plotinus himself not finding the administration of such a community an intolerable distraction from mystical speculation. But he may have felt that men like Zethus and Rogatianus had a contribution to make in an ideal community which was impossible in the violent and corrupt ambitions of Rome.

Not long after, another piece of Utopia burst into the practicalities of Rome. The old gods had lost their power. The divinity of the emperor could not unite the empire in a half-century which saw some twenty-five emperors and literally innumerable pretenders: we can name eighteen in the brief reign of Gallienus alone, and tradition speaks of a dozen more. The Persians had flourished in a religion which exalted Light against Darkness. The centre of gravity within the empire had moved east, and Syria knew its sun-gods, and all the excesses of Elagabalus were insufficient to discredit them. In 274 Aurelian introduced the Sun as the supreme deity of Rome. At Emesa he claimed to have been sustained by the Sun's divine help.[77] In Rome he built a superb new temple to the Sun, who was declared 'Lord of the Roman Empire', *dominus imperii Romani*, and served by a new priestly college manned by senators. The issues behind this development were no doubt complex. The form of the cult was Roman, but it might forge together in Roman patriotism worshippers of Apollo, Mithras and Elagabalus, and we cannot escape the association with universalism, social justice, and the birth of a new age.

The emergence of Christianity to power meant one enormous change, which was at once theological, social, political and psychological. For the Greeks and Romans religion had been a function of the family, and of the extended family which was the state. Religion had sprung from social and political relationships, and it is not unjust to say that it had subserved them. For the Christians religion was independent of any particular political or social order, and, at least in theory, political and social thinking should be derived from religion, not the other way round.

But although the Christian Empire was in one sense a new beginning, in another it was a continuation, and Lactantius greets the establishment of Constantine in language which echoes Vergil: 'I begin my work under the auspices of your name, Constantine, Emperor Supreme, first of the Roman rulers to renounce error, first to know and honour the majesty of the one true God. For when that happiest of days shone on the earth in which Almighty God raised you to the blessed height of empire, you gave a splendid omen that your government would be wholesome and desirable for all your subjects by restoring routed and banished justice and thus expiating the fearful crime of other men. For this deed God shall give you happiness, virtue and length of days, that loyal to the same Justice which guided you in your youth, you may in old age hold fast the tiller of the state, and receiving the great charge from your father, transmit to your children the custody of the Roman name.'[78]

Constantine's family had in fact been worshippers of the Unconquered Sun, and it was from his family god of the Sun that the vision of the Cross had come to him. The two religions blurred and blended in his mind. He imposed solar militarism in place of Christian pacifism, and replaced Christian love with solar justice. Within a century Ambrose and Augustine are propounding a Christian philosophy of justice in Ciceronian terms (derived from the solar pantheism of the Stoics). Constantine erected his own statue in the new capital which he called New Rome and others nicknamed Constantine's City, Constantinople: it bore the rayed crown of the sun-god, made, as he believed, from the nails of the true Cross: syncretism could hardly go further. It must be from much this period that there comes the Vatican mosaic which shows Christ sweeping across the heavens in the sun-god's chariot. He is the Sun of Righteousness, that is the Sun of Justice. No one knows when Jesus was born, but Christmas was transferred to the winter solstice, the Sun's birthday. Constantine's god was always a god of Power, never of Love. The Christian Empire was still the City of the World.

Looking back after the sack of Rome in AD 410 Rutilius Namatianus was still able to echo Ovid:

> You created a single fatherland for varied peoples.
> It was worth losing the name 'unbeaten' to be under your sway.
> In offering those you conquered partnership in your own law
> you made a single city what was once a world.[80]

The Christian poet Prudentius too saw Rome's great achievement that though the nations differed Rome had been instrumental in bringing their ways and their usage, their tongues, their genius, their worship, into obedience to one law.[81]

CHAPTER XX

THE CITY OF GOD

ROME FELL TO ALARIC, and the echoes reverberated round the world. In Africa Augustine – if the sermon be his – spoke words of consolation to his horror-stricken congregation.[1] He has heard news of fire, looting and massacre, and wept at what he has heard. In Palestine Jerome learned the news and wrote: 'A terrible rumour has reached us from the West. Rome had been besieged; the citizens were driven to ransom their lives for money. Then, stripped of possessions as they were, they were again besieged; this time it was their lives not their property at stake. My voice sticks in my throat; tears choke the words as I dictate them. The city which had conquered the world has itself been conquered. Worse: starvation outran the sword; there were not many citizens left to take prisoner. The people were driven mad by starvation and turned to feed on horror; they tore one another limb from limb to provide meat. Even the mother did not spare the baby at her breast. 'In the night was Moab taken, in the night did her walls fall down.' 'O God, the heathen have come into thine inheritance; thy holy temples have they defiled; they have made Jerusalem an orchard. The dead bodies of thy servants have they given to be meat unto the fowls of the heaven, the flesh of thy saints unto the beasts of the earth. Their blood have they shed like water, and there was none to bury them.'[2] 'If Rome can perish,' he asked, 'what can be safe?'[3] Pelagius was actually in Rome at the time, and described the scene he saw. 'It happened only recently, and you yourself heard. Rome, the mistress of the world, trembled with terror on hearing the warcry of the trumpets and the ululations of the Goths. At that moment where was the aristocracy? Where were the upper classes, so proud of their distinctions? Everyone was huddled together, terror-struck; every home was racked with grief; terror stalked around and held us all in its grip. The spectre of death moved before all our faces alike.'[4]

The Christians voiced their horror. The pagans were struck dumb. The calamity was too shocking; their grief was too deep for words. Rutilius Namatianus as prefect in 414 must still have been helping the recovery; but in his poem *On His Return* he does not allude to the fall of Rome. Zosimus wrote his history of Rome's decline in the 420s but he does not carry his story as far as the siege. The general attitude of the pagans was perhaps that of Macedonius, vicar of Africa. He writes in courteous acknowledgement of the first four books of *The City of God*, but at the same time expresses his regret that Augustine has chosen to advert to the unhappy subject of Rome's fall.[5]

Some pagans blamed the Christians for the disaster.[6] Christianity, they said was a way of life incompatible with the normal obligations of citizenship, and the Christian refusal to meet evil with evil, and renunciation of violence meant that Christians had stood aside alike from military service and from the exercise of those magistracies which might involve capital punishment. Christianity, the argument ran, was politically and socially irresponsible. Celsus had said much the same thing two centuries and more earlier. Alongside this was the fact that the pagans had always seen Rome's destiny as a religious destiny. The *pax Romana* depended on the *pax deorum*. The Christians had turned men aside from the gods of the state, the ancient gods, and disaster was bound to ensue. It was obvious for all to see that the major calamities had come under the governance of those emperors who had forsaken the old gods and turned to Christianity.

These and similar complaints were voiced to Augustine by a non-Christian named Volusianus and a Christian named Marcellinus. Augustine's immediate reaction is contained in two long letters to his correspondents.[7] Fundamentally Augustine is saying two things. First, the story of calamity belongs to the decline of paganism rather than to the emergence of Christianity. It is the immoralities of the pagans not the moralities of the Christians which bear the guilt: witness their own writers, Sallust, say, or Juvenal.[8] The world's day is drawing to its close, and the natural and humanly caused calamities are a sign of this; but they are also a sign of the imminence of a new age, the everlasting blessedness of the heavenly city. Yet in this situation the unbelievers continue to rail against Christ's Church; and she shows what she is by patient endurance. The second affirmation is a thought unexpected. It is that the qualities criticized in Christianity are approved by the pagans themselves in themselves. Thus Cicero commended in Caesar that he would forget nothing but the wrongs done to him.[9] What is this but turning the other cheek? It is perhaps not the best of answers, of itself innocent, but tending to accommodate the Church to the state, especially as he goes on to insist that if all men were as the Christians taught them to be, it would be the salvation of the empire. In the long term, no doubt, but the New Testament promises no such facile or short-term success. Between the Sermon on the Mount and worldly wisdom there is a great gulf fixed.[10]

Augustine knew that a longer and more considered answer was called for. It took him the best part of fifteen years from inception to completion. He called it *The City of God: Against the Pagans*, or, for short, *The City of God*, and addressed it to Marcellinus. It is one of the most monumental and influential works ever written. In *Retractations* he gives a summary account of how he came to write it.[11]

'At the point when Rome fell by storm to the Goths under King Alaric, the worshippers of false gods of all sorts (whom we commonly call "pagans") made an attempt to attribute this disaster to the Christian religion, and surpassed themselves in their biting and bitter blasphemies against the true God. This kindled my zeal for the household of God. I began to write *The City of God* as an answer to their blasphemous misrepresentations. This work occupied me for several years; there were other problems pressing on me, to which I had to give priority. But I finally completed *The City of God* in twenty-two books. It had been a major undertaking. The first five books are directed against the argument that worldly prosperity depends on pagan polytheism, and that all the calamities around us have arisen from its suppression. The next five answer those who admit that such calamities in varying forms always have been and always will be our human portion, but who claim that polytheistic worship and its attendant sacrifices are a valuable investment against the life beyond the grave. These ten books then refute these idle and unchristian views. I wanted to anticipate the criticism that I exposed the errors of others without declaring my own position. The last twelve books are directed expressly to this, though of course I make my own position plain when appropriate in the first ten, and criticize my opponents' standards in the last twelve. The first four of these contain an account of the origin of the two cities, the city of God and the city of this world. The next four describe their history or progress, the last four their proper ends. The whole twenty-two books treat of both cities, but take their title from the better of the two: *The City of God*.'

A letter from Augustine to a priest named Firmus, discovered only in this century, is of considerable interest, though it adds little to our knowledge.[12] Firmus has asked for a copy of *The City of God*. Augustine sends him an unbound copy. To bind it in one volume would be clumsy. The obvious solution is to make two volumes of it. 1–10 will then give the refutation of the pagans and 11–22 an exposition of Christianity. If Firmus wants smaller units he could turn it into five volumes, 1–5 refutes the idea that worship of the pagan gods brings happiness or success here on earth; 6–10 refutes the idea that it brings happiness in the hereafter; 11–14 expounds the origin of the city of God; 15–18 its progress; 19–22 its appointed destiny. This reinforces the passage in *Retractations*; at the same time it gives a very clear outline of the work as Augustine planned it.

The contrast between the two cities had been part of his thought for many years. In the end it is only an adaptation of the pagan fable of the two ways, attributed in its most familiar form, 'Heracles' Choice', to the sophist Prodicus.[13] Jesus too sets a clearcut antithesis between the narrow gate of life and broad gate of destruction,[14] and this is taken up and elaborated by the early Fathers.[15] Also relevant is the Stoic antithesis which we have seen in Marcus Aurelius between the city of Cecrops and the city of Zeus. Seneca too had drawn out the two citizenships, one universal, natural and inclusive, the other limited, accidental and exclusive.[16] In taking it up, Augustine is the inheritor of both pagan and Christian wisdom, and he has made the theme his own. The antithesis appears first in 388, where the contrast is drawn between the lovers of things temporal and the lovers of things eternal.[17] A couple of years later a similar line is drawn between the mass of the wicked, the men of this world, and the succession of those devoted to the one God.[18] By the turn of the century the antithesis has begun to take the form of the two cities: 'There are two cities, one of the wicked, the other of the holy, and both extend from the beginning of mankind to the end of time. Physically they intermingle; spiritually they are separate – and will further be physically separated on the Day of Judgement.' Augustine takes as names and types of the two cities Jerusalem and Babylon, but we must remember that Babylon is also not infrequently in Christian writings a symbol for Rome.[19] At much the same time he began his commentary on *Genesis*. In this he contrasts two loves. The first is sacred, socially constructive, pursuing the common good for the sake of the fellowship of heaven, obedient to God, quiet and peaceable, preferring truth to false praise, friendly, desiring for others what it desires for itself, seeking the good of the neighbour. This is the love of the good angels. The second love is ugly, selfish, ambitious and authoritarian, usurping the place of God, restless, troublesome, hungry for praise, envious, forcing the neighbour for its own ends. This is the love of the evil angels. These two loves mark off from one another the two cities, the one of the righteous, the other of the wicked. Augustine expresses his intention to develop this last theme.[20] This promise is fulfilled in *The City of God*.[21]

Society to Augustine is a superficial whole, but beneath the surface it is split into two. The division goes back to the beginning of mankind, to the quarrel between Cain and Abel; Cain built a visible city, but Abel was a sojourner, and citizen of an invisible and eternal city.[22] (The division goes back even beyond that, into the angelic realm, as Augustine argues in the eleventh book.) The city associated with Abel is the City of God, the city to which the Scriptures bear witness, of which 'glorious things are spoken'.[23] Its motive power is that love of God which leads to indifference to self.[24] In it all is good, all righteous, all loving. Its origin is in God; its wisdom is in the light from God; its happiness rests in the enjoyment of God. 'It is, it sees, it loves. Its strength is in God's eternal nature, its light in God's truth, its joy in God's goodness.'[25] The city associated with Cain contains all that is evil, including the Devil. Its motive power is that love of self which leads to indifference to God. Mankind is then divided into two sorts, those who live as followers of God and those who live as followers of man. 'Mystically we call them two cities, that is, two human societies, one predestinated to reign eternally with God, the other to undergo eternal punishment with the devil.'[26] Augustine says that the two are temporarily mixed but will be isolated from one another at the end of time. The distinction between the two cities is the cardinal point in Augustine's analysis of all social institutions.

It is important to see that though Augustine sometimes speaks as if the City of God were equated with the Church this is not really part of his thought. The City includes among its citizens the good angels and the saints of past generations who are not visible members of the Church and even among the persecutors there are some saints; the Church is thus but one part of the City of God. But also the Church itself has in its members some who are not members of the City.[27] The Church therefore, while associated with the City of God in

Augustine's mind, is not identical with it. Similarly when Augustine speaks of the *civitas terrena*, the City of the World, his mind often turns to the Roman Empire. But the City of the World is not identical with the State. The City of the World contains all that is evil. But the state is not absolutely evil, despite Augustine's innuendo that it began in fratricide and continued that way;[28] on the contrary it is relatively good;[29] it is superior to anarchy. Absolute righteousness is impossible on earth even for the saints. Private property and political power are not found in the City of God; they arise from selfishness and greed. But owing to original sin, communism and anarchy are not practicable. Private property thus is relatively justifiable; it takes the sting out of greed; it is better than absolute sinfulness. Political power is justifiable in so far as it helps the individual to suppress the ambition for more power. The state therefore has its place in helping individuals in their pilgrimage to the City of God. To the Romans in fact Augustine has a delightful ambiguity. He is liable to impugn their morals and to treat them as a modern Babylon; the quarrel of Romulus and Remus is a quarrel between one evil and another.[30] But the Roman Empire grew under the Providence of God to control the evils of the world, to give a due though worldly reward in a moral order to self-sacrifice and other virtues, even when directed to limited ends, and for the genuine value of Roman universalism.[31]

Augustine's treatment owes a certain debt to Plato, as does all his thought, but Jaeger is wrong in saying that he took Plato's Republic and Christianized it into the City of God.[32] Plato shaped an ideal state by the light of reason, but Augustine is more interested in his censorship of immoral poetry than in other aspects of his society.[33] Augustine had assimilated a deal of Platonism, and it is even possible that he took the name 'City of God' directly or indirectly from Plato.[34] But he is not greatly interested in Plato's political thought. He alludes to *Timaeus* far more than to *The Republic*, and within *The Republic* is primarily interested in such topics as the immortality of the soul. He took his Platonism primarily from Plotinus, who had played down the Master's political concerns. The truth is that though Augustine is in his own way shaping the ideal society, that way is very different from Plato's.

Augustine's ideal society then is not found in visible institutions, but in the vision of the City of God. But this City is not divorced from life on earth. In the first place it is a genuine community. We might even say that it is *the* genuine community, the real thing which people are vainly searching for in their other forms of association. Its cement, its point of unity is the common love and worship of God; this common love and worship constitutes the community; Augustine says again and again that the members of the City of God 'enjoy community with God and with one another in God'.[35] Secondly in the City of God and in the City of God alone are realized the two great values of Justice and Peace. Here Augustine takes up the object of Plato's ideal society (and indeed Cicero's), and the greatest constructive claim of the Roman Empire, and claims that the City of God is needed for their full realization.

Cicero, it will be remembered, defined a state as the state or concern of the people.[36] Rome never conformed to that definition. Not for the obvious reason that it was never within the power of the people as a whole, but because Cicero also defines a people in terms of a common sense of justice. Rome had never known true justice. Augustine maintains this both theologically and practically: theologically in that he does not believe that true justice is possible apart from belief in the true God; practically in that Rome conquered by military power, and there was no justice there. 'Set justice aside then,' he says in the best known chapter of the whole work, 'and what are kingdoms but gangs of robbers on a large scale?' He tells the story of the pirate saying to Alexander 'I cause trouble with one small ship and am called a pirate; you cause trouble with a powerful fleet and are called an emperor.'[37] Important to see that Augustine, here as often, has Plato in mind. Plato thought that justice might be seen writ large in the state;[38] Augustine asserts that it is injustice which is so magnified. The difference between Plato and Augustine is in fact that although Plato believed in a transcendent order he in fact identified justice with the order of the state. But Augustine, in the Christian tradition and with the Stoics before him, starts from the universal order, the universal law. It follows that 'true justice exists only in that state whose founder and director (rector) is Christ, if it is all right to call it a state, since we cannot deny that it is a state or concern of the people.'[39]

Augustine's discussion of peace is one of the profoundest parts of The City of God.[40] The mystic meaning of Jerusalem is 'vision of peace' (this is not quite right, but the root meaning is there), and peace is the end of the Heavenly City. All men seek peace. Men go to war in order to achieve peace, a different peace from their present state but peace nonetheless. But human peace may be unjust, and the peace of wickedness does not deserve the name peace at all. 'The peace of the body is an orderly organization of its parts; the peace of the irrational soul is an orderly tranquillity of its appetites; the peace of the rational soul is an orderly harmony of knowledge and action; peace between body and soul is an orderly life and health of the living creature; peace between man and God is an orderly obedience in faith under an eternal law; peace in the home is an orderly agreement between those who live there as to who shall give orders and who obey; peace in the state is an orderly agreement between citizens as to who shall give orders and who obey; the peace of the Heavenly City is a perfectly orderly and perfectly harmonious community in the enjoyment of God and in mutual enjoyment through union with God; universal peace is a tranquillity achieved by order. Order is the allocation of things equal and unequal, each to its proper place.'[41] Every use of temporal things is related to the enjoyment of earthly peace in the Earthly City; in the Heavenly City it is related to the peace that is eternal. Peace is the fruit of love, love towards God and love towards the neighbour. Charity begins at home; the man who loves God will find the fruits of that love first in domestic peace. But he cannot rest there. He will be at peace, so far as in him lies, with all men, in the peace which men can have with one another, in ordered agreement, the order being to harm no man, and to give help wherever possible.[42] Clearly this peace does not consist in international organization. It is a personal commitment. But that personal commitment might lead to international organization and operate within the framework of international organization.

Rome fell; it had been built on violence, and in the end it reaped the harvest of violence.[43] But men survived, and built new cities and fresh communities. Utopia is nowhere. But men may live out the vision they have received in the community in which they find themselves. An earlier, unknown Christian writer had written: 'The distinction between Christians and the rest of mankind is not a matter of geography, linguistics or anthropology. They do not live in separate countries; they do not speak some curious language; they do not practise peculiar customs. . . . They live in states in different parts of the world, as each finds himself, and following the local practice in clothing and food and their general way of life, display the astonishing and admittedly unfamiliar character of their real citizenship. They live in their own fatherlands, but as resident aliens. They share in everything like citizens, and suffer everything like foreigners. Every foreign country is a fatherland to them and every fatherland a foreign country. . . . They live their lives on earth; their citizenship is in heaven. They observe the established laws and surpass them in their personal lives. . . . In a word, the Christians stand to the world as the soul stands to the body. They are spread through the cities of the world as the soul is spread through the limbs of the body. The soul dwells in the body, but is not of the body. The Christians live in the world, but are not of the world.'[44]

So too Augustine. 'So this Heavenly City lives on earth as an alien; it secures its citizens from every nation; it gathers its alien community from every language; it cares nothing about differences of custom, legislation or organization, which contribute to the search for earthly peace and its maintenance; it does not abrogate or destroy any of these, but rather preserves and follows them (for however different they are among different nations, they are directed to the identical end of peace on earth), provided only that they do not stand in the way of the religious worship of the one true God. So the Heavenly City in its pilgrimage on earth makes use of earthly peace; it cares about and actively fosters the working together of men's wills in matters which serve their mortal being in so far as accords with religious health; it links the earthly peace to the heavenly peace, the peace that is really the only peace for a rational being, a perfectly ordered and perfectly harmonious community in the enjoyment of God and in mutual enjoyment through union with God. . . . The Heavenly City, during its pilgrimage of faith, possesses this peace, and as a result of that faith lives a life of justice, as it links to the securing of that peace every good action towards God and the neighbour which it undertakes. For the life of any City is a life of community.'[45]

So we may say more widely, the ideal city lives in its citizens, here and now. '"You mean the city whose foundation we have just described," he said, "the one which exists only in words; I don't imagine it can be found anywhere on earth!" "Well," I replied, "perhaps there is a pattern of it in the heavens for anyone who is prepared to use his eyes, and using them to found a city in himself. It really doesn't matter whether the city exists or ever will exist. The man of real vision will live according to the citizenship of that city and of that city alone." '46

LIST OF PRINCIPAL
ABBREVIATIONS

ABSA *Annual of the British School at Athens*
Ael. Aelian
    HA Historia Animalium
    VH Varia Historia
Ael. Arist. Aelius Aristides
Aesch. Aeschylus
    Pers. Persae
Aeschin. Aeschines
Agatharch. Agatharchides
AJP *American Journal of Philology*
Alcm. Alcman
Alex. Aphr. Alexander of Aphrodisias
App. Appian
    BC The Civil War
Ap. Rhod. Apollonius of Rhodes
Apul. Apuleius
    Flor. Florida
Ar. Aristophanes
    Lys. Lysistrata
Arist. Aristotle
    Ath. Pol. Athenaion Politeia (Constitution of the
        Athenians)
    Met. Metaphysics
    NE Nicomachean Ethics
    Pol. Politics
    Rhet. Rhetoric
Arr. Arrian
    Anab. Anabasis of Alexander
    Epict. Discourses of Epictetus
Artemid. Artemidorus
Ath. Athenaeus
Aug. Augustine
    Cat.Rud. On the Catechising of the Unlearned
    CD The City of God
    C.Jul.Pel. Against Julian the Pelagian
    Ep. Letters
    Gen. ad litt. On Genesis word by word
    Lib.Arb. On Free Will
    Retract. Retractations
Aul. Gell. Aulus Gellius
    NA Attic Nights

BMC	*British Museum Catalogue of Coins*
Caes.	Caesar
	BC The Civil War
C.A.H.	*Cambridge Ancient History*
Callim.	Callimachus
	H. Del Hymn to Delos
CIA	*Corpus Inscriptionum Atticarum*
Cic.	Cicero
	Att. Letters to Atticus
	Cat. Speeches against Catiline
	De Am. On Friendship
	De Orat. On the Orator
	Fam. Letters to Friends
	Flacc. In defence of Flaccus
	Inv. On Invention
	Leg. Laws
	Leg. Agr. On the Agrarian Law
	ND On the Nature of the Gods
	Pro Lig. In defence of Ligarius
	Pro Marc. In defence of Marcellus
	QF Letters to his brother Quintus
	Rep. Republic
	Sest. In defence of Sestius
CIL	*Corpus Inscriptionum Latinarum*
Claud.	Claudian
	Nupt. Hon. et Mar. Marriage of Honorius and Maria
Clem. Al.	Clement of Alexandria
	Protr. Protrepticus
	Str. Stromateis (Miscellanies)
CP	*Classical Philology*
CQ	*Classical Quarterly*
CW	*Classical Weekly*
D.Chr.	Dio Chrysostom
Dem.	Demosthenes
	FL On the false legation
Did.	*Didache* (Teaching of the Twelve Apostles)
DK	Diels-Kranz. *Die fragmente der vorsokratiker*
D.L.	Diogenes Laertius
DS	Diodorus Siculus
Ep. ad Diognet.	Letter to Diognetus
Ep. Barn.	Letter of Barnabas
Epict.	Epictetus
	Man. Handbook
Epiphan.	Epiphanius
	Adv. Haer. Against All Heresies
Eur.	Euripides
	Andr. Andromache
	Supp. Suppliants
Eus.	Eusebius
	PE The Preparation of the Gospel
Ezek.	Ezekiel
F.Gr.H.	F. Jacoby *Fragmente der griechischen Historiker*

FHG	C. Müller *Fragmenta Historicorum Graecorum*
F.Ph.Gr.	F. Mullach *Fragmenta Philosophorum Graecorum*
Gen.	Genesis
Gnom. Vat.	*Gnomologium Vaticanum*
Hdn.	Herodian
Hdt.	Herodotus
Hellan.	Hellanicus
Heraclit.	Heraclitus
Hes.	Hesiod
	WD Works and Days
Hesych.	Hesychius
	De Vir. Ill. On famous men
Hipp.	Hippocrates
	Aer.Aq.Loc. Airs, Waters, Places
	Anc.Med. On Ancient Medicine
Hom.	Homer
	Il. Iliad
	Od. Odyssey
Hor.	Horace
	CS Carmen Saeculare
	Epod. Epodes
	Od. Odes
HP	*Herculaneum Papyri*
HSCP	*Harvard Studies in Classical Philology*
HTR	*Harvard Theological Review*
Iambl.	Iamblichus
	V.Pyth. Life of Pythagoras
IG	*Inscriptiones Graecae*
ILS	*Inscriptiones Latinae Selectae*
Ins. v. Perg.	*Inschriften von Pergamum*
Is.	Isaiah
Isoc.	Isocrates
	Antid. Antidosis
	Panath. Panathenaicus
	Phil. Philip
Jer.	Jeremiah
JHS	*Journal of Hellenic Studies*
Jn.	The Gospel according to John
Jos.	Josephus
	Ant. Jewish Antiquities
J.Ph.	*Journal of Philosophy*
JRS	*Journal of Roman Studies*
Jul.	Julian
	Or. Orations
Jul.Laod.	Julian of Laodicea
Just.	Justin
Lact.	Lactantius
	Inst. Div. Divine Institutes
Liv.	Livy
Lk.	The Gospel according to Luke

Luc.   Lucan
                   BC Civil War
                   VH True History
Lucr.   Lucretius
M.A.   Marcus Aurelius
Max. Tyr.   Maximus of Tyre
Mk.   The Gospel according to Mark
Mt.   The Gospel according to Matthew
Mus. Ruf.   Musonius Rufus
Nic. Dam.   Nicolaus Damascenus
Orig.   Origen
                   C.Cels Against Celsus
Oros.   Orosius
Orph.   Orpheus
                   Arg. Argonautica
Or.Sib.   Oracula Sibyllina
Ov.   Ovid
                   F. Fasti
                   Met. Metamorphoses
Paneg.Vet.   Panegyrici Veteres
Paus.   Pausanias
PBA   *Proceedings of the British Academy*
Pelag.   Pelagius
Phdm.   Philodemus
Philostr.   Philostratus
                   Imag. Imagines (Pictures)
Pind.   Pindar
                   Ol. Olympians
                   Pyth. Pythians
Plat.   Plato
                   Apol. Apology of Socrates
                   Hipp. Mai. Hippias Maior
                   Polit. The Statesman
                   Prot. Protagoras
                   Rep. Republic
                   Soph. Sophist
                   Theaet. Theaetetus
                   Tim. Timaeus
Plin.   Pliny
                   NH Natural History
Plot.   Plotinus
                   Enn. Enneads
Plut.   Plutarch
                   Alex. Life of Alexander
                   Cleom. Life of Cleomenes
                   Crass. Life of Crassus
                   De Alex.Fort. On Alexander's Fortune
                   Dem. Life of Demosthenes
                   Lyc. Life of Lycurgus
                   Mor. Moralia
                   Nic. Life of Nicias
                   Per. Life of Pericles

Q.Conv. Quaestiones Conviviales
Sert. Life of Sertorius
Tib.G. Life of Tiberius Gracchus

P.Oxy	*Papyri Oxyrhynchi*
Prud.	Prudentius
P.Ryl.	Papyri from the John Rylands Library, Manchester
Ps.	Psalms
Ps.Sol.	Psalms of Solomon
PW	Paully-Wissowa *Encyclop d. Klassischen Altertumswissenschaft*
Q.	Quintilian
Q.Curt.	Quintus Curtius
REG	*Revue des Etudes grecques*
Rev.	The Revelation of John the Divine
Rh.Mus.	Rheinisches Museum
Riv.di fil.	*Rivista di filologia*
Rut. Nam.	Rutilius Namatianus
Sall.	Sallust

Cat. The War with Catiline

Schol.	Scholia
Sen.	Seneca

Ben. On Benefits
Clem. On Clemency
Ep. Letters
Tranq. An. On Tranquillity of Mind

Serv.	Servius
Sext.Emp.	Sextus Empiricus
SHA	Scriptores Historiae Augustae
SIG	Sylloge Inscriptionum Graecarum
Soph.	Sophocles

Ant. Antigone

Steph.Byz.	Stephanus of Byzantium
Stob.	Stobaeus
Strab.	Strabo
Suet.	Suetonius
SVF	*Stoicorum Veterum Fragmenta* (Fragments of the Ancient Stoics)
Tac.	Tacitus

Ann. Annals
Germ. Germania

Thuc.	Thucydides
Tyrt.	Tyrtaeus
V.	Vergil

Aen. Aeneid
Ecl. Eclogues
G Georgics

Val. Max.	Valerius Maximus
Vell.Pat.	Velleius Paterculus
Xen.	Xenophon

Anab. Anabasis
Hell. Hellenica

Mem. Memorabilia
Oec. Oeconomicus
Resp.L. Respublica Lacedaemoniorum
Symp. Symposium

Zech.   Zechariah

NOTES
CHAPTER I

1 For a far more detailed treatment of this than I am able here to give it see J. L. Myres, *Geographical History in Greek Lands* (Oxford 1953): M. Cary, *The Geographic Background of Greek and Roman History* (Oxford 1949).
2 M. Rostovtzeff, *Orient and Greece*, p. 181, cited T. B. L. Webster, *Political Interpretations in Greek Literature* (Manchester 1948).
3 V. Ehrenberg, *Aspects of the Ancient World* (Oxford 1946), 37. The whole chapter repays careful study.
4 ibid. p. 41.
5 (Cic). *Ad Fam.* 4, 5, 4.
6 Hom. *Il.* 2, 100 ff.
7 ibid. 12, 321.
8 Hom. *Od.* 6, 12.
9 ibid. 8, 41.
10 ibid. 13, 14.
11 Hom. *Il.* 2, 211 ff.
12 Hom. *Od.* 2, 25 ff.
13 T. B. L. Webster, *Political Interpretations in Greek Literature*, 7.
14 Hom. *Il.* 8, 18–27.
15 ibid. 1, 423.
16 ibid. 13, 7.
17 ibid. 14, 153 ff.
18 ibid. 21, 383 ff.
19 ibid. 1, 423 cf. 23, 20–6.
20 K. H. W. Völcker, *Ueber homerische Geographie and Weltkunde* (Hanover 1830), 46–7.
21 Hom. *Od.* 1, 23–4 cf. 4, 83–4.
22 Hdt. 3, 17–18.
23 Hom. *Od.* 6, 43–6.
24 ibid. 13, 125 ff.
25 ibid. 9, 106 ff.
26 ibid. 6, 4–6.
27 ibid. 7, 104 ff.
28 ibid. 7, 112 ff.
29 ibid. 8, 558 ff.
30 ibid. 8, 246 ff. It is worth a passing note that Alcinous is speaking but despite what he says about clean clothes Nausicaa has had to remind him to get his washed – a happy touch.
31 ibid. 7, 155 ff.
32 ibid. 7, 11.

CHAPTER II

1 A. O. Lovejoy and G. Boas, *Primitivism and Related Ideas in Antiquity* contains an important chapter on this subject with an invaluable collection of passages. E. E. Sikes's pioneering *The Anthropology of the Greeks* (London 1914) is unfortunately not much to our purpose.
2 Hor. *Epod.* 16, 39 ff.
3 Plut. *Sert.* 8. See p. 157.
4 Isid. *Etym.* 14, 6, 8.
5 Mela 3, 36–7.
6 Aesch. fr. 196.
7 Strab. 11, 4, 3.
8 Ver. *Ecl.* 4, 18 ff.
9 Ver. *G.* 2, 136 ff.
10 Hom. *Il.* 13, 5–6; Strab. 5, 73; Aesch. *fr.* 198; Ath. 6, 2265; (Scymnus) *Orb. Descr.* 853; Strab. 7, 303; Justin *Hist. Phil. Epit.* 2, 2; (Anacharsis) *Ep.* 5; Cic. *T.D.* 5, 32, 90.
11 Hellan. fr. 96.
12 Solinus *Coll., App.* 22, 12–5.
13 Tac. *Germ.* 46; Plin. *NH* 6, 13.
14 Pind. *Pyth*, 10, 41.
15 Plin. *NH* 4, 12.
16 Callim. *H. Del.* 282.
17 Agatharch. *Lib. Jun. Phil.* 4 ff.
18 Scylax *Periplus* 112 cf. Hdt. 3, 20.
19 Strab. 11, 4, 4.
20 See Roy Walker *The Golden Feast* (London 1952), an advocate's book, but not unscholarly; also J. Haussleiter, *Der Vegetarismus in der Antike* (Berlin 1935).
21 Porph. *De abst.* 2, 20–1.
22 DS 3, 23 ff.
23 Hom. *Od.* 9, 82–105.
24 Hes. *WD* 109 ff.
25 ibid. 233.
26 Hdt. 1, 66.
27 Lucr. 5, 937.
28 Ver. *G.* 1, 7; 1, 147–9.
29 (Orph) *Arg.* 1142 ff.
30 Ov. *Met.* 15, 96.
31 Porph. *De abst.* 4, 6–18.
32 Hom. *Il.* 13, 6.
33 Aesch. *fr.* 196 cf. Steph. Byz. s.v. Αἰθίοψ.
34 id. *fr.* 198.

35 D. Chr. 69, 6.
36 Justin *Hist. Phil. Epit.* 2, 2.
37 Strab. 11, 4, 4; Ath. 12, 524c.
38 Agatharch. *De Mari Erythro* 49.
39 Strab. 44, 25.
40 Steph. Byz. sv, Αἰθίοψ.
41 (Scymnus) *Orb. Descr.* 420 ff.
42 Nymphodorus in *Schol. ad* Ap.
Rhod. 2, 1010.
43 Polyb. 4, 20.
44 Tac. *Ann.* 3, 26.
45 fr. 24 Wehrli.
46 fr. 49 Wehrli.
47 Theopompus in Mueller, *FHG*
I, 319.
48 Hdt. 1, 216.
49 ibid. cf. Ephorus ap. Str. 7, 3, 9.
50 ibid. 4, 104.
51 ibid. 4, 180.
52 Arist. *Pol.* 2, 1262 a 19.
53 Plin. *NH* 5, 8, 45; Pomp. Mela
I, 8, 45; Solinus 30, 2.
54 Jacoby *F. Gr. H.,* n. 90, 104 cf.
Ephorus ap. Str. 7, 3, 9.
55 *F. Gr. H.* 90, 103(d).
56 DS 3, 15, 1; 3, 17, 1.
57 DS 3, 24, 1.

58 DS 3, 24, 1.
59 DS 3, 32, 1.
60 Solinus *App.* 22, 15.
61 Clem. Al. *Str.* 3, 515.
62 Ath. 13, 517 D.
63 Ath. 13, 555 C.
64 Aug. *CD* 18, 9.
65 Dittenberger *SIG*, 126, 7.
66 Pind. *P.* 10, 37 ff.
67 Ael. *HA* 11, 1.
68 DS 2, 47, 1–6.
69 Polyb. 4, 20–1.
70 Paus. 10, 5, 7–9; Mela, 3, 37;
Call. *H.Del.* 280–99.
71 Polyb. 4, 20–1.
72 Nic. Dam. in Stob. 44, 25; Favonius in Steph. Byz. sv. Αἰθίοψ.
73 Phil. *Quod omn. prob.* 12.
74 Hdt. 4, 53.
75 Mela, 1, 117.
76 Aesch. *PV* 447 ff.
77 Plat. *Prot.* 320 c ff.
78 ʼHipp. *Anc. Med.* 3, 26.
79 Lucr. 5, 1011 ff.
80 Cic. *Sest.* 42, 91–2; *Rep.* 3, 1,
1 etc.
81 Ath. 14, 660 ff.

CHAPTER III

1 There are many useful accounts, including the standard histories. It would be hard to better Victor Ehrenberg, *The Greek State* (Oxford 1960), whose guidance I have largely followed.
2 A. W. H. Adkins, *Merit and Responsibility* (Oxford 1960); *Moral Values and Political Behaviour in Ancient Greece* (London 1972).
3 Hes. *WD* 313.
4 Tyrt. 10, 2.
5 e.g. *Ol.* 2, 56; *Pyth.* 10, 71.
6 H. Collitz, *Sammlung der griechischen Dialekt-Inschriften* (Göttingen 1884–1915), 1152.
7 *IG* 12, 2, 6.
8 Ar. *Pol.* 1322b29.
9 Hdt. 5, 92.
10 See J. Ferguson, *Moral Values in the Ancient World* (London 1958) 19–23.
11 P. N. Ure *The Origin of Tyranny* (Cambridge 1922) is controversial but

still useful. A. Andrewes, *The Greek Tyrants* (London 1956) is the best modern treatment.
12 Plat. *Rep.* 8, 562A.
13 Thuc. 3, 82.
14 L. Whibley, *Greek Oligarchies* (Cambridge 1896) remains as useful as anything.
15 T. R. Glover, *Democracy in the Ancient World* (Cambridge 1927).
16 Thuc. 8, 97.
17 Arist. *Pol.* 4, 1296 a 38.
18 Aesch. *Pers.* 241–2.
19 ibid. 491 ff.
20 Hdt. 3, 80–2.
21 For contrasting views see G. W. Bowersock, 'Pseudo-Xenophon' *HSCP* 71 (1966) 33–55, who proposes a date about 443; A. W. Gomme, *More Essays in Greek History and Literature* (Oxford 1962), who puts it 420–15.
22 Ar. *Pol.* 3, 1279 b.
23 Thuc. 2, 35–46.

24 Plut. *Per.* 11.
25 Thuc. 6, 36–40.
26 Plat. *Rep.* 6, 488A–489A; R. Bambrough, 'Plato's Political Analogies' in P. Laslett, *Philosophy, Poli-*

tics and Society (Oxford 1956), 98–115.
27 M. Gigante, 'Il frammenti fiorentino di un dialogo politico', *Aegyptus* 28 (1948), 195–8.
28 Xen. *Mem.* 4, 6, 12.

CHAPTER IV

1 Pavel Oliva, *Sparta and her Social Problems* (Amsterdam and Prague 1971) is to my mind the most important recent treatment and shows a comprehensive familiarity with primary and secondary sources, and good judgement. The modern literature includes two large studies in English: K. M. T. Chrimes, *Ancient Sparta* (Manchester 1949) and H. Michell, *Sparta* (Cambridge 1952). This last has a useful select bibliography. G. L. Huxley's austere *Early Sparta* (London 1962) does not add much. There are shorter, but palmary, sketches by W. G. Forrest, *A History of Sparta 950–192 BC* (London 1968) and A. H. M. Jones, *Sparta* (Oxford 1967). F. Kiechle, *Lakonien und Sparta* (Munich 1963) should also be consulted. There have been important articles by A. J. Toynbee, 'The Growth of Sparta' *JHS* 33 (1913), 249 ff. and A. Andrewes, 'Eunomia' *CQ* 32 (1938), 89 ff.; also (though controversial) N. G. L. Hammond, 'The Creation of Classical Sparta' in *Studies in Greek History* (Oxford 1973), 47–103; also a number of articles by V. Ehrenberg. The mellifluous appraisal of W. Pater, *Plato and Platonism* c. viii is still worth reading. W. den Boer, *Laconian Studies* (Amsterdam 1954) contains a valuable discussion of some of the problems and a good bibliography. Pioneering work on the influence of Sparta was done by F. Ollier in his still fascinating *Le Mirage Spartiate* (2 vols. Paris 1933–43). See also E. N. Tigerstedt, *The Legend of Sparta in Classical Antiquity* Vol. I (Stockholm 1965) with very full notes and an excellent bibliography (esp. pp. 311–13). For more modern influences see E. Rawson, *The Spartan*

Tradition in European Thought (Oxford 1969). Of the early documents Xenophon, *Constitution of Sparta*, Aristotle, *Politics* and Plutarch, *Life of Lycurgus* and *Ancient Customs of the Spartans* are the most important, together with historical evidence from Herodotus, Thucydides, Xenophon and other of Plutarch's lives.
2 See the curiously naïve identification by Gilbert Murray in World War II of England with Athens and Germany with Sparta (*Greek Studies* Oxford 1946, 192–212).
3 Ollier op. cit. n. 1 above, I, 197 ff; Tigerstedt, pp. 240 ff.
4 Ar. *Birds* 1281–3.
5 Aeschin. *In Tim.* 173.
6 See pp. 130 ff.
7 Rawson, p. 171.
8 A. J. Toynbee, *A Study of History* IV (London 1939), 1 ff.
9 Plut. *Lyc.* 15.
10 Arist. *Pol.* 1294 B.
11 Plat. *Laws* 4, 712 D.
12 Huxley p. 65 cites the Vix crater to the contrary. But it is doubtful if this is Spartan at all. See M. Guarducci, 'L'alfabeto del cratere di Vix' *Rend. della Classe di Sc. mor., stor. e filol. dell'Accademia dei Lincei* 18 (1963), 3–19.
13 Alcm. *fr.* 1, 64 ff.
14 cp Hom. *Il.* 6, 130; 7, 142; Hdt. 1, 65–6; Paus. 1, 20, 3; 2, 15, 3; 5, 5, 5.
15 Plut. *Lyc.* 1.
16 Xen. *R. Lac.* 10, 8; Ephorus ap. Strab. 10, 4, 18; Arist. ap. Plut. *Lyc.* 1.
17 Forrest pp. 55–58.
18 Michell pp. 101–4. There are other views. See Oliva, pp. 23–8.
19 Hdt. 5, 75; Thuc. 5, 75; Xen. *Hell.* 5, 3, 10.
20 Plut. *Lyc.* 26.
21 Chrimes, p. 421. 28, is however

itself a powerful number, the sum of its parts $(1 + 2 + 4 + 7 + 14)$.

22 Arist. *Pol.* 2, 1270 B.

23 Isoc. 12, 154; Dem. 20, 107; Polyb. 6, 45; DH 2, 14; Plut. *Lyc.* 26.

24 Chrimes, p. 410.

25 Plut. *Lyc.* 6 cp Hom. *Il.* 18, 497 ff.

26 Aeschin. *In Iim.* 153; Plut. *Mor.* 800 C.

27 Michell p. 144.

28 Tyrt. *fr.* 4 B, tr. B. Perrin.

29 Michell pp. 118 ff.; Chrimes, pp. 402 ff.

30 Plut. *Cleom.* 10.

31 Thuc. 1, 87; Xen. *Hell.* 2, 2, 19; Plut. *Agis* 9.

32 D.S. 13, 106; Plut. *Lys.* 16; *Agis* 16.

33 Ath. 12, 550 C.

34 Plut. *Lyc.* 28.

35 Xen. *Resp. L.* 8, 4.

36 Plut. *Mor.* 254 cf Schol. ad Thuc. 1, 84.

37 Plut. *Cleom.* 9.

38 Thuc. 1, 131; 8, 11; Xen. *Hell.* 3, 1, 1; 6, 4, 17; Plut. *Lys.* 19.

39 Cic. *Rep.* 2, 23.

40 Xen. *Hell.* 3, 3, 8; G. Glotz in Daremberg-Saglio, *Dictionnaire des Antiquités* s.v. Ekklesia.

41 Arist. *Pol.* 2, 1270 A 37.

42 Plut. *Lyc.* 8.

43 Chrimes, p. 350.

44 Hdt. 7, 234.

45 ibid. 9, 10.

46 Thuc. 5, 68; Xen. *Hell.* 4, 2, 16.

47 Xen. *Hell.* 6, 4, 15.

48 Isoc. *Panath.* 255; 257.

49 Ar. *Pol.* 2, 1270 A 31.

50 Xen. *Hell.* 5, 3, 16.

51 Plut. *Mor* 238 A; Stob. *Flor.* 40, 8 (233).

52 Xen. *Resp. L.* 10, 7.

53 Arist. *Pol.* 2, 1271 A; 1272 A.

54 e.g. Hdt. 7, 134.

55 Plat. *Alc.* 1, 122 C.

56 Plut. *Lys.* 18.

57 But see G. Dickins in *ABSA* 13 (1906–7), 173.

58 Hdt. 9, 35; Plut. *Mor.* 218 B; 230 D; *Dion* 17.

59 Thuc. 5, 74; Xen. *Hell.* 1, 1, 35; 3, 2; 6, 5; *C.I.A.* 2, 50.

60 Xen. *Mem.* 1, 2, 61; Cratinus apud Ath. 4, 138 E; Schol. ad Ar. *Pax* 622; Plut. *Agis* 29; Philostratus *Vit. Ap.* 258; M. Aur. 11, 24.

61 Thuc. 2, 39 tr. A. E. Zimmern cf 1, 144.

62 e.g. Hdt. 3, 148; Ar. *Birds* 1012; Arist. fr. 543 R; Theopompus in Jacoby, *F. Gr. H.* n. 115, 178.

63 Plut. *Lyc.* 27 cf *Mor.* 238 E.

64 Xen. *Resp. L.* 14 cf. Plut. *Mor.* 217 D.

65 Plut. *Lyc.* 12 as against Schol. ad Plat. *Laws* 633 A.

66 Plut. *Lyc.* 12.

67 Ath. 4, 141 A ff tr. C. B. Gulick. Cited Michell p. 292.

68 Plut. *Mor.* 218 B.

69 id. *Lyc.* 12; *Mor.* 46 C–D.

70 C. Seltman, *Women in Antiquity* (London 1956), 70.

71 Plat. *Laws* 7, 806 A.

72 Pind. apud Ath. 14, 613.

73 Alcm. *fr.* 1.

74 Plut. *Lyc.* 14.

75 C. Seltman op. cit. p. 67 citing S. de Beauvoir, *The Second Sex*.

76 Plut. *Lyc.* 14–5; Theocr. 18, 23 cf. two Spartan bronzes reproduced by C. Seltman op. cit.

77 cf. Eur. *Andr.* 595 ff.

78 Ath. 13, 566 A; F. Wehrli, *Herakleides Pontikos* (Basle 1953).

79 Ar. *Lys.* 78 ff. tr. P. Dickinson.

80 Michell p. 53.

81 Xen. *Resp. L.* 2, 7 f; Plut. *Lyc.* 15 cf. Nicol. Damas. in Jacoby, *F. Gr. H.* n. 90, 103 $(144)^2$.

82 Polyb. 12, 6.

83 Hdt. 5, 41.

84 Plut. *Lyc.* 16, 1.

85 Isoc. *Panath.* 209; Plut. *Mor.* 237 A; *Lyc.* 16.

86 Plato. *Hipp. Mai.* 285 C.

87 Ath. 14, 632 F.

88 Plut. *Arist.* 17; *Lyc.* 18; *Mor.* 239 D; Xen. *Resp. L.* 2, 9; Nic. Dam. *fr.* 1032 apud *F. Gr. H.* n. 114, 11; Lucian *Anacharsis* 38; Philostr. *V. Ap.* 6, 20; Cic. *T.D.* 2, 14, etc.

89 Michell pp. 177 ff.; Plut. *Lyc.* 17; Xen. *Resp.L.* 2, 7–8.

90 Xen. *Resp. L.* 3, 5.

91 Xen. *Resp. L.* 2, 12 ff.; Plut.

Mor. 237 B; Lyc. 18, 4; Ael. V.H.
3, 10, 12.
92 Michell p. 197.

93 W. Pater, *Plato and Platonism* 3
(London 1901), *c*. viii ad fin.

CHAPTER V

1 D.L. 1, 12.
2 Clem. Al. *Strom.* 1, 59.
3 Plat. *Prot.* 342 E tr. W. K. C.
Guthrie.
4 id. *Rep.* 9, 587 D cf. 1, 336 A.
5 Plut. *Mor.* 385 E.
6 The traditions are usefully collected in F. Mullach *F. Ph. Gr.* I pp.
203–236.
7 Arist. *Met.* 1, 983 B 20.
8 Hdt. 1, 170. See E. A. Freeman,
History of Federal Government (London and Cambridge 1863), I pp 187 ff.
9 Ausonius *Sent. Sept. Sep.*
10 R. D. Hicks *Diogenes Laertius*
(Loeb), I p. xix.
11 See I. M. Linforth, *Solon the
Athenian* (Berkeley 1919); W. J.
Woodhouse, *Solon the Liberator* (Oxford 1938); C. Hignett, *A History of
the Athenian Constitution* (Oxford
1952); F. E. Adcock in *CAH* IV
c. 2; W. Jaeger, *Solons Eunomie* (Berlin 1926); N. G. L. Hammond 'The
Seisachtheia and the Nomothesia of
Solon' *JHS* 60 (1940) 71–83.
12 Solon *fr.* 1 tr. R. Lattimore. For
a fuller examination see T. B. L.
Webster *Greek Interpretations* (Manchester 1942) pp. 13–24.
13 Arist. *Ath. Pol.* 5.
14 Solon *fr.* 3 apud Dem. *F.L.* 254;
summary translation by J. A. Sy-
monds.
15 Solon *fr.* 24 apud Arist. *Ath. Pol.*
12 tr. R. Lattimore.
16 Solon *fr.* 5 apud Arist. *Ath. Pol.*
12 tr. G. Highet.
17 cf. Arist. *Ath. Pol.* 9, 1.
18 C. Hignett, *History of the Athenian Constitution*, p. 106.
19 *C.A.H.* IV p. 57.
20 D.L. 1, 76.
21 Hdt. 3, 50–3; 5, 92; D.L. 1, 94;
Nic. Damasc. *frr.* 58–60.
22 H. T. Wade-Gery in *C.A.H.* III,
553.

23 Stob, 3, 1, 172 ff.
24 *C.A.H.* III, 568.
25 D.L. I, 68.
26 D.L. I, 68,
27 Timaeus apud Clem. Al. *Strom.*
1, 353; Plut. *Mor.* 175 E cf. Arist.
Met. 3, 1010 A 4.
28 J. Burnet, *Greek Philosophy* (London 1914), 58.
29 Heraclit. *fr.* 121.
30 D.L. 8, 52, 63 ff.
31 D.L. 8, 66.
32 Arist. *Met.* 1, 985 B 23.
33 The best work on this has been
done in America. See K. von Fritz,
Pythagorean Politics in Southern Italy
(New York 1940): E. L. Minar, *Early
Pythagorean Politics in Practice and
Theory* (Baltimore 1942). See also
A. Delatte, *Essai sur la politique pythagoricienne* (Liège 1921).
34 Porph. *V. Pyth.* 9.
35 Plat. *Rep.* 10, 600 A 9.
36 Iambl. *V. Pyth.* 17.
37 ibid. 137.
38 ibid. 249 cf. D.L. 8, 15.
39 Polyb. 2, 39. For the date see
Minar pp. 77–8 as against von Fritz
pp. 78–9; 97–9, who argues for 445.
40 e.g. A. Krische, *De Societatis a
Pythagora in urbe Crotoniatarum con-
ditae scopo politico* (Göttingen 1830).
41 See E. Rohde, 'Die Quellen des
Iamblichos in seiner Biographie des
Pythagoras', *Rh. Mus.* 26 (1871),
554–76; 27 (1872), 23–61.
42 G. Thomson, *Aeschylus and
Athens*² (London 1946), 213 ff.
43 von Fritz, pp. 91 ff.
44 J. Burnet, *Early Greek Philosophy*⁴
(London 1930), 89 ff.
45 D.L. 8, 3 tr. R. D. Hicks.
46 G. Thomson, *Aeschylus and
Athens*, 216–17.
47 See my edition of Plato *Republic
X* (London 1957), notes on 595 A 7,
600 B 2, 605 B 5; *Moral Values in the*

Ancient World (London 1958), 25–7.
Also E. J. Urwick, *The Message of Plato* (London 1920); S. Radakrishnan, *Eastern Religions and Western Thought*² (Oxford 1940).
48 Polyb. 2, 39; cf. von Fritz pp. 97–8.
49 Aristox. *frr.* 18, 19 cf. Soph. *Ant.* 672.
50 W. L. Newman, *The Politics of Aristotle* (Oxford 1887), 1, 377.
51 Porph. *V.P.* 22.
52 D.L. 8, 79 ff.
53 J. Burnet, *Early Greek Philosophy*⁴ (1930), p. 276.
54 D.S. 15, 57.
55 Arist. *Rhet.* 2, 1398 B.
56 See V. Ehrenberg, 'The Foundation of Thurii', *AJP* 69 (1948), 49–70. For a popular account, K. Freeman, *Greek City States* (London 1950) 23–40.
57 Arist. *Pol.* 2, 1267 B 22.
58 ibid. 1267 B 29.
59 ibid. 1267 B 30 ff.; *De Cael.* 268 A 10 ff. cf. D.L. 9, 46; Harpocration s.v.
60 ibid. 1268 A 6; cf. D.S. 10, 9, 2.
61 cf. Eur. *Supp.* 428 ff.
62 See I. Lana 'L'Utopia di Ippodamo di Mileto', *Riv. di Filos.* 40

(1949), 125–51. Also his *Protagora* (Turin, 1950).
63 D.L. 9, 55.
64 e.g. T. Gomperz, *Greek Thinkers* (E. T. London 1906), 1, 438; K. Freeman, *Greek City-States*, 28; A. Menzel, 'Protagoras als Gesetzgeber von Thurii', *Ber. u.d. Verhandlungen der k. Sachsischen G. der Wiss. zu Leipzig* phil-h-klasse 62 (1910), 191–229.
65 Arist. *Pol.* 1266 A 38 ff. See also H. C. Baldry, *Ancient Utopias* (Southampton, 1956) for some characteristically sensible remarks; and J. Pečirka, 'Aristophanes Ekklesiazusen und die Utopien in der Krise der Polis' *Wiss. Zeitschr. der Humboldt – Univ. zu Berlin: Gesellsch. und sprachwiss.* 12 (1963), 215–19 for some speculative suggestions.
66 So Susemihl and Hicks *ad loc.*
67 e.g. A. Böckh, *Die Staatshaushaltung der Athener*³ (Berlin, 1886) 1 p. 65; W. Roscher, *Leben Werk und Zeitalter des Thukydides* (Göttingen, 1847) p. 247; H. Henkel, *Studien zur Geschichte der griechischen Lehre vom Staat* (Leipzig 1872), 165.
68 Arist. *Pol.* 2, 1266 B 29.
69 ibid. 1267 A 13.

CHAPTER VI

1 For the fragments see F. Decleva Caizzi, *Antisthenes: Fragmenta* (Milan 1966).
2 Plat. *Theaet.* 149 a ff.
3 Apul. *Flor.* 1, 2.
4 Xen. *Mem.* 1, 1, 6.
5 Plat. *Lach.* 187 e.
6 Xen. *Mem.* 1, 6, 15.
7 Plat. *Apol.* 30 e.
8 Ar. *Birds* 1282. See above p. 29.
9 Plut. *Nic. 13.*
10 Aeschin. *In Tim.* 173
11 Some sentences in the above paragraph are taken from the introduction to my edition of Plato, *Republic X* (London 1957).
12 D.L. 6, 103.
13 ibid. 6, 15–18.
14 Ath. 5, 220 c.

15 *The Suda*; D.L. 6, 9; Ath. 5, 220 c.
16 Xen. *Symp.* 4, 61; D.L. 3, 35; 6, 7.
17 Ath. 5, 220 c; 11, 507; D.L. 3, 35; 6, 7.
18 S. F. Dummler, *Antisthenica* (Berlin, 1882), 63.
19 E. de Strycker, 'Antisthène ou Thémistius', *Archives de Philosophie* 12 (1936), 181–206.
20 U. von Wilamowitz-Moellendorf, *Platon* (Berlin 1920).
21 A. E. Taylor, *Plato, The Man and his Work*⁴ (London 1937), 331 n. 1.
22 H. Von Arnim, *Leben und Werke des Dio von Prusa* (Berlin 1898), 32–6.
23 D.L. 6, 14; F. Sayre, *Diogenes of Sinope* (Baltimore 1948), 50, 70.

24 ibid. pp. 50, 52; D. R. Dudley, *History of Cynicism* (London, 1937), 14.
25 D.L. 6, 15.
26 ibid. 21; 1; 2.
27 D. R. Dudley, *History of Cynicism*, 13.
28 Hesych. *De Vir. Ill.* 7.
29 Plut. *Lyc.* 30.
30 Jul. *Or.* 6, 190 D; D.L. 7, 3.
31 Ath. 11, 508 C.
32 id. 5, 220 E. Reading *phronimos* for *nomimos*.
33 Arist. *Pol.* 3, 1284 A 15.
34 D.L. 6, 8.
35 Stob. 4, 8, 31.
36 Arr. *Epict.* 4, 6, 20; M. Aur. 7, 36; Plut. *Alex.* 41; D.L. 6, 3.
37 Stob. 4, 4, 28.
38 D.L. 6, 12.
39 ibid. 6.
40 ibid. 5.
41 Plat. *Polit.* 267c ff; *Rep.* 2, 372a ff.
42 Plut. *De Alex Fort.* 16.
43 D.L. 6, 15.

44 Arr. *Epict.* 3, 24, 67 ff.
45 Xen. *Symp.* 4, 34 ff.
46 Stob. 3, 1, 28.
47 ibid. 3, 10, 41.
48 ibid., 4, 9, 10.
49 ibid. 4, 13, 41; Hesych. *De Vir. Ill.* 7; D.L. 6, 1; F. Sayre, *The Greek Cynics* (Baltimore, 1948), 53.
50 Plat. *Rep.* 2, 372c, 1.
51 Arist. *Pol.* 2, 1274b 9–14 cf. 1266a 30.
52 Schol. Lips. on Hom. *Il.* 15, 123.
53 D.L. 6, 11; Jul. 7, 217 A; Epiphan. 3, 26; Xen. *Symp.* 3, 4; Hesych. *De Vir. Ill.* 7.
54 *Gnom. Vat.* 2.
55 Xen. *Symp.* 2, 10; Ath. 12, 534 E.
56 Xen. *Symp.* 4, 61 ff.
57 Stob. 2, 31, 33; 2, 31, 68; 2, 31, 76; Hesych. *De Vir. Ill.* 7.
58 D.L. 6, 10 cf. Xen. *Symp.* 2, 12; 3, 4.
59 Xen. *Symp.* 4, 64.
60 ibid. 2, 9–10.
61 D.L. 6, 12.

CHAPTER VII

1 The arguments against Xenophon's authorship are well presented in K. M. T. Chrimes, *Ancient Sparta* (Manchester 1949), pp. 490–9; see also ibid. *The Date and Authorship of the Respublica Lacedaemoniorum* (Manchester 1948).
2 Xen. *Oec.* 7, 30–6.
3 ibid. 7, 6.
4 Ath. 10, 427 f.
5 See J. Luccioni, *Xenophon: Hieron* (Paris N.D. *c.* 1947).
6 Xen. *Hiero* 6, 4.
7 ibid. 7, 12.
8 The most useful studies are L. Castiglioni, 'Studi Senofontei V', *Rendiconti della r. Acad. dei Lincei* (1922), 34–56; W. Henkel, *Studien zur Geschichte der griechischen Lehre vom Staat* (Leipzig 1872), 136 ff.; J. Luccioni, *Les idées politiques et sociales de Xénophon* (Paris 1947); D.L. 3, 34 cf. Plato *Laws* 3, 694c.
9 e.g. 1, 4, 21; 7, 1; 7, 5.

10 e.g. 1, 3, 2; 7, 5, 60; 8, 1, 40; 8, 2, 8.
11 8, 7, 17–22.
12 8, 1, 14; 8, 2, 5, etc.
13 1, 1, 5.
14 1, 6, 8.
15 See e.g. 1, 6, 9; 8, 5, 2–16.
16 8, 2, 24–5.
17 8, 6, 17–18.
18 e.g. 2, 2, 20; 2, 3, 4; 3, 3, 6; 8, 1, 39.
19 e.g. 8, 1, 19–20, 34–5.
20 8, 2, 27–8.
21 8, 2, 2.
22 e.g. 7, 2, 28; 7, 3, 14.
23 8, 1, 43–4; 8, 2, 4.
24 1, 2, 2–3.
25 1, 2, 6–14; 7, 5, 78–9.
26 7, 5, 72–86.
27 1, 6, 2–6.
28 8, 1, 23–5.
29 3, 1, 38.
30 2, 2, 17; 2, 3, 1.
31 8, 8.

CHAPTER VIII

1 D.L. 3, 1.
2 Plat. *Ep.* 7, 324 B.
3 Xen. *Hell.* 1, 7.
4 Aeschin. 2, 76; 3, 150; Arist. *Fr.* 1532 and schol.
5 Plat. *Ep.* 7, 324B–326B. I assume in common with most scholars that this is genuine. For a contrary view see G. Ryle, *Plato's Progress* (Cambridge 1966).
6 Aeschin, 1, 173.
7 D.L. 3, 6.
8 Plat. *Ep.* 7, 325 D–6 B.
9 G. R. Levy, *Plato in Sicily* (London 1956) offers an attractive and scrupulous reconstruction of these encounters.
10 J. Ferguson, 'Plato and Phaedo', *Museum Africum* 1 (1972) 9–17.
11 Plat. *Apol.* 40 C ff; 42 A.
12 Plat. *Laches* 191 E.
13 D.L. 3, 6.
14 Ath. 11, 506 E. 508 D.
15 *Adv. Col.* 32.
16 ibid.
17 D.L. 3, 46.
18 Cic. *De Orat.* 1, 89; Plut. *Dem.* 5.
19 Plut. *Princ. Inerud.* 1.
20 D.L. 3, 23.
21 P. M. Schuhl, 'Platon et l'activité politique de l'Académie', *REG* 59 (1946), 46–53.
22 The only good edition in English is an old one: J. Adam, *The Republic of Plato* (Cambridge 1902). The best translation is assuredly F. M. Cornford, *The Republic of Plato* (Oxford 1941). For guidance R. L. Nettleship *Lectures on The Republic of Plato* (London 1901) is still as useful as most. N. R. Murphy, *The Interpretation of Plato's Republic* (Oxford 1951) is the most important recent treatment. I have not myself found R. C. Cross and A. D. Woozley, *Plato's Republic* (London 1966) as illuminating as these. Two books, politically critical of Plato, though sometimes misrepresenting him, are important: R. H. S. Crossman, *Plato Today*[2] (London 1959); K. R. Popper, *The Open Society and Its Enemies*[4] (London 1962).

Recent articles are usefully represented in G. Vlastos *Plato II* (New York, 1971). To these may be added R. S. Bluck, 'Plato's Ideal State', *CQ* 9 (1959), 166–8; R. Demos, 'Paradoxes in Plato's Doctrine of the Ideal State', *CQ* 7 (1957), 164–74; R. S. Brumbaugh, 'A New Interpretation of Plato's Republic' *J.Ph.* 64 (1967) 661–70.
23 D. J. Allan in his edition disagrees.
24 The interaction is explored in T. J. Andersson, *Polis and Psyche* Göteborg 1971).
25 See E. J. Urwick *The Message of Plato* (London 1920) 24; G. R. Morrow, *Plato's Law of Slavery* (Urbana 1939), 130; W. L. Newman, *The Politics of Aristotle* (Oxford 1887), I, 143; G. Vlastos, 'Slavery in Plato's Thought', *Phil. Rev.* 50 (1941), 289–305; ibid. 'Does Slavery exist in Plato's Republic?' *CP* 63 (1968), 291–5.
26 See J. Ferguson, *Moral Values in the Ancient World* (London 1958) 24–52.
27 E. J. Urwick, *The Message of Plato* (London 1920).
28 Arist. *NE* 1, 1097a 8.
29 Arist. *Pol.* 2, 1262b 16.
30 Pl. *Rep.* 8, 546 A ff.
31 Pl. *Rep.* 6, 511 A ff.
32 *Historical Essays and Studies*: appendix.
33 Pl. *Soph.* 248 E ff.
34 Pl. *Rep.* 9, 592 A.
35 *Phil.* 3, 20.
36 Pl. *Rep.* 9, 597 B.
37 ibid.
38 *Ep.* 7, 329 A.
39 ibid. 330 B.
40 Pl. *Ep.* 7, 340 B – 345 A.
41 The principal primary sources are Plutarch *Dion*; Nepos *Dion*; Diodorus Siculus; and Plato's *Letters*. There is a valuable study in H. D. Westlake, *Essays on the Greek Historians and Greek History* (Manchester 1969), 251–64. The whole story of Dion is imaginatively reconstructed

by Mary Renault in her striking novel, *The Mask of Apollo.*

42 Pl. *Ep.* 7, 334 C.

43 ibid 337 B.

44 ibid. *Ep.* 8.

45 R. S. Bluck, *Plato's Seventh and Eighth Letters* (Cambridge 1947), Appendix I and II.

46 Stob. *Fl.* 43, 129, 132–4; 46, 61.

47 For: A. Delatte, *Essai sur la Politique Pythagoricienne* (Liège-Paris 1922); E. L. Minar, jr., *Early Pythagorean Politics in Practice and Theory* (Baltimore 1942). Against: A. Rivaud, 'Platon et la "politique Pythagoricienne"' *Mélanges Glotz* II (Paris, 1932), 779–92; W. Theiler, 'Sur la politique Pythagoricienne', *Gnomon* 2 (1926), 147–56.

48 Minar pp. 86–94.

49 For details see J. B. Skemp, *Plato's Statesman* (London 1952), an admirably judicious work.

50 Plato *Pol.* 301 D-E.

51 ibid. 308 D.

52 ibid. 311 A.

53 ibid. 290 C.

54 ibid. 290 B.

55 ibid. 287 B ff.

56 ibid. 289 D–E.

57 ibid. 268 D–274 D.

58 G. M. A. Grube, *Plato's Thought* (London 1935), 279.

59 op. cit. 52–3.

60 Plat. *Tim.* 19 B.

61 See G. E. L. Owen's now famous 'The Place of the *Timaeus* in Plato's Dialogues', *CQ* 3 (1953), 79–95.

62 Plat. *Tim.* 23 B ff.

63 ibid. *Critias* 110 E.

64 ibid. 110 C.

65 See P. Friedländer, *Plato I: An Introduction* (E. T. London 1958), pp. 314–22; H. Herter, 'Platons Atlantis' *Bonner Jahrb.* 133 (1928), 28–47; ibid. 'Die Rundform in Platons Atlantis und ihre Nachwirking in der Villa Hadrians' *Rh M* 96 (1953), 1 ff. There is an interesting general study of the myth in P. Vidal-Naquet, 'Athènes et L'Atlantide. Structure et signification d'un mythe platonicien' *REG* 77 (1964), 420–44. See also, among some general remarks, K.

Kerenyi, 'Ursinn und Sinnwandel des Utopischen' in *Vom Sinn der Utopie* Eranos-Jahrb. 1963 (Zürich 1964), 1–29.

66 ibid. 120 A ff. tr. J. Ruskin, *The Crown of Wild Olive* §83.

67 There is an excellent edition, E. B. England, *The Laws of Plato* (Manchester 1921); a comprehensive study, G. R. Morrow, *Plato's Cretan City* (Princeton 1960); a convenient translation, Plato *The Laws* tr. T. J. Saunders (Harmondsworth 1970).

68 1, 625 B.

69 2, 654 C ff.

70 8, 848 D; 9, 860 E; 11, 919 D; 12, 946 B, 969 A.

71 O. Kern, *Inschriften von Magnesia am Maeander* (Berlin 1900), 17.

72 C. Ritter, *Platon* I (Munich 1910) 87–8.

73 4, 709 E.

74 5, 739 B.

75 5, 737 E.

76 Morrow p. 113.

77 5, 736 E.

78 5, 745 C.

79 e.g. 6, 755 E, 764 A, 768 A.

80 Arist. *Pol.* 1266 a 5.

81 6, 781 B.

82 6, 766 A.

83 7, 796 E ff., 809 A ff.

84 7, 794 D ff.

85 7, 804 D ff.

86 7, 817 E ff.

87 H. Cairns, 'Plato's Theory of Law' *Harvard Law Review* 56 (1942), 359–87; P. Friedländer, *Plato I: An Introduction* (London 1958), 285–313; Morrow, 241–96.

88 9, 862 C.

89 There are useful studies in O. Reverdin, *La Religion de la Cité Platonicienne* (Paris 1945); F. Solmsen, *Plato's Theology* (New York 1942); G. N. Belknap, *Religion in Plato's States* (Portland 1935); Morrow, 399–499.

90 10, 885 B.

91 1, 632 C; 10, 908 A, 909 A; 12, 951 D.

92 12, 951 D–E, 961 A–B.

93 1, 644 D; 7, 803 C; 7, 804 B.

94 7, 819 A.

95 1, 643 B.
96 5, 729 B.
97 5, 730 C.
98 5, 731 D.
99 1, 636 D; 2, 653 A.
100 2, 653 C.
101 F. M. Cornford, *The Unwritten*

Philosophy (Cambridge 1950), 67.
102 See especially G. R. Morrow, 'Plato and the Rule of Law' *Phil. Rev.* 59 (1941) 105–26; G. Vlastos, *Plato* II (New York 1971), 144–65.
103 4, 715 D.
104 3, 693 B.

CHAPTER IX

1 *CAH* 6, 353.
2 This paragraph is based on E. Barker, *The Politics of Aristotle* (Oxford 1952) xxi.
3 Arist. *Ath. Pol.* 42, 3–5; Plato *Laws* 740–2.
4 *CAH* 6, 440.
5 *Pol.* 1, 1255 a 21 ff.
6 ibid. 7, 1330 b 32–1331 b 3.
7 ibid. 1331 b 16.
8 *NE* 1, 1094 a 1.
9 *Pol.* 1, 1252 a 1.

10 ibid. 1253 a 3.
11 1261 b 33.
12 1262 b 15.
13 1263 b 22.
14 1324 a 24.
15 1326 a 35 ff, cf. *N.E.* 1170 b 32.
16 1290 b 40.
17 1331 b 18.
18 1332 a 40.
19 1338 a 22.
20 1339 a 9.
21 1341 b 35.

CHAPTER X

1 D.L. 6, 80.
2 D.L. 5, 43.
3 Philodemus *H.P.* 339 col. VII.
4 D.L. 6, 48; D. Chr. 8, 9; Diog. *Ep.* 17.
5 F. Sayre, *Diogenes of Sinope* (Baltimore 1938), 95.
6 ibid. p. 79.
7 ibid. p. 122; *The Suda* s.v. Diogenes.
8 Ar. *Pol.* 1266 a 30.
9 W. W. Tarn, 'Alexander, Cynics and Stoics', *AJP* 60 (1939), 41–70.
10 K. Von Fritz, 'Quellen – Untersuchungen zu Leben und Philosophie des Diogenes von Sinope', *Philologus* supp 18 (1926).
11 D.L. 6, 20; *The Suda* s.v. Diogenes cf. C. T. Seltman, *Riot in Ephesus* (London 1958), 135 ff.
12 Stob. 3, 9, 46; cf. 3, 24, 14.
13 D.L. 6, 28.
14 D. Chr. 6, 25.
15 Stob. 13, 43; D. Chr. 8, 7–8; 9, 4; 10, 5.
16 U. von Wilamowitz-Moellendorff, *Aristotle und Athen* II, 24; D.L. VI. 41.
17 Stob. 3, 7, 46.

18 D. Chr. 10, 5.
19 ibid. 8, 14.
20 D. Chr. 6, 1.
21 D.L. 6, 63; Lucian *Vit. Auct.* 8.
22 D. Chr. 9, 12; Jul. 7, 238A.
23 D.L. 6, 39.
24 Jul. 7, 239.
25 D.L. 6, 38.
26 W. Windelband, *History of Philosophy* II, 8.
27 Max. Tyr. 36, 5.
28 D.L. 6, 93.
29 Plut. *Lyc.* 31.
30 Diog. *Ep.* 27.
31 D.L. 6, 59.
32 Ar. *Rhet.* 3, 1411 a 24.
33 Stob. 3, 13, 43.
34 D. Chr. 8, 11.
35 D.L. 6, 27.
36 Stob. 2, 31, 75; D.L. 6, 68.
37 D.L. 6, 80.
38 Stob. 4, 32, 21.
39 D.L. 6, 98.
40 D. Chr. 4, 92.
41 D.L. 6, 30.
42 D.L. 6, 48.
43 Stob. 4, 29, 19; 4, 29, 57.
44 D.L. 6, 73 cf. 104.
45 D. Chr. 4, 30.

46 Stob. 4, 34, 72.
47 D. Chr. 4, 29 ff.
48 Plut. *Mor.* 439 E.
49 D.L. 6, 70; D. Chr. 4, 56.
50 D. Chr. 4, 17; 10, 17. Philo, *Quod Omnis Probus liber sit* 21.
51 D.L. 6, 30; 6, 70.
52 D. Chr. 4, 14; D.L. 6, 76.
53 D. R. Dudley, *A History of Cynicism* (London 1937) p. 38.
54 D.L. 6, 23, 34–5, 48–9, 70–1, 90; D. Chr. 6, 8–9; Stob. 2, 31, 87; 3, 7, 17.
55 Stob. 4, 33, 26.
56 D.L. 6, 43, 50, 66.
57 D.L. 6, 38, 60, 63; Sen. *Ben* 54, etc.
58 K. von Fritz op. cit. (n. 10)
59 Arrian *Epict.* 4, 1. 29–31.
60 W. Gomperz, *Greek Thinkers* (ET. London 1906) 2, 160.
61 D.L. 6, 28, 34, 86.
62 D. Chr. 4, 131–2.
63 D. Chr. 4, 131–2.
64 K. von Fritz, op. cit. pp. 59, 60.
65 D.L. 6, 25–6, 29–30, 40–1, 53–4,

58, 67, 74–6; D. Chr. 10, 17 ff.; Max. Tyr. 32, 9; 36, 6; Stob. 3, 3, 52; *The Suda* s.v. Diogenes.
66 D.L. 6, 72.
67 D.L. 7, 131.
68 Philodemus col. ix.
69 D. Chr. 6, 31; Max. Tyr. 36, 5.
70 D. Chr. 9, 1.
71 Lucian *Quomodo Historia* 3.
72 D. Chr. 6, 16–17, 34, 51; D.L. 6, 50; 6, 72.
73 D.L. 6, 50.
74 Stob. 4, 31, 88.
75 Diog. *Ep.* 36.
76 Stob. 3, 10, 45, cf. 57.
77 D. Chr. 4, 92; 6, 34; 6, 49.
78 D.L. 6, 73.
79 Jul. 6, 209 c.
80 Ath. 4, 159 C; Philodemus col. xiv.
81 Plat. *Laws* 5, 742 A.
82 D.L. 6, 72.
83 K. von Fritz op. cit. pp. 59–60.
84 D. Chr. 10, 16.
85 ibid. 8, 14; D.L. 6, 73.

CHAPTER XI

1 For the facts see W. W. Tarn, *Alexander the Great* I (Cambridge 1948); W. Wilcken, *Alexander the Great* (New York 1967); A. R. Burn *Alexander the Great and the Hellenistic World* (London 1947). Also more recently J. R. Hamilton, *Alexander the Great* (London 1973) and R. Lane Fox, *Alexander the Great* (London 1973). (Refs. due to Prof. Scullard.)
2 Ar. *Pol.* 1, 1252 b 9; 3, 1285 a 20; Plut. *Mor.* 329 B.
3 e.g. Isoc. *Antid.* 293–4; *Phil.* 154.
4 Plat. *Prot.* 337 C–E.
5 DK 87 B 44.
6 D.L. 6, 63.
7 W. W. Tarn, *Alexander the Great* II (Cambridge 1948), 399 ff.; H. C. Baldry, *The Unity of Mankind in Greek Thought* (Cambridge 1965) contrast p. 122 and p. 128.
8 G. Walser, 'Zur neueren Forschung über Alexander der Grossen', *Schweizer Beiträge zur alleminen Geschichte* 14 (1956), 156–89; G. Droysen,

Geschichte Hellenismus (Gotha, 1877–87).
9 W. W. Tarn, 'Alexander the Great and the Unity of Mankind', *PBA* 19 (1933), 123–66.
10 W. Kolbe, *Die Welt reichsidee Alexanders d. Grossen* (Frieburg 1935); C. A. Robinson jr., *Alexander the Great* (New York 1947).
11 G. Radet, *Alexandre le Grand* (Paris 1931).
12 W. Wilcken, *Alexander der Grosse* (Leipzig 1931).
13 A. R. Burn, op. cit. n. 1; F. Schachermeyr, *Alexander der Grosse, Ingenium und Macht* (Graz 1949); E. Badian, *Studies in Greek and Roman History* (New York 1964).
14 Plut. *Alex.* 27.
15 Arr. *Anab* 7, 8 ff. cf. Plut. *Alex.* 71; Q. Curt. 10, 2–3; D.S. 17, 109; Just. 12, 11 ff.
16 E. Badian, 'Alexander the Great and the Unity of Mankind' *Historia* 7 (1958), 425–44 (=*Alexander the Great,*

ed. G. T. Griffith (Cambridge 1966), 287 ff.)

17 Plut. *Mor.* 329 C.

18 See E. Schwartz 'Hekataeos von Teos', *Rh. M.* 40 (1885), 223–62, esp. 252–4; Tarn II, 438–9; Badian, 432–40.

19 Strabo 1, 4, 9; E. Schwartz op. cit.

20 D.S. 18, 4, 4. The authenticity is supported by H. Berve, 'Die Verschmelzungspolitik Alexanders des Grossen' *Klio* 31 (1938), 135–68, rejected

by Tarn, *Alex. the Great* II, 378–98.

21 Q. Curt. 6, 7 ff.; 8, 6 ff.; 10, 1.

22 Arr. *Anab* 1, 23; 2, 1.

23 ibid. 4, 20.

24 D.S. 17, 105, 6; Arr. 7, 4, 6.

25 Arr. 7, 6.

26 ibid. 7, 11.

27 e.g. Q. Curt. 4, 6, 29.

28 V. Ehrenberg, 'Die Opfer Alexanders an der Indusmündung' *Festschrift für M. Winternitz* (1933), 287–97; *Alexander and the Greeks* (Oxford 1938), 52–61.

CHAPTER XII

1 The best account is probably *Cambridge Ancient History* vols. 6–7.

2 *IG²*, IV, 1, 68; Plut. *Demetr.* 25; D.S. 20, 102–3; M. Kavvadias in *APX.EΦ.* (1918–19), 128; Daux, ibid. (1953–4), 245; M. Cary, 'A Constitution of the United States of Greece', *CQ* 17 (1923), 137–48.

3 There is an excellent account of him in W. S. Ferguson, *Hellenistic Athens* (London 1911), 38–94.

4 Syncellus 52.

5 Ath. 6, 245 A.

6 Plat. *Laws* 6, 752 E 1 ff; 755 B 3; Ar. *Pol.* 4, 1298 b 29; 6, 1323 a 8.

7 Philochorus *fr.* 143.

8 Philochorus *fr.* 143; Ath. 6, 245 A; Ar. *Pol.* 4, 1300 a 4; 6, 1323 a 4.

9 Eus. *PE* 2, 2, 29.

10 F. Jacoby F. Gr. H. n. 63 (1, 300 ff.); the main passage is D.S. 5, 41, 4 ff.

11 Strab 2, 104; 7, 299; Polyb. 34, 5, 10; Plut. *Mor.* 360 A.

12 Hdt. 4, 42; see L. Thompson and J. Ferguson, *Africa in Classical Antiquity* (Ibadan University Press 1969), 4.

13 For ancient references see Plin. *NH* 6, 34; 7, 57; 10, 2; Pomp. Mela 3, 8, 81; Lucr. 2, 417; V. G. 2, 159 (and Serv. and Jun. Phil. *ad loc*); 4, 379; Tib. 3, 2, 23; Ov. *Met.* 10, 309, 478; Claud. *Nupt. Hon. et Mar.* 94. Modern commentators have suggested sites from North America to Russia.

14 Steph. Byz. s.v.

15 Plut. *Mor.* 360 A.

16 Hom. *Od.* 7, 112 ff.

17 Plat. *Crit.* 114 E ff.

18 Many years ago, Prof. A. J. Beattie kindly gave me advice on these.

19 D.S. 5, 45, 3.

20 Arist. *Pol.* 2, 1267 b 33.

21 M. I. Finley, 'Utopianism Ancient and Modern' in K. H. Wolff and B. Moore, *The Critical Spirit: Essays in honor of Herbert Marcuse* (Boston 1967), 3–70.

22 Josephus *c. Apion* 1, 23.

23 D.S. 5, 44.

24 Plin. *NH* 10, 2.

25 Ath. 14, 658 ff.

26 Plin. *NH* 7, 57.

27 Hyginus *Astr.* 2, 42.

28 Lact. *Inst. Div.* 1, 11, 13.

29 Lucian *V.H.* 1, 25.

30 With Wesseling's reading of κοίλαις for κοιναῖς 'the men wore high boots'.

31 Arist. *Pol.* 2, 1262 b 37 ff.

32 Xen. *Anab.* 5, 4, 26; Strabo 16, 778.

33 There is a useful account of Euhemerus in R. v. Pöhlmann, *Geschichte der Sozialen Frage und des Sozialismus in der Antiken Welt* (Munich 1925) II, 293–305.

34 Ath. 3, 98 D.

35 For an attempt to be wiser than Apollo see O. Weinreich, *Menekrates Zeus und Salmoneus* (Stuttgart 1933), 108 ff.

36 W. W. Tarn, *Alexander the*

Great (Cambridge 1948) II, 429 ff.
37 H. C. Baldry, *The Unity of Mankind in Greek Thought* (Cambridge 1965), 124 ff.; I once took the other view, and here recant.
38 Clem. Al. *Protr.* 4, 36 A (from Aristus of Salamis); Plut. *Is. et Os.* 365 E (from Ariston: Ariston of Ceos? Or an error for Aristus?); Strab. 7, 331 fr 35; Plin. *NH* 4, 17.
39 Ptol. 5, 5, 6.
40 I am not aware of any recent study. See B. V. Head, *Historia Nummorum*² (Oxford 1911), 206. F. Imhoof-Blumer, *Monnaies Grecques* (Amsterdam 1883), 96–8; *BMC Macedon*, 133–4; P. Gardner, 'Ares as a Sun God and Solar Symbols' *Num. Chr.* 20 (1880), 49 ff; Ph. Lederer, 'Symbole der Aphrodite Urania', *Z. f. Num.* 41 (1931), 47 ff.
41 Jer. 7, 18; 44, 18, etc.

42 Hdt. 1, 105; Paus. 3, 23, 3.
43 Hdt. 4, 59.
44 op. cit. (n. 40).
45 In general see L. R. Farnell, *The Cults of the Greek States* (Oxford 1896–1909), 2, 626 ff.
46 Paus. 2, 5, 1; Strab. 732; Apul. *Met.* 11, 2; Hdn. *Ab Exc. Div. Marc.* 5, 6.
47 Pind. *fr* 107.
48 Xen. *Symp.* 8, 9; Plat. *Symp.* 180 D; Plot. *Enn.* 3, 5, 2; Paus. 8, 32, 2; 9, 16, 3.
49 op. cit. (n. 40).
50 W. Roscher, *Ausführliches Lexikon d. griechischen und römischen Mythologie*, s.v. βαίτυλος.
51 J. G. Frazer, *The Golden Bough* (1-vol. ed.) (London 1922), 330.
52 Max. Tyr. *Dial.* 38; Serv. ad V. *Aen.* 1, 719; Tac. *Hist.* 2, 3; Hdn. 3, 3.
53 *IG* 4, 1, 283.

CHAPTER XIII

1 D.L. 7, 1.
2 D.L. 7, 3; *The Suda* s.v. Zeno.
3 D.L. 7, 34.
4 *SVF* 1, 42.
5 D.L. 7, 4.
6 *P. Herc.* 339, 15.
7 H. C. Baldry, 'Zeno's Ideal State', *JHS* 79 (1959), 3–15.
8 Stob. 4, 1, 88.
9 Clem. Al. *Str.* 5, 12, 76 cf. Cic, *ND* 1, 14, 36.
10 J. Bidez, 'La Cité du Monde et la Cité du Soleil chez les Stoiciens', *Bull. Acad. Roy. de Belgique* 5 (1932), 244 ff.
11 Cic. *N.D.* 1, 14, 36.
12 cf. Cic. *Leg.* 1, 7, 23.
13 Plut. *Alex. Fort.* 329 A–B.
14 Ath. 13, 561 C.
15 D.L. 6, 15.
16 Phdm. *P. Herc.* 339, 11.
17 Plut. *Mor.* 1034 F cf. 1036 A; 1046 B; 1070 F.
18 Plat. *Laws* 778 C–D.
19 Plat. *Symp.* 180 D.
20 Heraclit. fr. 91.
21 Plut. *Lyc.* 31.
22 Epiphan. *Adv. Haer.* 3, 36.
23 Ath. 13, 561 C.

24 Plut. *Alex Fort.* 329 A–B.
25 Ath. 13, 561 C.
26 D.L. 6, 11–2; Plut. *Mor.* 1034 A.
27 Ath. 13, 561 C.
28 D.L. 7, 33.
29, 30 ibid.
31 W. W. Tarn, *Alexander the Great* (Cambridge 1948) II, 419.
32 D.L. 7, 32.
33 Arr. *Epict.* 3, 21, 19.
34 D.L. 7, 8.
35 L. Stein, *Die Erkentnisstheorie der Stoa* (Berlin 1888), 68–9.
36 D.S. 2, 29; B. Farrington, *Diodorus Siculus, Universal Historian* (Swansea 1937), 13–4.
37 cf. Plut. *Mor.* 78 E; 443 A; 1029 F; D.L. 7, 21; Ath. 14, 629 B.
38 W. S. Ferguson, *Hellenistic Athens* (London 1911), 129.
39 Plut. *Alex. Fort.* 329 A–B; D.L. 7, 33.
40 E. Bréhier *Chrysippe et l'ancien Stoicisme* (Paris 1951), 268.
41 J. Bidez op. cit. (n. 10), 32.
42 D.L. 7, 122.
43 D.L. 7, 32, 4; 7, 121; 7, 129; 7, 131; Plut. *Q. Conv.* 3, 6, 1; Orig. *C. Cels.* 7, 63.

44 Ath. 6, 233 B.
45 D.L. 7, 33.
46 Theodoretus *Gr. Cur.* 3, 74; Plut. *Mor.* 1034; Clem. Al. *Str.* 5, 12, 76; Orig. *C. Cels* 1, 5; Epiphan. *Adv. Haer.* 3, 36.
47 Stob. 3, 1, 179.
48 Philodemus col. 10, 3.
49 D.L. 7, 174–5; Plut. *Mor.* 1033 B cf. *The Suda* s.v. Cleanthes; Sen. *Tranq. An.* 1, 7.
50 Stob. 2, 7, 11.
51 Cleanthes *Hymn* 13; Cic. *ND* 1, 14, 37; D.L. 7, 139.
52 Plut. *Mor.* 923 A; D.L. 7, 174.
53 Jul. Laod. *Cat.* 1, 135.
54 D. Chr. 36, 39.
55 Malachi, 1, 8; 4, 2.
56 Paus. 2, 31, 8.
57 Artemid. *Oneirocr.* 2, 36.
58 Stob. 3, 4, 89.
59 Orig. *C. Cels.* 2, 12; D.L. 7, 179.
60 D.L. 7, 180.
61 D.L. 7, 188; Plut. *Mor.* 1044 F; Sext. Emp. *Adv. Math.* 11, 192; *Pyrrh. Hyp.* 1, 160; 3, 205, 246; Epiphan. *Adv. Haer.* 3, 39.
62 Plut. *Mor.* 1035 B.
63 Plut. *Mor.* 1076 A–F.
64 Plut. *Mor.* 1051 B.
65 Stob. 4, 4, 29.
66 Plut. *Mor.* 1040 C; 1046 B; 1070 D–F; D.L. 7, 129; Cic. *Fin.* 3, 26, 67.
67 Plut. *Mor.* 1041 F.
68 D. Chr. 36, 37 ff.: a passage based on Chrysippus.
69 D.L. 7, 185.
70 Plut. *Mor.* 1043 A–C cf. 1033 B–F.

71 D.L. 7, 122; Plut. *Mor.* 1043 C; 1060 B; Stob. 2, 7, 11m.
72 Philo, *Gig.* 67.
73 D. Chr. 36, 37 ff.
74 Alex. Aphr. *Quaest.* 4, 3.
75 Clem. Al. *Strom.* 7, 3, 1; D.L. 7, 91.
76 Porph. *Abst.* 3, 20.
77 Arr. *Epict.* 3, 21, 19.
78 D.L. 7, 200.
79 Q. 1, 1, 15–16.
80 Q. 3, 14; 10, 32; 11, 17.
81 Q. 1, 1, 4.
82 cf. Clem. Al. *Str.* 4, 8, 590–2; Lact. *Inst. Div.* 3, 25.
83 D.L. 7, 188.
84 D.L. 7, 188; Philod. col. 14; Epiphan. *Adv. Haer.* 3, 39; Sext Emp. *Adv. Math.* 11, 192–4.
85 Sen. *Ben.* 3, 22; Ath. 6, 267 B.
86 D.L. 7, 129.
87 Philo *Quod Omn. Prob. Lib.* 2, 452; Lact. *Inst. Div.* 3, 25.
88 Plut. *Mor.* 1044 B–D.
89 Cic. *Fin.* 3, 20, 67.
90 Cic. *Leg.* 3, 6, 14.
91 Cic. *ND* 1, 15, 40; Philod. *Piet.* 14; Marcian *Inst.* 1; Stob. 2, 7.
92 D.L. 7, 128; Cic. *Leg.* 1, 12, 33; *Fin.* 1, 16, 44; 3, 21, 71.
93 Cic. *Fin.* 3, 20, 67.
94 Clem. Al. *Str.* 4, 26 cf. D. Chr. 6, 20; Cic. *Leg.* 3, 5, 12.
95 Eus. *PE* 6, 264 B.
96 Philodem. col. 11.
97 G. Murray, *The Stoic Philosophy* (London 1915), 43.
98 M.A. 3, 11.
99 Arr. *Epict.* 1, 12, 7; Epict. *Man.* 25.

CHAPTER XIV

1 See T. S. Brown, 'Euhemerus and the Historians'. *HTR* 39 (1946), 259–76.
2 K. Trüdinger, *Studien zur Geschichte der griechischrömischen Ethnographie* (Basle 1918).
3 F. Jacoby *F. Gr. H.* 115, 75 (c); Ael. *VH* 3, 18 cf. Tert. *Pall* 2.
4 See F. Gisinger, *PW* s.v. Meropia; R. Hirzel, 'Zur Charakteristik Theopomps', *RhM* 47 (1892), 378–

89; E. Rohde, 'Zum griechischen Roman', *RhM* 48 (1893), 110–40; *Die griechische Roman³*, (Leipzig 1914). For general studies of Theopompus see G. Murray, *Greek Studies* (Oxford 1946), 149–70; A. Momigliano, 'Studi sulla Storiografia Greca del IV Secolo a.C: Teopompo', *Riv. di fil.* 9 (1931), 230–42, 335–53 (=Terzo contributo alla storia degli studi classici (1966), 367 ff;) K. v. Fritz, 'The

Historian Theopompos', *Am. Hist. Rev.* 46 (1941), 765-87.
5 e.g. 109 B.
6 Compare the description by Hanno. See L. Thompson and J. Ferguson, *Africa in Classical Antiquity* (Ibadan 1969), 5-7.
7 Jacoby *F. Gr. H.*, 32.
8 E. Schwartz s.v. Dionysius (109) *PW* 5, 929-30.
9 cf. D.S. 3, 57, 2; 3, 71, 5.
10 D.S. 3, 53, 4-6; Jacoby *F. Gr. H.*, 32, 7.
11 T. S. Brown, 'Euhemerus and the Historians', *HTR* 39 (1946), 259-274.
12 D.S. 3, 68, 4; Jacoby *F. Gr. H.*, 32, 8.
13 D.S. 2, 55-60.
14 The late Sir Richard Paget owing to a peculiarity of the voice-box, could sound two notes simultaneously. His daughter inherited the capacity, and they used to sing quartets.
15 E. Rohde, *Die griechische Roman*[3] (Leipzig 1914), 251-6.
16 Cleomedes, 1, 6, 31; H. J. Rose, 'The Date of Iambulos', *CQ* 33 (1939), 9-10.
17 Strab. 2, 97; W. W. Tarn, 'The Date of Iambulus: A Note', *CQ* 33 (1939), 193.
18 See chapter 16.
19 W. W. Tarn, *Alexander the Great* (Cambridge 1948), II, 411-14.
20 Lucian *Hermot.* 22; *VH* 1, 3, 6.

21 See c. 16 below.
22 Cic. *ND* 1, 14, 36; *Ac. Pr.* 2, 41, 126; Min. Fel. 19, 10; Tert. *Adv. Marc.* 1, 13.
23 Arr. *Epict.* 1, 16, 20.
24 Cic. *Fin* 3, 18, 60; Sen. *Ep.* 70.
25 Epiphan. *Adv. Haer.* 3, 36; Sext. Emp. *Adv. Math.* 11, 194; Lucian *Demonax* 66; Cic. *TD* 1, 43, 102-4.
26 Eur. *I.T.* 1193.
27 Schol ad Hom. *Il.* 1, 314.
28 D. Chr. 8, 14.
29 Arist. *Pol.* 2, 1261 a 35.
30 ibid. 1, 1256 a 1 ff.
31 ibid. 2, 1261 a 24.
32 Plat. *Pol.* 272 A.
33 Strab. 10, 5, 6 (486).
34 Jos. *Ant.* 1, 106; Müller *FHG* 2, 498 fr 4.
35 Hipp. *Aer. Aq. Loc.* 19; Philostr. *Imag.* 1, 29; Tac. *Germ.* 4, 2; Juv. 13, 163-6.
36 D.S. 2, 55.
37 D.S. 2, 60.
38 D.S. 2, 57.
39 D.S. 2, 58.
40 For Iambulus see also R.v. Pöhlmann, *Geschichte der Sozialen Frage und des Sozialismus in der Antiken Welt* (Munich 1925) II, 305-17. Pöhlmann calls him 'the Jules Verne of Marxism'. Also C. Mossé, 'Les utopies égalitaires à l'époque hellénistique' *Rev. Hist* 24 (1969), 300 ff.; J. Vogt, 'Sklaverei und Humanität', *Historia* Einzelschr. 8 (1972).

CHAPTER XV

1 For the economics of the period see especially F. M. Heichelheim, *An Ancient Economic History* III (Leyden 1970). U. Kahrstedt, *Geschichte des griechischrömischen Altertums* (Munich 1949); M. Rostovtzeff, *The Social and Economic History of the Hellenistic World* 3 vols (Oxford 1941).
2 Plut. *Agis* 5. There is no need with E. Meyer to disbelieve in Epitadeus. See P. Oliva (next note), pp. 188-92. For a sensible treatment of the special problems of Sparta see W. H. Porter (next note).

3 T. W. Africa, *Phylarchus and the Spartan Revolution* (Berkeley 1961) is an admirable monograph, though I cannot accept on the evidence his playing down of Sphaerus. P. Oliva, *Sparta and her Social Problems* (Amsterdam and Prague 1971) also examines the evidence fully, and has an excellent account of sources both primary and secondary. B. Shimron, *Late Sparta: The Spartan Revolution 243-146 BC*, Arethusa Monographs III (Buffalo 1972) is as solid an account as one could wish, and has a first-class bibliography. M. Hadas, 'The Social Revolution in Third-Century Sparta' *CW* 26 (1932), 65–8, 73–6 is useful but derivative. Important articles include: A. Fuks, 'Non-Phylarchean Tradition in the Programme of Agis IV', *CQ* 12 (1962), 118–21; 'Agis, Cleomenes and Equality', *CP* 57 (1962), 16 ff.; 'The Spartan Citizen-Body in Mid-Third Century and its enlargement proposed by Agis IV', *Athenaeum* 40 (1962), 244–63; B. Shimron, 'Polybius and the Reforms of Cleomenes III' *Historia* 13 (1964), 147–55; E. Gabba, 'Studi su Filarco', *Athenaeum* 35 (1957), 1–55; P. Cloché, 'Remarques sur les règnes d'Agis IV et de Cléomène III', *REG* 56 (1943), 53–71; F. W. Walbank, 'The Spartan Ancestral Constitution in Polybius' in *Ancient Society and Institutions: Studies presented to Victor Ehrenberg*, 303–12; K. von Fritz, *The Theory of the Mixed Constitution in Antiquity* (New York 1954), 96–114; W. H. Porter 'The Antecedents of the Spartan Revolution of 243 BC', *Hermathena* 34 (1935), 1–15.

4 Mahaffy once said that this was the only attempt in Greek history to realize these famous catchwords: see *What have the Greeks done for Modern Civilization?* (New York 1909), 186.
5 Plut. *Agis* 8.
6 ibid. *Lycurg.* 8.
7 ibid. *Agis* 5.
8 Plut. *Agis* 4, 6, 9–10, 19.
9 T. W. Africa *Phylarchus and the Spartan Revolution*, 18 ff.; cf. ibid. 'Stoics, Cynics and the Spartan Revolution', *Int. Rev. Soc. Hist.* 4 (1959), 465 ff.
10 D.L. 7, 4.
11 Plut. *Cleom.* 11.
12 Plut. *Lycurgus* 1, 3.
13 Polyb. 4, 35, 14.
14 Plut. *Cleomenes* 13, 2.
15 B. V. Head, *Historia Nummorum²*

(Oxford 1911), 436.
16 Polyb. 5, 39, 6.
17 F. Ollier 'Le Philosophe Stoicien Sphairos et l'Oeuvre réformative des rois de Sparte Agis IV et Cléomène III', *REG* 49 (1936) 536–70; *Le Mirage Spartiate*, II, (Paris 1943), 99–122; see also H. Hobein in *PW* s.v. Sphairos.
18 D.L. 7, 37.
19 ibid. 7, 178; Ath. 4, 141 C.
20 D.L. 7, 177; Ath. 8, 354 E cf. Cic. *T.D.* 4, 24, 53.
21 W. W. Tarn, *Alexander the Great* II (Cambridge 1948), 425.
22 Plut. *Cleom.* 2, 11.
23 Plut. *Cleom.* 10.
24 *A.P.* 7, 709.
25 Plut. *Cleom.* 11.
26 Polyb. 20, 6, 4.
27 ibid. 2, 48, 4; 2, 50, 2; 2, 65.
28 Cercidas *Mel.* 6.
29 Africa, op. cit. p. 20.
30 Cercidas *Mel.* 2.
31 Plut. *Cleom.* 14.
32 ibid. 33.
33 ibid. 39.
34 See Naomi Mitchison's remarkable novel *The Corn-King and the Spring-Queen* (London 1931).
35 Plut. *Cleom.* 20.
36 ibid. 1–2.
37 Polyb. 4, 35, 6–15.
38 F. W. Walbank *ad loc.*
39 Polyb. 4, 81.
40 See J. Mundt, *Nabis: Koenig von Sparta* (Diss. Münster 1903); V. Ehrenberg, 'Nabis' *PW* cols. 1472–3; B. Shimron, 'Nabis of Sparta and the Helots', *CP* 61 (1966), 1–7; id. *Late Sparta: The Spartan Revolution 243–146 BC*, Arethusa Monographs III, (Buffalo 1972); M. Hadas, 'The Social Revolution in Third-Century Sparta', *CW* 26 (1932), 74–6.
41 For his sons see Liv. 32, 38, 3. For the Helots: Shimron op. cit. n. 40. For the redistribution of families: Polyb. 6, 13, 6.

CHAPTER XVI

1 Plut. *Tib. G.* 8.
2 Cic. *De Am.* 11, 37

3 A. J. Toynbee, *A Study of History* (London 1939), 5, 179–80.

4 D. R. Dudley, 'Blossius of Cumae', *JRS* 31 (1941), 94 ff. See also T. S. Brown 'Greek Influences on Tiberius Gracchus' *CJ* (1941-2), 471 ff.
5 Liv. 23, 7 ff.
6 Liv. 27, 3 ff.
7 Cic. *De leg. agr.* 2, 93.
8 Plut. *Tib. G.;* 8 cf. Val. Max. 4, 7, 1.
9 ibid. 17.
10 Cic. *De Am.* 11, 37.
11 Polyb. 1, 1, 5.
12 H. H. Scullard, *From the Gracchi to Nero*[3] (London 1959), 6.
13 Plin. *NH* 18, 6, 7, 35.
14 Caes. *B.C.* 1, 17; Cic. *Leg. Agr.* 3, 8; Plin. *NH* 33, 135.
15 For recent accounts see D. C. Earl, *Tiberius Gracchus* (Brussels 1963) and review by P. A. Brunt in *Gnomon*, 3 (1965), 189-92; A. E. Astin, *Scipio Aemilianus* (Oxford 1967); H. C. Boren, *The Gracchi* (New York 1968) with useful bibliography.
16 Plut. *Tib. G.* 5-7.
17 Plut. *Tib. G.* 8, 4.
18 App. *BC* 1, 11, 5; Plut. *Tib. G.* 9, 2 (though Plutarch's addition of financial compensation is not supported elsewhere).
19 The sequence of events is controversial. See e.g. R. M. Geer, 'Plutarch and Appian on Tiberius Gracchus' in L. W. Jones, *Classical and Mediaeval Studies in honour of E. K. Rand* (New York 1938), 105-12.
20 For the work of the commission see J. Carcopino, *Autour des Gracques*[2] (Paris 1967).
21 Esther V. Hansen, *The Attalids of Pergamon* (New York 1947) pp. 134, 138.
22 T. W. Africa, 'Aristonicus, Blossius and the City of the Sun', *Int. Rev. Soc. Hist.* 6 (1961), 110.
23 Strabo, 13, 4, 2.
24 J. L. Ussing, *Pergamos, dens Historie og Monumenter* (Berlin 1899), 70.
25 P. Foucart, 'La formation de la province romaine d'Asie', *MAI* 37 (1904), 302, refuted by G. Cardinali, 'La morte di Attalo III la rivolta d'Aristonico', *Saggi di Storia Antica e di*

Archeologia offerti a G. Beloch (Rome 1910).
26 Th. Mommsen, *History of Rome* (E. T. London 1911), 3, 74.
27 *Ins. v. Perg.* 249 l.7. Cf. Greenidge and Clay, *Sources of Roman History*[2] (ed. rev. by E. W. Gray, Oxford 1960), 11 ff.
28 Florus 1, 35.
29 *Ins. v. Perg.* 249 ll.5-6.
30 T. W. Africa, op. cit. n. 22 above, p. 119.
31 Plut. *Tib. G.* 15.
32 Cic. *De Am.* 37; Val. Max. 4, 7, 1 as against Plut. *Tib. G.* 20.
33 Plut. *Tib. G.* 20.
34 Justin 36, 4, 6 but cf. Vell. Pat. 2, 4, 1; Strabo 14, 1, 38.
35 D. Magie, *Roman Rule in Asia Minor to the End of the Third Century After Christ* (Princeton 1950), 1, 32; 148.
36 1, 35, 20.
37 Appian *BC* 1, 18. As against G. Cardinali, op. cit. n. 24 above, pp. 294-9.
38 Strabo 14, 1, 38.
39 Justin 37, 1.
40 Florus 1, 35, 20.
41 Attalus II.
42 W. Dittenberger *OGIS* 338. Translation in T. W. Africa, op. cit. n. 22 above, 113-4. See further Esther V. Hansen, *The Attalids of Pergamon* (New York 1947), 142 ff.
43 Plut. *Tib. G.* 21; Val. Max. 5, 3, 2e.
44 Aul. Gell. 1, 13.
45 Strabo 14, 1, 38.
46 Strabo 14, 1, 38.
47 *OGIS* 339; Esther V. Hansen, *The Attalids of Pergamon* (New York 1947), 145.
48 Eutropius 4, 20.
49 Plut. *Tib. G.* 20.
50 Florus 1, 47, 12; Plin. *NH* 33, 149.
51 Florus 1, 35, 20.
52 W. W. Tarn and G. T. Griffith, *Hellenistic Civilization*[3] (London 1952), 55.
53 Soph. (?) fr. 1017.
54 T. W. Africa, op. cit. n. 22 above, pp. 120 ff., cf. M. Rostovtzeff,

The Social and Economic History of the Hellenistic World² (Oxford 1952), 808; J. W. Swain, 'Antiochus Epiphanes and Egypt' *C. Ph.* 39 (1944), 78.
55 J. Bidez, 'La Cité du Monde et la Cité du Soleil chez les Stoiciens', *Bull. Acad. Roy. Belg.* Lettres 518 (1932), 291, cf. J. Beloch, 'Sozialismus und Kommunismus im Alterthum' *Zeitschr. für Socialwissenschaft* IV (1901), 360; R. von Pöhlmann, *Geschichte der sozialen Frage und des Sozialismus in der Antiken Welt³* (Munich 1925) 1, 404 ff.

56 T. W. Africa, op. cit. n. 888 above, 122-3. For other important treatments of Aristonicus see F. Börner, *Untersuchungen über die Religion der Sklaven in Griechenland und Rom* III (Akademie der Wiss, und Lit., Mainz); *Abh. des geistes – und sozial wissenschaftlichen Klassen* 1961 no. 4; J. C. Dumont, 'A propos d'Aristonicos' *Eirene* 5 (1966), 189–96; V. Vavřínek, *La révolte d'Aristonicos* (*Rozpravy Československé Akadémie Věd*, 1957 no. 2); J. Vogt 'Sklaverei und Humanität', *Historia* Einzelschr. 8 (1972) 61-8.

CHAPTER XVII

1 The most comprehensive treatment I know is in J. Klausner, *The Messianic Idea in Israel* (E. T. London 1956). My own thinking was much influenced by two books: H. W. Robinson, *The Religious Ideas of the Old Testament* (London 1913); R. H. Charles, *Religious Development Between the Old and New Testaments* (London 1914).
2 *Gen.* 2, 8-3, 24.
3 *Gen.* 4, 14-15.
4 *Gen.* 2, 15.
5 *Ps.* 48, 1-3.
6 *Ezek.* 28, 12-15. The reading is uncertain, the general sense clear.
7 *Is.* 51, 3.
8 *Is.* 2, 2-4.
9 *Enoch* 8, 1.
10 *Is.* 11, 1-9.
11 *Is.* 35, 1-10. These last paragraphs are indebted to W. O. E. Oesterley, *The Evolution of the Messianic Idea* (London 1908).
12 *Amos* 5, 18.
13 H. Gressmann, *Der Ursprung der israelitisch-jüdischen Eschatologie* (Göttingen 1905).
14 *Amos* 5, 17.
15 *Amos* 6, 1-7.
16 *Amos* 5, 24.
17 *Is.* 9, 6-7; 11, 1-9; 32, 1-8.
18 *Jer.* 23, 5-6.
19 *Jer.* 31, 31-3.
20 *Lk.* 17, 21.

21 1 *Enoch* 48, 10; 38, 2; 40, 5; 48, 2; cf. *Mk.* 8, 29; *Acts* 3, 14; *Lk.* 9, 55; *Mk.* 10, 45.
22 1 *Enoch* 52, 6-9.
23 *Ps. Sol.* 17-18.
24 Phil. *De praem. et poen.* 15; *De execr.* 9.
25 *Is.* 45, 1.
26 *Zech.* 3, 8; 6, 9-14.
27 *Zech.* 8, 1-23.
28 So the Syriac version; the Hebrew has a more military tone.
29 1 *Macc.* 14, 8-14.
30 *Test. Levi* 8, 14-15; 18, 2-9; *Test. Jud.* 24, 1-2.
31 *Acts* 5, 35-9.
32 S. Yeivin, *The War of Bar-Cochba* (Jerusalem 1946), 74-80.
33 The literature is large, and much of it unreliable. The texts are conveniently found in English in T. H. Gaster, *The Scriptures of the Dead Sea Sect* (London 1957). M. Burrows, *The Dead Sea Scrolls* (London 1956) is also very sound. Extremer views such as those of J. M. Allegro, *The Dead Sea Scrolls* (Harmondsworth 1956) have not been sustained by other scholars.
34 S. G. F. Brandon, *Jesus and the Zealots* (Manchester 1967) sees rightly the political involvement, but imposes on it a violence of his own invention. J. H. Yoder, *The Politics of Jesus* (Grand Rapids 1972) offers a

magisterial corrective. See also J. Ferguson, *The Politics of Love* (Cambridge 1973).
35 *Is.* 42, 1-4; 49, 1-6; 50, 4-9; 52, 13-53, 12. See T. W. Manson, *The Servant Messiah* (Cambridge 1953). Also the superb chapter in C. H. Dodd, *The Founder of Christianity* (1971), pp. 99-118.
36 *Lk.* 1, 46-55, 68-75.
37 *Lk.* 4, 16-21.
38 *Mk.* 1, 15.
39 *Mt.* 12, 28.
40 *Mt.* 6, 10.
41 *Lk.* 4, 5-8; 19, 41-4; *Mt.* 26, 52.
42 e.g. *Lk.* 13, 18-9; *Mk.* 4, 26-19.

In general see C. H. Dodd, *The Parables of the Kingdom*[3] (London 1942).
43 *Mt.* 5, 1 ff.
44 *Acts* 4, 32-5.
45 *Mt.* 10, 5-6.
46 *Mk.* 7, 24-30 (a fascinating story which probably points this way); 7, 31 (a very odd route unless Jesus is deliberately going through Gentile territory); *Jn.* 4, 7-9; 12, 20-3; *Mt.* 28, 19.
47 C. H. Dodd, *History and the Gospel* (London 1938).
48 *Mt.* 5, 45.

CHAPTER XVIII

1 DS 34-5, 2, 19.
2 Oros. 5, 9, 4.
3 DS 34-5, 2. In general the slavewars are well treated by J. Vogt, 'Die sklaverei im utopische Denken der Griechen', *Riv. stor. dell' ant.* 1 (1971) 19-32; 'Sklaverei und Humanität', *Historia* Einzelschr. 8 (1972), 131-40. I am grateful to Prof. H. H. Scullard for drawing my attention to the article.
4 *BMC, Sicily*, 9, 13.
5 36, 1-11.
6 This has led some critics to suspect 'doublets': more probably the second consciously followed the patterns of the first. See A. Giacobbe, 'Sulle duplicazioni delle guerre servili in Sicilia', *Rend.* 1 (1925), 655 ff.: L. Pareti, 'I supposti 'sdoppiamenti' delle guerre servili in Sicilia', *Riv. Fil.* 5 (1927), 44 ff.
7 DS 36, 7, 3.
8 There is an intelligent study in modern political terms in F. A. Ridley, *Spartacus* (London 1944). The detailed problems are well treated in T. Rice-Holmes, *The Roman Republic and the Founder of the Empire* (Oxford 1933) vol. I. The events were fully treated in Sallust *Hist.*, a tradition partly reflected in App. *Bell. Civ.* and Plut. *Crass.*; another tradition less favourable to Spartacus will be found in Florus.

9 Plut. *Crass.* 8.
10 A. Koestler, *The Gladiators* (London 1939).
11 The primary sources are Plut. *V. Sert.*: App. *BC* 1, 108-15: Sall. *Hist.* 1, 2; Liv. *Epit.* Plutarch and Sallust represent a sympathetic tradition, Appian and Livy an unsympathetic one. For a modern treatment see A. Schulten, *Sertorius* (Leipzig 1926).
12 Sall. *Hist.* 1, 90.
13 Plut. *Sert.* 8-9.
14 T. Mommsen, *The History of Rome* (Clinton 1958), 228.
15 We are well endowed with primary sources, notably Sall. *Cat.* and Cic. *Cat.* The best secondary treatment is probably still E. G. Hardy, *The Catilinarian Conspiracy* (Oxford 1924). See also J. Vogt, *Cicero und Sallust über die catilinärische Verschwörung* (Frankfurt 1938).
16 See *CAH* IX 491-3.
17 The literature is vast. Enough here to mention L. A. Thompson, 'Cicero the Politician' in J. Ferguson, *Studies in Cicero* (Rome 1962) 35-79, a masterly summary; and the recent R. E. Smith, *Cicero the Statesman* (Cambridge 1966); D. A. Stockton, *Cicero: A Political Biography* (Oxford 1971). The most important account of his political ideals is H. Stasburger, *Concordia Ordinum: Eine Untersuchung*

zur Politik Ciceros (Amsterdam 1956 (1931)).
18 Cic. *Att.* 1, 16, 11; 2, 1, 8.
19 Cic. *Flacc.* 7, 15–18.
20 Cic. *Rep.* 2, 33, 57 Cic. *Fam.* 1, 9, 21; *Sest.* 45, 96–48, 103 (the fullest working-out); Ch. Wirszubski, 'Cicero's *Cum Dignitate Otium*: A Reconsideration', *JRS* 44 (1954), 1–13.
21 G. H. Sabine and S. B. Smith, *Marcus Tullius Cicero: On the Commonwealth* (Columbus 1929). There is no comparably useful edition of *The Laws*. Useful articles include three papers by R. Heinze reprinted in R. Heinze, *Vom Geist des Römertums* (Leipzig-Berlin 1938). W. W. How, 'Cicero's Ideal in his *De Republica*', *JRS* 20 (1930), 24 ff.; C. W. Keyes, 'Original Elements in Cicero's Ideal Constitution', *AJP* 13 (1921), 309–23.
22 The date is established from the letters: QF 2, 12, 1; 3, 5, 1 ff.; *Att.* 4, 16, 2; 5, 12, 2; 6, 1, 8; 6, 2, 3; 6, 3, 3; *Fam.* 8, 1, 4.
23 *Rep.* 1, 10, 15.
24 1, 21, 34.
25 1, 25, 39.
26 1, 32, 49.
27 1, 45, 69–46, 70.
28 Tac. *Ann.* 4, 33.
29 2, 42, 69.
30 2, 44, 70 cf. Aug. *CD* 2, 21.
31 Aug. *C. Jul. Pel.* 4, 12, 60.
32 Cic. *Rep.* 3, 8, 12–18, 28 cf. Lact. *Inst. Div.* 5, 16, 5–13.
33 3, 22, 33.
34 3, 23, 34.
35 4, 5, 6.
36 4, 7, 7.
37 6, 1, 1.
38 Schol. ad Cic. *Inv.*; see Sabine and Smith (op. cit. n. 21), p. 250.
39 See Th. Zielinski, *Cicero in Wandel der Jahrhunderte*³ (Berlin 1912); R. Reitzenstein, 'Die Idee des Principates bei Cicero und Augustus', *Nachrichten von der Gesellsch. der Wissensch. zu Göttingen* (ph. hist. kl.) (1917), 399 ff.; 436 ff.; E. Meyer, *Caesars Monarchie und das Principat des Pompejus*³ (Stuttgart-Berlin 1919);

R. Heinze, 'Ciceros "Staat" als politische Tendenzschrift' *Hermes* 59 (1924), 73–94.
40 Cic. *Rep.* 5, 6, 8 Stob. 48, 61.
41 Cic. *Rep.* 2, 25, 46.
42 Schol. ad Cic. *Inv.* (n. 38 above).
43 For Panaetius: G. Galbiati, *De fontibus M. Tullii Ciceronis librorum qui manserunt de re publica et de legibus quaestiones* (Milan 1916), 364–97. For Antiochus: A. Laudien, 'Die Composition und Quelle von Ciceros I Buch der Gesetze', *Hermes* 46 (1911) 108 ff.
44 *Laws* 1, 4, 14.
45 1, 6, 19.
46 1, 13, 37.
47 1, 18, 49.
48 2, 7, 15.
49 See B. Farrington, *Science and Politics in the Ancient World*² (London 1965), where this point is soundly made among others less sound.
50 *Laws* 2, 10, 23.
51 3, 5, 12.
52 3, 1, 2.
53 3, 2, 5; 3, 5, 12.
54 3, 3, 7.
55 3, 10, 23–5.
56 3, 4, 10; 3, 18, 40.
57 3, 20, 46.
58 R. Reitzenstein, *Drei Vermutungen zur Geschichte der römischen Litteratur* (Marburg 1894), 1–31.
59 But see A. du Mesnil's edition (Leipzig 1879) for an alternative view.
60 Cic. *Rep.* 6, 1, 1; R. S. Rogers, *Studies in the Reign of Tiberius* (Baltimore 1933).
61 3, 22, 33.
62 Plin *NH* 7, 31.
63 The best modern study is M. Gelzer, *Caesar, Politician and Statesman* (ET Oxford 1968).
64 Caes. *BC* 1, 9, 2.
65 Cic. *Pro Marc.* 8, 25.
66 R. Syme, *The Roman Revolution* (Oxford 1939), 52, 194.
67 An immense amount has been written on this, and other, far less plausible identifications have been made. See D. A. Slater, 'Was the Fourth Eclogue written to celebrate

the marriage of Octavia to Mark Antony? – A literary parallel', *CR* 26 (1912), 114–19. In general see J. B. Mayor, W. Fowler, R. S. Conway, *Vergil's Messianic Eclogue* (Oxford 1907); E. Norden, *Die Geburt des Kindes* (Leipzig 1924); J. Carcopino, *Virgile et le mystère de la IVe Églogue*³ (Paris 1930); H. J. Rose, *The Eclogues of Vergil* (Berkeley 1942); A. Alfoldi, 'Der neue Weltherrscher der vierten Ekloge Vergils', *Hermes* 65 (1930), 369–80.
68 T. F. Royds, *Virgil and Isaiah* (Oxford 1918); H. W. Garrod, 'Note on the Messianic Character of the Fourth Eclogue', *CR* 9 (1905), 37–8.
69 Jos. *Ant.* 15, 370.
70 ibid. 15, 342.
71 V. *Ecl.* 4, 4–10.
72 T. E. Page, *Virgil: Bucolics and Georgics* (London 1898), 129.
73 V. *Ecl.* 4, 46–7

74 The last phrases are repeated from my *The Heritage of Hellenism* (London 1973), as are some subsequent phrases.
75 W. W. Tarn in *CAH* 10, p. 111.
76 *Or. Sib.* 3, 367–80; ll 371–2 defective; ll 377–8 transposed; tr. in *The Heritage of Hellenism* (London 1973), 68. For the oracles see also J. Lindsay, *Cleopatra* (London 1970) ch. 15; also M. Grant, *Cleopatra* (London 1973) (refs. due to Prof. Scullard).
77 W. W. Tarn, '*Alexander Helios and the Golden Age*', *JRS* 22 (1932), 135–60.
78 H. J. Rose, 'The departure of Dionysos', *Ann. Arch. Anthr.* 11 (1924), 25 ff.
79 W. Spiegelberg, 'Aegyptologische Mitteilungen', *Sitz. Bay. Akad.* (1925), 2.
80 Hor. *Od.* 1, 37, 25–32.

CHAPTER XIX

1 L. S. Mazzolani, *The Idea of the City in Roman Thought* (ET London 1970) is highly relevant.
2 Ov. *F.* 2, 683–4.
3 V. *Aen.* 1, 278–9.
4 Tib. 2, 5, 23 cf. Ov. *F.* 3, 72.
5 L. Waddy, *Pax Romana and World Peace* (London 1950) is worth reading on this.
6 E. Birley at the Classical Association 1973.
7 Cic. *Att.* 14, 12, 1; Suet. *Jul.* 80.
8 Suet. *Aug.* 40.
9 Dessau *ILS* 206; 212; Tac. *Ann.* 11, 23–5.
10 Plin. *Ep.* 10, 5–7.
11 M. Hammond, *The City in the Ancient World* (Cambridge Mass. 1972), p. 287; to whom these pages are generally indebted.
12 B. Farrington, *Diodorus Siculus: Universal Historian* (Swansea 1937).
13 M. I. Finley, *The Greek Historians* (London 1959), 15.
14 DS 3, 12–14; 5, 35–8.
15 5, 41–6; 2, 55–60.
16 Zosimus 2, 5–6; *CIL* 6, 32, 323; Hor. *CS*. There is an admirable

secondary account in W. W. Fowler, '*The Carmen Saeculare* of Horace and its Performance, June 3rd, 17 BC', *Roman Essays and Interpretations* (Oxford 1920), 111–26, which I follow here.
17 I have taken some sentences of the above from a forthcoming paper on 'Communication and Propaganda in the Graeco-Roman World'. For the altar see G. Moretti, *L'Ara Pacis Augustae* (Rome 1938).
18 Any attempt at a comprehensive rehabilitation of Nero is misguided. We are fortunate in the reliable B. H. Warmington, *Nero: Reality and Legend* (London 1969).
19 Einsiedeln Eclogue tr. in my *The Heritage of Hellenism* (London 1973) 69–70.
20 Luc. *BC* 1, 60–2 cf. (Sen.) *Ludus* 4, 1.
21 Sen. *Clem.* 1, 1, 2–4.
22 J. Ferguson, *Moral Values in the Ancient World* (London 1958), 102–17.
23 Suet. *Nero* 10.
24 Tac. *Ann.* 14, 11.
25 E. M. Sandford, 'Nero and the

East', *HSCP* 48 (1937), 75–103; M. P. Charlesworth, 'Nero: Some Aspects', *JRS* 40 (1950), 69–76. cf. Suet. *Nero* 57.
26 Sen. *Ep.* 73 is a fascinating apologia; also *De Otio* 31.
27 M. Rostovtzeff, *Social and Economic History of the Roman Empire* (Oxford 1926), 108. See also R. Mac-Mullen, *Enemies of the Roman Order* (Harvard 1967) ch. II (ref. due to Prof. Scullard).
28 Sen. *Ben.* 2, 20; Mus. Ruf. apud Stob. *Fl.* 46, 67
29 Plut. *Cato* 25, 37; Mart. 1, 8, 1–2; Arr. *Epict.* 1, 1, 26; Juv. 5, 16.
30 DC 61, 15.
31 Tac. *Ann.* 6, 22.
32 See Tac. *Hist.* 4, 5–11; 4, 40–4; 4, 53; there is supporting material in Suet. *Vesp.* and Dio Cassius. There is a useful account of Helvidius in D. R. Dudley, *A History of Cynicism* (London 1937), 132–7.
33 E. Gibbon, *The Decline and Fall of the Roman Empire*, c. iii.
34 Plin. *NH* 27, 1, 1, 3.
35 Ael. Arist. *To Rome* 60; 64–66, 97, 104. See J. H. Oliver, 'The Ruling Power', *Transactions of the American Philosophical Society*, 43, 4 (1953); M. Hammond, op. cit. (n. ll), 30.
36 Lucian, *VH* 1, 7.
37 ibid. 1, 20, cf. DS 5, 43, 2.
38 ibid. 2, 5.
39 ibid. 1, 34; DS 5, 42, 6 ff.
40 Lucian, *VH*, 1, 3.
41 ibid. 4 cf. Schol. ad loc.; Plat. *Rep.* 10, 614 A.
42 ibid. 1, 11; DS 2, 58. 5.
43 ibid. 1, 13.
44 Lact. *Inst. Div.* 3, 23, 41.
45 Lucian, *VH* 22; DS 2, 56.
46 ibid. 2, 5.
47 ibid., 2, 7, 17.
48 ibid. 2, 19; DS 2, 58, 1.
49 ibid. 2, 47; DS, 2, 60, 1.
50 *P. Ryl.* 77.

51 *P. Oxy.* 1, 40.
52 *P. Oxy.* 13, 1415.
53 A. Birley, *Marcus Aurelius* (London 1966) is the most useful recent study and has a good bibliography. See also A. S. L. Farquharson, *The Meditations of the Emperor Marcus Aurelius*, 2 vols. (Oxford 1944).
54 F. W. H. Myers, *Essays: Classical* (London 1897), 178.
55 SHA *Marcus*, 27, 7; Just. *Apol.* 1, 3.
56 MA 9, 29.
57 ibid. 5, 17; 9, 18, cf. DC 71, 34, 4.
58 ibid. 1, 14.
59 ibid. 4, 23, cf. 2, 16; 3, 11; 4, 3; 4, 29; 5, 22; 6, 54.
60 ibid. 6, 44; 2, 5.
61 ibid. 3, 5.
62 ibid. 6, 24.
63 ibid. 6, 36.
64 ibid. 6, 30.
65 ibid. 4, 49.
66 DC 78, 9, 4–5; *Dig* 1, 5, 17; for an apparent exception see *P. Giessen* 40.
67 SHA *Caracalla* 2.
68 A. Alföldi, 'Insignien und Tracht der römischen Kaiser;, *Röm. Mitt.* 50 (1935), 1–171, esp. 107 ff.
69 *CIL* 3, 2.
70 Paneg. Vet. 10, 35.
71 Porph. *V. Plot.* 1.
72 ibid. 2.
73 Plot. *Enn.* 1, 2, 1–3; 1, 3, 6; Plat. *Rep.* 4, 427E–434D; Ambrose *Lib. V. in Lucam*. See J. Ferguson, *Moral Values in the Ancient World* (London 1958), c. iii.
74 Porph. *V. Plot.* 7.
75 ibid. 12.
76 ibid. 7,
77 SHA *Aur.* 25, 4–6.
78 Lact. *Inst. Div.* 1, 1, 13–6; even if this is an interpolation, it remains an example of Christian continuity.
79 Rut. Nam. 1, 63–6.
80 Prud. *Peristeph.* 2, 413 ff.

CHAPTER XX

1 Aug. *De urbis excidio*, 2, 3.
2 Jerom. *Ep.* 127 cf *Is.* 15, 1; *Ps.* 78, 1–3; 79 1–3.
3 ibid. 123, 16.

4 Pelag. *Ep. ad Demetriadem* 30.
5 Aug. *Ep.* 154.
6 Aug. *Ep.* 136.
7 ibid. 137, 138.
8 Aug. *CD* 2, 19.
9 Cic. *Pro Lig.* 12, 35.
10 1 *Cor.* 1, 18–25.
11 Aug. *Retract.* 2, 69.
12 C. Lambot, 'Lettre inédite de S. Augustin relative au *De civitate Dei*' *Rev. Bén.* 51 (1939), 109–21.
13 Xen. *Mem.* 2, 1, 21–34.
14 *Mt.* 7, 13–14.
15 *Did.* 1, 1; *Ep. Barn.* 18–20.
16 MA 4, 23; Sen. *De Otio* 31.
17 Aug. *Lib. Arb.* 1, 15.
18 ibid. *Ver. Rel.* 27.
19 ibid. *Cat. Rud.* 19, 31; 27, 37 cf. *Rev.* 14, 8; Aug *CD* 18, 2.
20 id. *Gen. ad. litt.* 12, 15; 20. I owe some of these references to G. E. McCracken's introduction to the Loeb edition.
21 The literature is immense. I have found particularly useful: R. H. Barrow, *Introduction to St. Augustine. The City of God* (London 1940); N. H. Baynes, *The Political Ideas of St. Augustine's 'De Civitate Dei'* (Bell 1936) (= *Byzantine Studies* (1955), 288 ff.); J. H. S. Burleigh, *The City of God* (London 1949), pp. 153–84; G. Combés, *La Doctrine politique de Saint Augustin* (Paris 1927); J. N. Figgis, *The Political Aspects of St. Augustine's City of God* (London 1921); M. B. Foster, *Masters of Political Thought, I, Plato to Machiavelli* (London 1947), pp. 196–227; E. Gil-

son, *Introduction à l'étude de la Philosophie de Saint Augustin* (Paris 1931); C-V. v. Horn, *Die Staatslehre Augustins nach de Civitate Dei* (Breslau 1934); R. Niebuhr, 'Augustine's Political Idealism' in *Christian Realism and Political Problems* (London 1954). P. Brown's otherwise excellent *Augustine of Hippo* (London 1967) has less on *The City of God*.
22 Aug. *CD* 15, 1 ff.
23 11, 1.
24 14, 28.
25 11, 24.
26 15, 1.
27 1, 35.
28 15, 5.
29 15, 4.
30 e.g. 2, 21; 4, 3; 15, 5; 18, 2.
31 5 *passim*, esp. 5, 17.
32 W. Jaeger, *Paideia: The Ideals of Greek Culture*[3] (Oxford 1946), II, 77.
33 2, 14; 8, 13.
34 Plat. *Laws* 4, 713 A.
35 e.g. 19, 13; 19, 17.
36 2, 21; 19, 21; cf. Cic *Rep.* 1, 21, 34.
37 4, 4.
38 Plat. *Rep.* 2, 368D.
39 2, 21.
40 19, 11–4.
41 19, 13.
42 19, 14.
43 19, 7.
44 *Ep. ad Diognet.* 5–6.
45 19, 17.
46 Plat. *Rep.* 9, 592 A–B. See L. S. Mazzolani, *The Idea of the City in Roman Thought* (ET London 1970), 276.

INDEX